D1367430

THE CHILDREN'S CHOIR

Volume II

NANCY   POORE   TUFTS

The

Children's

Choir

Volume II

Dedicated to the late RUTH KREHBIEL JACOBS

FORTRESS PRESS   Philadelphia, Pennsylvania

THE CHILDREN'S CHOIR

Volume II

Copyright, 1965

FORTRESS PRESS

First Printing

FORTRESS PRESS   2900 Queen Lane   Philadelphia, Pa. 19129

.63717

Foreword

There are thousands of boys and girls in the world today whose lives are being enriched through the educational, musical, and spiritual leadership of many choir directors who have been helped through the Choristers Guild. The Guild has played a big part in the training of these young people by bringing many new and workable ideas to many of these dedicated music directors. These same boys and girls, upon reaching maturity, will make more useful citizens because of the guidance of these dedicated leaders.

NITA AKIN, *President*
Choristers Guild

"MOST OF US SPEND OUR LIVES MAKING SMALL TOKEN PAYMENTS, AND NEVER COMING INTO POSSESSION OF THE TREASURE. AND HOW WE ENVY THE COURAGEOUS FEW WHO VENTURED EVERYTHING . . . AND GAINED EVERY-THING."

From the writings of RUTH KREHBIEL JACOBS

L'envoi

"In vain our labors are, whate'er they be,
Unless God gives
THE BENEDICITE."
—HERRICK

RUTH KREHBIEL JACOBS
1897–1960

Preface

The phenomenal growth in numbers of children's choirs, their use of better music, their enthusiastic acceptance by the church as an important part of church life, their growth in quality of singing and of music use, and their acknowledgement as an essential element in Christian education—all contrast markedly with the state of affairs only a few years ago. Many children's choirs then existing were haphazard in their direction and organization; ministers often would not even tolerate them in a regular church service, let alone encourage their formation. Enthusiasm started many choirs; but also, many soon faded away. Children were not challenged, and parents showed little interest.

In spite of the unfavorable atmosphere, rays of hope for better children's choirs became brighter. Among the brightest of such hopes was Ruth Krehbiel Jacobs and the Choristers Guild which she founded in 1949. Ruth Jacobs, in years of experimentation and development, had evolved a workable method of building and maintaining successful children's choirs—an approach set forth in a small book published in 1948 entitled *The Successful Children's Choir*. The Choristers Guild grew out of the many requests for advice and help which came to Mrs. Jacobs. The responses, both general and specific, were first published in the *Choristers Guild Letters* which have been issued monthly ever since to members of the Guild. It is probably quite reasonable to state that Ruth Jacobs and the Choristers Guild have had a greater impact on the growth in numbers and quality of children's choirs than any other individual or instrumentality.

The Choristers Guild is dedicated to the firm conviction expressed in its slogan *"Christian Character Through Children's Choirs."* In its work the children's choir combines two of the most powerful forces known to man—religion and music. Since the answer to a worthwhile and meaningful children's choir lies in the hands of adults, it becomes readily apparent that the director must be completely dedicated and thoroughly trained. Children, particularly present-day boys and girls, need the challenge of the difficult but possible. Children in a choir can sing good music well in generally excellent tone-quality if the leadership demands it. *The limitations of children's choirs are generally those of their directors!*

During the past fifteen years the Choristers Guild through its annual nation-wide seminars, regional workshops, monthly *Letters,* and personal contacts has provided help and training for those directors who desire to increase their effectiveness with children's choirs. Many leaders in the children's choir field have heartily endorsed the work of the Guild and have aided it to grow into the leading position it now occupies in a highly specialized field.

This book attempts to increase the amount of self-help through reading available to the children's choir director. The enthusiastic response of choir directors to Volume 1 of *The Children's Choir* implies a similar success for Volume 2. The first volume contains material published in the *Choristers Guild Letters* from the first issue in September 1949 to that of June 1957. This second volume continues with material from the issues of recent years. This material has been selected and compiled by Nancy Poore Tufts, a long-time close personal friend and associate of Ruth Jacobs, and of mine as well. Mrs. Tufts has herself contributed much of the success of the *Guild Letters* in promoting handbell choirs by her series "Tintinnabulations." Her devotion to the task of selection and compilation from the great amount of material in the *Letters* arises from a deep sense of dedication to the Guild tenet "Christian Character Through Children's Choirs."

Practically all the material in this volume has been written by actual successful practitioners of the art of directing children's choirs. It has been tried in the crucible of actual weekly rehearsals. It works! Launched on the sea of books it bears the eager hope that it will help give our boys and girls the opportunity they deserve of learning Christian attitudes by doing.

This volume is dedicated to the memory of the late Ruth Krehbiel Jacobs, who provided such a large measure of impetus and leadership for the present improved status of children's choirs.

ARTHUR LESLIE JACOBS

March 1965

Contents

The Choristers Guild

The Choristers Guild is an organization dedicated to the development of "Christian Character Through Children's Choirs." It was started in 1949 to help church musicians with the many problems of maintaining a children's choir. Churches that expected an inclusive choir program were increasing; schools were graduating church music majors without training in children's choir techniques; and both churches and directors were at a loss as to objectives and methods.

Realizing the great potential influence of the children's choir movement, the Choristers Guild has undertaken to give it purposeful leadership. Its program has come to include:

The *Choristers Guild Letters,* published monthly (September to June), is filled with suggestions and practical advice on the many subjects related to children's choir work such as discipline, organization, selection of music, rehearsal plans, hymn-learning, parent co-operation, equipment, sight-singing, tone, etc.

The Choristers Guild also promotes:

Better standards of achievement through the Guild Merit System;

A distinctive pin award which may be earned by all choristers. This pin is recognized as indicating personal accomplishments;

Choristers Guild chapters for the encouragement of local directors;

Progressive material for children's choir notebooks;

Short seminars in all parts of the country;

1

Summer schools;

Children's choir festivals.

It is the Guild's firm belief that the choir can be a profound factor in the religious growth of children. It teaches them to give themselves wholeheartedly to group endeavor; it gives them happy associations with the church; it trains them in the fundamentals of leadership: regularity, loyalty, dependability, and idealism; it teaches them the great song literature of the church; it provides a satisfying means of self-expression; and through a responsible part in the service of worship it opens the door to the experience of worship.

Furthermore, the children's choir bridges denominational differences, as it can be a means of tying together the far corners of the whole Christian world.

The children's choir is a powerful Christian tool, and the Choristers Guild is dedicated to its use in the intelligent shaping of worthy Christian leadership. Working together toward that objective are dedicated ministers, teachers, and musicians in all the states of the Union, and in many foreign countries. The directed efforts of a world-wide association can accomplish things that are impossible for an individual, or any number of unorganized individuals.

If the Choristers Guild is to realize its full potential, it must appeal to the faith and generosity of a large number of people. Each of us can help in our own way, with Contributing memberships, special gifts, and by interesting others in the movement.

GUILD MEMBERSHIP

Membership in the Choristers Guild is open to all people interested in children's choirs and their potential influence on Christian education. Annual dues are $4.00, which entitle one to receive the *Choristers Guild Letters,* published from September to June.

Members who are actively in charge of a choir are encouraged to:

Reach as many children as possible.

Present worthy music, adequately prepared.

Encourage reverence.

Use the choir as a means of character development.

Make the choir a religious, artistic, educational, and recreational influence in the lives of the children.

Support the purposes of the Choristers Guild.

2

CONTRIBUTING MEMBERS

A gift of $10.00 or more a year makes one a Contributing Member. Both organizations and individuals may become Contributing Members.

The children's choir represents a tremendous character influence. It works with two of the greatest powers known: religion and music. It works through the strongest moral force known to society—the Christian church. The Contributing Member has a keen awareness of his personal obligation to the present and the future, to others and to himself. Because of that awareness, he is constantly improving his methods, enlarging and deepening the meaning of the choir experience, and supporting the Choristers Guild's efforts to knit together in one universal movement the scattered seeds of growth. It is the Contributing Member who will bring that goal in sight.

VOTING MEMBERS

Voting Members are those who have been Contributing Members for five successive years. They are entitled to attend the annual meeting and to have a voice in determining the policies of the Guild.

All memberships are annual and run from September to September. The *Choristers Guild Letters* are mailed to all members.

SPECIAL MEMBERSHIP CLASSIFICATION

Three additional classifications of membership have been approved by the Board of Directors. These are:

Subscribing Memberships	$ 25.00
Patron Memberships	$100.00
Life Memberships	$500.00

Subscribing, Patron, and Life members have all the benefits available to Regular and Contributing members. Life members are recognized in a special manner by the officers of the Board of Directors.

REGARDING GIFTS

The Guild is recognized by the Internal Revenue Service of the United States Treasury Department as a non-profit religious and educational organization. Because of this, contributions and gifts to the Guild are tax-deductible on one's personal income tax returns. Professional musicians also may list the cost of membership as a deduction under the heading of professional organizations.

THE CHORISTERS PIN
The Suggested Merit System

75 credits for 100% attendance at rehearsals and performances.

50 credits for 85% attendance at rehearsals and performances.

25 credits for a complete and neat notebook.

25 credits for 100% attendance at church school.

15 credits for 85% attendance at church school.

25 credits for good behavior.

> (It is suggested that a child be given a demerit if he needs to be reprimanded. Ten demerits should disqualify him for these credits.)

15 credits for bringing a new member.

> (Granted only if new member remains through the season; no more than 15 credits granted in any one year.)

This system is based on a nine months' season of regular weekly rehearsals. To earn a pin a chorister must earn 100 credits during the year. The virtue of the system is that it is impossible to earn a pin without being regular, and it is also impossible to earn one by attendance only.

The Chorister Pin is the first-year award in a choir.

Each successive year the pin may be returned to the Guild to have a pearl set in it, or a note-guard added.

Other awards are also available to members for use with their choirs: distinctive cross, patches, books, etc.

CHORISTERS GUILD CHAPTERS

With the growth of Guild membership in various communities has come the formation of local chapters for mutual encouragement and more purposeful local action. That every chapter may honestly bear the name of the Choristers Guild, and worthily serve its high purposes, the following conditions are required:

There shall be a minimum membership of five.

The official title shall be: The (city or area) Chapter of the Choristers Guild.

Every member shall be a member of the national organization.

At least four meetings shall be held annually.

The Chapter shall promote an annual children's choir festival.

A yearly report shall be made to the Choristers Guild national officers.

4

Chapters fulfilling these conditions shall be entitled to use the Choristers Guild letterhead design and other official insignia.

Suggestions of worthy topics for chapter meetings will be sent upon request made to the national office.

CHORISTERS GUILD OFFICE

The Choristers Guild was incorporated under the laws of the state of Tennessee. Because of this it is necessary to maintain a legal office in that state. The operational headquarters is at:

440 Northlake Center
Dallas, Texas 75238

Dr. Federal Lee Whittlesey is the Executive Secretary-Treasurer of the Guild and responsible for the daily operation of the office. Any communications about the Guild should be addressed to him at the Dallas office.

The Value
of Children's Choirs

The Value to the Child

"IS IT REALLY IMPORTANT THAT MY CHILD
SINGS IN THE CHOIR?"

A Psychologist says: "The children who have received extensive training in children's choirs grow up to become happy, well-adjusted adults on a higher percentage rate than do those having no choir experience. I would say that the reason for this is that the principles of music and harmony which are learned in choir work become part of the child and are subconsciously carried over into his everyday life."

DR. GEORGE CRANE

A Doctor says: "Singing helps to develop and strengthen the lungs and respiratory organs and helps the entire body resist disease."

DR. J. H. MOORE

An Educator says: "We are only beginning to learn that the right kind of music and singing taught to children while they are young has the power to change the course and destiny of their lives."

DOROTHY BROMBLEY

A Sociologist says: "Music and singing are extremely beneficial, not only to the well-being of a person physically and spiritually, but in every experience a person may have, whether public or private."

DR. J. J. DAVIS

7

A Philosopher says: "Because music has so much to do with the molding of the character, it is necessary that we teach it to our children."

ARISTOTLE (320 B. C.)

A Criminologist says: "The child who receives music training and who finds joy in singing and making music will not make mischief. The girls who sing and play the piano do not pick your pocket; the boy who sings and draws the violin bow is not the boy who draws the gun."

J. EDGAR HOOVER

A President says: "Music and singing make for better citizenship; they drive out envy and hate, they unify and inspire. Music is the one common tie between races and nations."

WOODROW WILSON

A Minister says: "Our little children we instruct chiefly by hymns, whereby we find the most important truths most successfully insinuated into their minds."

JOHN WESLEY

The Bible says: "Train up a child in the way he should go, and when he is old he will not depart from it." (Proverbs 22:6)

YOUR CHILD NEEDS MUSIC

MUSIC helps the child to enjoy the group. One of the best ways to establish a feeling of friendliness among a group of adults is to have them sing a familiar song. This also holds true for children.

MUSIC is a medium of expression. One of the most important phases of personality development is self-expression. Music encourages both group participation and self-expression.

MUSIC helps the child to discover beauty. Children's eyes are very sensitive to bright and beautiful colors. We should also develop their sensitivity to beautiful musical sounds.

MUSIC helps to encourage the child's imagination, to take his mind away from the here and now.

MUSIC helps the child to discover the joy of creating. With television, and various other entertainments, our modern tendency is to sit and watch. We need to continue to stimulate the creative desire in our children. A child needs and deserves the opportunity to develop musically according to the capacity. By singing songs and hymns of other lands, a child gains a feeling of warmth for other peoples and nations.

8

MUSIC is very definitely essential to the worship experience of your child. The depth of his musical worship experience is dependent upon the training your child receives before he reaches adulthood.

Dr. Irving Wolfe
Peabody College
Nashville, Tennessee

CHILDREN AND SINGING

Giving musical advice is one thing I prefer not to do; however, because some parents say, "Can't Johnnie begin to sing later on when he is 10 or 11?" I think it would be helpful for parents interested in the subject of "Children and Music" to know that correct singing habits and use of the voice are more naturally achieved when begun in childhood and continued. The discouragement that comes with the necessity of unlearning incorrect vocal habits has prevented many people from enjoying, later in life, the fine expressions which singing brings.

If you are wondering about which musical instrument a child should study first, I would recommend the voice. My reasons are:
1. It is the finest and most beautiful musical instrument there is, and the most natural.
2. It is the most personal, therefore the most expressive.
3. It has no age limitations and is adaptable to any social, cultural, or religious medium such as singing at home, in a community group, or in a church choir.
4. One can have personal acquaintance with the world's treasury of music and literature, thus finding joy and inspiration in living.
5. Technically, singing is the least complicated.

Edward Johe, *Minister of Music*
First Congregational Church
Columbus, Ohio

The Value to Church

THREE DIMENSIONS

(Service to the Church through the Medium of Children's Choirs)

When an individual joins the church, he promises to support it with his prayers, his presence, his gifts, and his service.

9

Participation in the choir program should be something that is accepted as naturally as attendance at church school. Life was three-dimensional long before the movies thought of the term; it has length, breadth, and depth. Our concern seems to be in that order: length, or health ("How are you?"); breadth, or mind ("Have you read the latest books?"); but for the spirit—silence! Yet it is the spirit that makes one stand out in a crowd. None of these areas is ever static; there is constant progress or retrogression.

This same emphasis is reflected in the care of our children. We see to it that they have expert medical attention; we expect them to avail themselves of compulsory education. But when it comes to things of the spirit we say, "I don't want to force him."

You may be familiar with J. Edgar Hoover's answer to the often-asked question: "Shall I force my child to go to Sunday school and church?" "Yes!" And with no further discussion about the matter! Startled? Why?

How do you answer Junior when he comes to the breakfast table Monday morning and announces rebelliously, "I'm not going to school today!" You know—he *goes!*

How do you answer Junior when, threatened with illness, he says, "I'm not going to take my medicine!" You know—he *takes* it!

Why all this timidity, then, in the realm of spiritual guidance and growth? Going to wait and decide what church he'll go to when he's old enough? Quit your kidding! You didn't wait until he was old enough to decide to go to school and get an education, or until he could make up his mind as to whether he wished to be a clean person or not, or whether he wished to take the medicine that would make him well.

Afraid he'll succumb to the old-wives' tale about "too much religion when I was young; parents made me go" sort of gag? Look about you: the story is demonstrably and obviously false despite its currency. Do you suppose that because you insist over his protests he will turn into a bathless Groggins when he is 21?

What shall we say when Junior announces he doesn't like Sunday school and church? That's an easy one. Be consistent! Just say, "Junior, in our house we all attend Sunday school and church, and that includes you." Your firmness and example here furnishes a bridge over which youthful rebellion may travel into rich and satisfying experiences in personal religious living.

"The parents of America may strike a most effective blow against the forces which contribute to juvenile delinquency, if the mothers and fathers will take their children to Sunday school and church regularly."

It is our challenge to make of church music an equally rich and satisfying experience—one in which all children and youth will participate.

The conflicts and stresses of our day are greater than ever before in history. There are conflicts that hang threateningly over everyone. Not the least one of us can escape the fog of fear that blots out the sky.

In its groping the world has turned to religion. Suddenly people outside the church are saying hopefully that the only thing that can save the world is a practical application of the principles of Jesus. And they are turning to the church to produce that kind of leadership.

The church has been groping, too, and often losing sight of its goal: namely, a generation of people, leaders and followers, with sound education in the principles of Christianity, a conviction of the value of these principles, and the stamina to live by them.

To approach that goal, we need to make every educational resource of the church productive. Frequently one of the most subtle powers within the church—the choir—is overlooked.

Children of today have so many secular organizations angling for their time that the church is frequently crowded out completely. It is not surprising that a child should think of the church as the place where the Cubs or Brownies meet. It is difficult to understand how the church can so casually sell its birthright. The children's choir can and should use as wide a range of activities as any secular organization. It can provide recreation, drama, and opportunity for personal achievement, in addition to a sound musical education. The choir, and the choir only, can deepen religious awareness through a responsible part in services of worship. If it is true that 85% of the Episcopal clergy started their training as choir boys, we need no further proof of the influence the choir has in molding the thoughts and lives of children.

Leaders are greatly concerned about the large percentage of teenagers who drift away from the church. All kinds of activities have been devised to hold their interest, but the best sustaining force of all is the choir because it meets the problem before it arises.

The program of graduation, the pride in reaching each successive stage of the choir scale, with the adult choir at its peak, the habits of regular service and punctuality and responsibility started with the children—all these are positive factors in counteracting the indifference of adolescence.

11

A sound and controlling personal religion cannot be inherited. In that area every successful man is a self-made man. He must find and develop his own peace of mind and heart. The concentrated quiet that a good choir imposes on its members during the service of worship is the finest seedbed for the growth of religious maturity. There will be occasional moments when worship suddenly becomes more than a formal pattern of words, and those moments will be a greater influence for the inclusion of religion in his life than the most convincing of reasonable arguments.

NORMA LOWDER
Bellaire Methodist Church
Bellaire, Texas

IN SEARCH OF WORSHIP

We speak glibly of the experience of worship as one of the major values of the choir for our children. But what *is* worship? There are probably as many and varied concepts of worship as there are types of services of worship. I venture to say that not one of us can construct from our own observation and experience a satisfying definition of worship. It is well-nigh impossible to dissociate our idea of worship from the worship customs in which we were reared. And there is no end to the variations in those customs, from the Quaker Meeting in which no word is spoken or sung to the highly formalized ritual of the Catholic or Episcopal or Lutheran Church. Each of the two extremes and all the variations between represent different concepts of worship.

Just what *is* worship?

Is it a carefully organized series of acts planned to induce a series of emotions?

Is it a program of sacred words, spoken and sung?

Is it a familiar ritual?

Is it an atmosphere that permits private communion or meditation, or is it the meditation itself?

Is it a sermon with varied preliminaries?

We could go to the dictionary for our definitions of worship, but whom would that satisfy? Our children can learn a definition without the discipline of regular choir attendance and experimentation. And that definition will not be static; it will change with our growing understanding. A philosopher has said that a creed marks the spot where a man stood growing. The same may be true of our under-

12

standing of worship. Unless it becomes richer and deeper it ceases to exist.

Worship is not confined to the Christian religion. Some kind of worship of some kind of deity is a part of every religion ever known. Would it be possible, do you suppose, for a Christian to experience worship in the rites of some completely foreign religion? And on the other hand, how often does the person who attends church faithfully every Sunday have an experience more profound than that provided by any other social gathering of like-minded people?

And if we are concerned with the reality of worship, then certainly as leaders in worship we should concern ourselves with a consideration of the essentials of worship. What *are* the essentials? And can we free ourselves enough from acceptance of the customary to consider our services of worship critically and objectively?

Anthems? Are they essential? Accepted, yes, but essential? If so, what do they contribute? Or what should they contribute?

Hymns? Every one of us is concerned that our children should know the great hymns and sing them vigorously and fervently and with increasing understanding. Are they an essential or only an habitual part of worship? We often complain of the minister's or congregation's abuse of hymns, but visiting many services in many parts of the country makes me wonder if we musicians are not the chief offenders. Recently in a morning service I attended, the final hymn, a rather reflective one, was played in a sharply staccato manner, quite obviously to keep the choir together in the recessional. Is that use, or abuse? And how often does one hear a painfully slow, long-faced "Amen" at the close of a stirring hymn or response! The hymns and anthems, whether they are essential or superfluous, are our personal responsibility. And it is our responsibility also to see that they contribute something of unmistakable value.

If the children's choir is to fulfill the claim of encouraging a sense of worship, then we must take the blinders off our eyes. We may never find a completely satisfying definition of worship, but perhaps in the honest attempt we will come closer to more meaningful use of the elements of worship.

It will be a difficult and probably life-long undertaking, like Sir Launfal's search for the Holy Grail, but we can make a beginning by setting ourselves three assignments.

We will train ourselves to think and to observe with an open and an active mind. We will cut the shackles of habit, of confusing the customary and the right.

13

We will resolve to discard anything that suggests showmanship. Banish the thought of "Now the choir will perform for us." Banish, too, the smug pleasure in the minister's praise of an anthem from the pulpit. And banish still deeper in limbo such "cute" contrivances as the use of children's "action songs" in the service!

These two assignments are difficult enough, but the third is even more so. We must *experience* worship; we must know what it is and what it means before we can kindle it in others.

What is worship?—"Seek, and ye shall find."

RUTH KREHBIEL JACOBS

DECISIONS

(Summary of a talk given by RUTH KREHBIEL JACOBS to 300 boys, girls, and parents during a March seminar held in Birmingham, Michigan, by ROLAND CRISCI, Minister of Music, Redford Presbyterian Church, Detroit.)

Remember the game called "London Bridge"? Two people join hands to make a bridge under which all the others are to pass. When one is caught, he is to make a choice between two very desirable wishes. For boys the wishes might be for a palomino horse with a silver saddle or a beautiful boat that could sail the seven seas. For girls the choice might lie between a child-size doll house or the gorgeous clothes of a princess.

All of life's choices are not so fabulous, yet our life *is* a constant choosing process. In making the right choices we are building our own "London Bridge" of the strong and lasting material known as *character*. Decisions may be such as these:

"Shall I skip choir today to play or watch TV, or shall I be present because I am needed and am expected to attend the rehearsal?"

"Shall I look in the book for the answer on this exam in order to make a good grade, or shall I be honest and take the lower grade, but study harder for the next exam?"

All decisions have their importance from such lesser ones to greater decisions concerning the acquiring of material or spiritual wealth. Decisions motivated by material ends have often led to bribery, robbery, tyranny, national disputes, even bloodshed. When we make the wrong decisions, we are tearing down our "London Bridge," our character, instead of building it.

Surely choices begin in childhood. The right choices should be encouraged and exemplified by parents and leaders. Parents want

14

their children to make a triumphant success in society, but parents often fail to realize that helping them make the right choices as children will determine their future success.

Today's youth is already an important part of our future world citizenship. Young people, prepared with a strong "London Bridge" of good character built upon right choices, will be entrusted with the positions of great responsibility.

"Blessed are the pure in heart, for they shall see God." (Matthew 5:8)

READERS DENY CHOIR WORK A MERE ACTIVITY FOR CHILDREN

Among the children's choir directors groups in the country, one of the oldest and most active is the Choristers Guild chapter of Lynchburg, Virginia. The members of the chapter have their problems as do you and I. All children's choir directors must at some time or other face the challenge of this modern day which relegates the church to a second or third place in the lives of both adults and children. Bishop Pike, of the Episcopal Diocese of California, has forcibly brought this situation to our attention in a recent issue of *Look* magazine.

The following clipping from the Lynchburg *News* states the case in another way. This clipping was sent me by Madeline Ingram, who wrote that a committee worked hard to express exactly the feelings of the Guild members. Reading it will help you. (R. K. J.)

TO THE EDITOR OF THE *NEWS*:
Sir:

The issue of your paper dated November 6 carried a report by Miss Robin Gross of the growing concern of the Lynchburg Elementary School Principals over the maze of "activities" surrounding the lives of young children in today's society. May we say that we, too, are much aware of the terrific pace today's children have to follow. It is a factor with which we also have constantly to deal.

We would take exception, however, with reporter Gross and the principals. Listed in the article among the various activities crowding the lives of children were church choir rehearsals. Our objection is based on the fact that youth choirs in Lynchburg are not a mere activity. They represent, rather, what has grown to be a vital part of the over-all program of Christian education within churches, as well as a means of active participation in the worship of God not otherwise available to children.

15

Parents in our city have come to recognize the educational and spiritual values of youth choirs, as can be seen obviously in the steady growth of these organizations during the past 20 years.

These values can be fully revealed to any who will see, during the coming Christmas season, when hundreds of children will not merely perform, but re-tell through music the story of the birth of Christ. The same is true for Lent, Easter, and other special seasons. In some churches the children's choirs are a part of every service of worship.

And for more than 20 years these young choristers have extended their talents beyond the doors of individual churches as they have joined together for the annual Junior Choir Festival. For nearly 10 years high schoolers have done the same thing in annual presentations of the Gymanfa Ganu.

This education has two purposes: first, a better understanding of God through the study of music; secondly, an active part in guiding self and others in worship through messages based on music.

Indeed it is true that our children are heavily burdened with activities. But let us not classify church choirs in such a category any more than we would Sunday school or services of worship.

LYNCHBURG CHORISTERS GUILD
(By Mrs. C. R. HUGHES, *Secretary*)

MUSIC CONTRIBUTES TO CHRISTIAN GROWTH
(A Report by DR. ARTHUR LESLIE JACOBS)

The General Assembly of the National Council of Churches in the U. S. A., of which the Council of Religious Education is a member body, met in December 1960 in San Francisco. My chief interest lay in the meetings of the Council. In just one afternoon those interested in the educational field had, unhappily, to choose between 24 separate topical meetings! For the first time, to my knowledge, music was officially included under the heading "Music Contributes to Christian Growth." The session was very ably handled by Mr. and Mrs. Richard Alford, who have built up the effective music program now operating in the First Methodist Church, Glendale, California. About 30 enthusiastic persons attended the session.

Unhappily, some religious education leaders still view music with suspicion. However, the attitudes of both groups, religious education directors and musicians, are becoming more Christian. Real respect and cooperation are growing, to the immense benefit of youngsters everywhere.

The use of the regular denominational hymnal was stressed, and much of the meeting centered around ways to use it. Mr. Alford outlined on the board what actually most denominational hymnals can teach youngsters. It can stress and teach:

The Consciousness of God	The Christian Church
The Life of Jesus	The Christian Family
A Christ-like Character	The Plan of the Universe
The Social Order	The Bible

Our job as Christian music educators is to put the hymnal into its proper focus. Part of this focus is to get the hymnal back into use in the homes of our boys and girls. A father singing "O God, our help in ages past," even in the shower, has a greater influence than anyone can imagine. Christian attitudes are quite largely caught rather than taught in the home. The songs and hymns which children learn do help to formulate their attitudes. As much as possible, boys and girls should learn the folk songs of other nations to stimulate the feeling of a world together. A good book to use for this purpose is *The Whole World Singing* by Edith Lovell Thomas (Friendship Press).

The change in attitudes towards music generally in the children's field has been a gradual one and is not yet complete. It is with modest pride that the Choristers Guild can state that the late Ruth Krehbiel Jacobs, through the influence of the Guild, helped to bring about such change. In the words of Dr. Edwin Dahlberg, immediate past-president of the National Council, speaking to us educators: "We must be something better than our best, for it is a sin to be just average."

Such a gathering was, for me, at once challenging, stimulating, and sobering. Ten thousand people should have been in attendance instead of some thirty-five hundred. We all need to be jolted, and jolted hard at times. Sorry is the individual who never feels the need to get out of his own little domain occasionally. Honestly, most of us fear to learn something new! Then there exists the tremendous divisiveness among Christians. We cast suspicious glances at the other fellow because he crosses a "t" or dots an "i" in a theologically different fashion from us. The singing of praises to God with hymns and spiritual songs may yet prove to be our most powerful adhesive and cohesive force. So you and I and children's choir directors face a stupendous task and duty with our children.

17

TO WHOM DOES THE CHOIR BELONG?

How do we speak of the Choir—as "mine" or "ours"? To whom do those pronouns refer? Who engaged us to be choir directors? To whom are we responsible for what we do with this office?

Each church musician would do well to answer some such questions at the opening of the fall season. A square look at the particular organization is imperative so that we may see clearly the fellowship and labors to which it has admitted us; to discover anew its chief function and the part we are to render toward its fulfillment, understanding our specific relationship to all the other members of its working forces.

Suppose we begin by stating our own concept of the church and its unique mission to society. Do we believe with Paul that it is the "household of God . . . with Christ Jesus as the cornerstone; in him the whole structure is welded together and rises into a sacred temple in the Lord, and in him you are yourselves built into this to form a habitation for God"? (Ephesians 2:19-22)

The welding together of the structure, in Paul's view, precedes the rising of the sacred temple. This image of wholeness with every member fitting into his proper place is good to hold in mind constantly, if the beauty and symmetry of the structure is preserved as it steadily rises according to the architect's design. No one section is unduly important or prominent, and yet each one is indispensable if kept in balance with the entire building.

"To form a habitation for God" is here made the supreme function of the church, the "household of God," which can be realized only as we learn and practice the art of being "welded together." We belong to it, according to this blueprint, rather than its belonging to us.

In another realm we take for granted that a manufacturer's plant is planned, equipped, and operated to make a carefully designed product. No department is allowed to work without consultation and co-operation with all the others. Each group is trained to do its part toward turning out the desired article. In the church, can her supreme end be achieved with any less foresight, supervision, and teamwork? Music is only one means to the achievement, set within the larger framework of Christian education, which in turn is one aspect of the church's over-arching building plans for God's habitation.

In the light of the importance and subtle nature of the church's task more, rather than less, is required of her in the organizing and working together of the staff—ministers of preaching, teaching, and music-making—if the choir, for example, performs its obligation in the

18

inclusive process of Christian nurture and worship to the glory of God and the education of children.

How can any music director get the distorted picture of himself which leads him to speak of a choir as "mine" or to reach the strange conclusion that he can conduct the musical portion of the church's production program without regular consultation with the Master-builder, the minister, and with his assistants, the foremen of the various construction units? Without this procedure, what provision can be made for an adequate check and balance on what must be a joint effort?

Some glimpses of integration of thought and activity in erecting the "sacred temple" that are now in progress may offer clues as to how to better our own ways of cultivating unity in our differing situations.

SETTING UP SCHEDULES: One minister and the director of music prepare together a year in advance an entire list of sermon themes and musical items that will harmonize with those themes.

A community church staff, after repeated attempts, secures from the public-school teachers an agreement to clear one afternoon a week after school to allow children's choir rehearsals to be held undisturbed by other demands.

Church-school study and music periods are jointly decided upon by leaders of each so as to supplement and complement both and to avoid conflicts of interest at any point.

CHOIR MEMBERSHIP: Choirs are open to all members of respective departments rather than to the most talented few, merely as the church recognizes its responsibility to follow the psalmist's democratic request: "Let the people praise thee, O God; let *all* the people praise thee." (Ps. 67:3)

CHURCH, SCHOOL, AND CHOIR—O N E HOUSEHOLD: Knowing the necessity of the church to see itself as a household comprised of all ages, a certain minister with the aid of his assistants works long and diligently to obtain one eleven o'clock Sunday service a year for observance of Church School Day as a substitute for the former Vesper service, used for this purpose when children are weary and a small congregation looks upon it as something extra to attend rather than a central and essential gathering of the entire household. In this are dramatized prime aspects of the study and musical education program: "The Bible in Our Church,"—living pictures of the sanctuary mosaics; "The Glorious Company,"—a presentation of the history of the Christian church, and other such features.

DEDICATION OF CHOIR IN CHANCEL TO MUSICAL MINISTRY: Through the combined concern of the music committee, minister, and choral director the children, youth, and adult choristers are commissioned for singing service by the church, assembled in Sunday morning worship. This is the form in which it has come to be expressed:

Choral Director: Your directors of music present you, the members of the Carillon and Crusader Choirs (Juniors and Junior High Girls at 9 o'clock; Pilgrim Fellowship and Chancel Choirs at 11 o'clock), on this first Sunday in Lent to be consecrated to the musical ministry of our church.

Minister: The church welcomes each one and all of you with gratitude for the important part your singing lends to our common worship. We unite silently with you as you sing your prayer that you may become worthy to offer music unto God.

Choristers (singing): "God of all lovely sounds, grant us a share

(Poem by Anne Lloyd)   In thy great harmonies of earth and air.
(Music—Dickinson)   Make us thy choristers, that we may be
                      Worthy to offer music unto thee."

Minister: God gives to us richly all things to enjoy. The earth is full of the loving-kindness of the Lord.

Choristers (spoken): We will sing to the Lord as long as we live!

Minister: Enter into his presence with songs of praise. Worship the Lord in the beauty of holiness.

Choristers: We would worship in his presence evermore and never forget the wonders he does.

Minister: Remember that the Son of Man comes not to be served, but to serve and to give his life for many.

Choristers: We would be ministers of life to all who hear us sing.

Minister: The Eternal inspires and consecrates you to comfort those who mourn and to give beauty for ashes and the garment of praise for the spirit of heaviness.

Congregation: Let us teach and help one another along the highway with psalms and hymns and Christian songs, all singing God's praises with joyful hearts. And whatever work we may have to do, do everything in the Name of the Lord Jesus.

Minister: Now to Him who by his power within us is able to do far more than we ever dare to ask or imagine—to Him be glory in the church through Jesus Christ forever.
All: Amen.

To whom does the choir belong? To the church that brought it into being. Its members and leaders are dedicated to the holy service of forming a "habitation for God" with all its household welded together, rising into a "sacred temple in the Lord."

EDITH LOVELL THOMAS

THE MEANING OF CHOIR MEMBERSHIP

The difference between being just a choir member and a *good* choir member lies within the definition of membership itself: what it means to each of us and how we treat it. Here are ten points which spell out choir membership.

M usic is the fundamental of choir membership. It is both cause and effect; it is the reason for being and the stimulus for participation.

E njoyment is the heart of choir membership. It is that intangible and contagious attitude which springs from within and is transmitted to those around us.

M inistry is the purpose of choir membership. It is the opportunity to give meaning to music; it is the reaching-out process through which our goal can be achieved.

B eauty is the soul of choir membership. Music without sound is beauty without being. Neither composer nor conductor can achieve beauty without the performer, who must re-create and bring it to life.

E nrichment is the result of choir membership. It is the inward satisfaction derived from the outward expression.

R esponsibility is the substance of choir membership. It is an obligation to church and to self which must be accepted willingly and prayerfully.

S ervice is the privilege of choir membership. It is the giving, which in turn allows us to receive.

H oliness is the spirit of choir membership. It is the impulse of Christian fellowship that transforms a group of voices into a great choir.

I nterest is the motivation for choir membership. It can be sustained only through active participation.

P articipation is the core of choir membership. It is the means of fulfillment; it is the dividing line between being just a choir member and being a *good* choir member.

> CLARK HILTON, *President*
> *of the Cathedral Choir*
> RICHARD ALFORD, *Minister of Music*
> First Methodist Church
> Glendale, California

The Value to the Home

"WANTED! PARENTS!"

Here is a strong plea from a strong Christian leader. Can you use it for the parents of your choir children?

WANTED! PARENTS!

Who will be as diligent in getting their children to church school as they are in getting them to weekday school. The church asks for only one day; the other for five days. Surely their spiritual development, their awakening wonder about God, the moral decisions they will face all their lives merit whatever help the church can give now. These areas of query and growth must be one-fifth as important, surely, as the reading, basketball, and the rest of the fine things every good school helps our children to know and do! Only the church seeks to do this spiritual job.

WANTED! PARENTS!

Who will themselves set the example for their children by going to church with them. What we do weighs a thousand times as much as what we say. And it is also important that we say grateful and positive things about the church in front of these children of ours. A disdainful, carping parent can turn a child's mind and heart forever from or even against the church. It is a pretty serious thing to do, this poisoning of a child's mind. It is a wonderful thing to do, however, to lead your own children toward God.

WANTED! PARENTS!

Who will honestly face the fact that scores of people (usually busy parents too) have volunteered and served faithfully for years to help your children—all of them. Turn about is fair play. It is a blessed thing to give as well as to receive, and most people who begin by giving time and strength and talents sacrificially for their own child—and other children too—end up confessing that they have received far more than they have given.

WANTED! PARENTS!

Who are aware that they will have these children of theirs for but a few swiftly passing years and who will, while the time is now, hopefully and lovingly help the church to help them. The dividends in wonderful young adults are astronomical when parents do cooperate, just as regrets can be sad when we let the chance go by and have to live with remorse. It is not "too late" now. Some day—and how the days and years fly by!—it *will* be too late. Wanted! Parents who care enough!

BOYNTON MERRILL

TWELVE RULES FOR RAISING DELINQUENT CHILDREN
(Reportedly published by the Police Department of Houston, Texas)

1. Begin with infancy by giving the child anything he wants. In this way he will grow up to believe the world owes him a living.
2. When he picks up bad words, laugh at him. This will make him think he's cute. It will also encourage him to pick up "cuter" phrases that will blow off the top of your head later on.
3. Never give him any spiritual training. Wait until he is 21 and then let him "decide for himself."

23

4. Avoid use of the word "wrong." It may develop a guilt complex. This will condition him to believe, later, when he is arrested for stealing a car, that society is against him and he is being persecuted.

5. Pick up everything he leaves lying around—books, shoes, clothing. Do everything for him so he will be experienced in throwing responsibility on others.

6. Let him read any printed matter he can get his hands on. Be careful that the silverware and drinking glasses are sterilized, but let his mind feast on garbage.

7. Quarrel frequently in the presence of your children. In this way they will not be too shocked when the home is broken up later.

8. Give a child all the spending money he wants. Never let him earn his own. Why should he have things as tough as you had them?

9. Satisfy his every craving for food, drink, and comfort. See that every sensual desire is gratified. Denial may lead to harmful friction.

10. Take his part against neighbors, teachers, and policemen. They are all prejudiced against your child.

11. When he gets into real trouble, apologize for yourself by saying, "I never could do anything with him."

12. Prepare for a life of grief. You will be most apt to have it!

The Value
of Good Leadership

COMMITMENT

I wonder how many of us are totally *committed?* Committed to what? I wish I knew. When I hear of music directors at odds with the Christian education director, it is difficult to doubt their commitment to anything beyond their own program. The director who binds his choirs to himself with a blind loyalty that makes progress impossible for his successor, what is *his* commitment? The director who gets by with as little preparation as possible, the director who makes no effort to improve, the one who sees only the flaws in his associates: what would happen if they should experience an unmistakable sense of commitment? What would happen to you and to me if our eyes were suddenly opened to the meager quality of our service and our dedication? And if we had the courage to pledge ourselves to a life of total commitment?

You have known perhaps two or three people, and so have I, whose very presence made one feel nobler and more worthy, people who without a word made you conscious of depths in your own self that you seldom sounded and of which you were hardly even aware. That is the power of total commitment, and it is a power that is available to everyone of us if we are willing to pay the price.

And the price? The price is a different one for every person. The price is the relinquishing of those very habits, desires, ambitions that

25

stand between us and total commitment. I know very well what the price is for me; and you probably know equally as well. Most of us spend our lives making small token payments, and never coming into possession of the treasure. And how we envy the courageous few who ventured everything—and gained everything!

"Either Christ is God, and Savior and Lord, or he isn't. And if he is, then he has to have all my time, all my devotion, all my life." And once having accepted this commitment, he directs our work. Life is a complicated mass of interrelated people. Every one of us is affected by the lives of many people. We cannot determine arbitrarily the lives that will be influenced by ours, or how, or when. But only when we permit a spirit greater than ourselves to express itself through us are we fulfilling the specific purpose for which we were created.

Christianity needs that kind of leadership. Nothing else is good enough. The church needs it in every area of its efforts. Church music needs it. "Christian character through children's choirs" becomes something more than a slogan when it is the field in which a total commitment directs us to work. It is said that every great achievement is the lengthened shadow of one man. But only when he becomes the shadow of a greater Being does his own shadow fall clearly and beneficently upon humanity. "All—or not at all."

RUTH KREHBIEL JACOBS

✕ PERSONAL INVENTORY

If you were not satisfied with your choir last season; if the attendance was not what you had hoped for, and discipline left something to be desired; if the children's response was half-hearted; then check your stock of the following:

1. ENTHUSIASM: Can you get excited about your work? Or is it an endurance contest? If you find it dull and depressing, you can be sure it is the same for the children. How you feel about your work is as important as how much you know about it. And how you feel about it is sure to be reflected in the children. You have a job that is worth getting enthusiastic about. Enjoy the fine experiences it brings you, and learn to forget the little irritations. What happens in rehearsal may influence a whole life.

2. CAN YOU OVERLOOK? Benjamin Franklin once said, "There is a time to wink and a time to see." Learn to distinguish between natural ordinary wiggling and intentional disturbance.

26

3. INTERESTING: Discipline, anyhow, is a sign of failure. If you could make the work interesting enough, there would be little trouble. More work and less worry! Learning music can be either exciting or dull. What it is to you, it will surely be to the children too.

4. HUMOR: If you can't see a joke, work on yourself until you can. If something funny happens in rehearsal, enjoy the situation and let everybody also enjoy it too. It's much better for everybody to laugh together than for some to be laughing at others. The better your sense of humor, the more you will enjoy your children.

5. HUMAN: Don't set yourself up as infallible. If you make a mistake, admit it. Keep a kindly human attitude. An act of kindness brings more respect than harsh disciplinary measures. More is accomplished through love than fear.

Every children's choir director should possess these five qualities in some degree. If you are dissatisfied with your choir, it will pay to take inventory of your supply of these five qualities.

ADAPTED BY R. K. J.

"HOW FAR DO YOU KNOW?"

It is a good question for each one of us to ponder at times. Recently propounded in the Guild office by an eight-year-old, it has set me to some contemplation. Sylvia, one of the numerous youngsters in the neighborhood who visit us more or less regularly, asked the secretary to sew some clothing for her doll. The secretary, Lora Krehbiel, Ruth's niece, thought a moment to reply: "In so far as I know, I can." Sylvia meditated a moment to come back with, in a completely serious manner: "How far do you know?" Who says that children do not touch upon the foibles of adults with profound statements or questions?

"How far do you know?" Once in awhile every one of us is faced with a situation, the solution to which places us in a dilemma. But of course none of us knows what the morrow may bring of sorrow, or despair, or even that we shall be living. Very often, however, we toss off an "As far as I know" as a stock answer when we actually do *not* know and should say so. Then again, we employ the phrase to put off the making of a decision. Then yet again, the phrase may be a deception when we really want and should say "No." Human fraility leads us to adopt the path of least resistance.

In so far as their spiritual and moral strength permits, leaders of children must follow a positive course. No group of people dare tamper with, twist, or put off the truth less than those who dare to lead boys and girls. No group is more privileged than children's choir directors, and none works with more powerful tools: religion and music.

He who leads a child helps fashion the future. Many an adult enjoys the creative occupation of raising beautiful flowers, of making furniture, of building a boat, or sewing a dress. What greater joy of creation, however, can anyone be privileged to enjoy than the building of Christian character in a child?

The children's choir director is God's interpreter. God's truth must continually be evidenced. Let me repeat the quotation from *World Scouting* by George S. Benson: "Great ideals and principles do not live from generation to generation just because they are right, and not even because they are carefully legislated. Ideals and principles continue from generation to generation only when they are built into the hearts of children as they grow up."

ARTHUR LESLIE JACOBS

YOUTH LEADERSHIP AND YOU

Creative ideas do not spring from groups; they spring from individuals. Being creative doesn't mean being different; it means the ability to see situations clearly and to meet them constructively.

The secret of your success lies chiefly with *you*. Those who achieve great things not only have high intellectual traits but also have persistence of motive and spirit, confidence in their abilities, and great strength of character.

At the beginning of every undertaking you are confronted with two ways of attacking it. One is with doubt and uncertainty; the other is with courage and confidence. To a certain extent you create or destroy the power by which to accomplish what you undertake. One mental approach strengthens and energizes, the other weakens and paralyzes.

A leader is a person who has influence with other people which causes them to:

1. Listen and agree on common goals;
2. Agree to follow leadership upon advice;
3. Go into action toward these goals.

To qualify as a youth leader, one must be worthy of emulation by the children. He must be a good citizen and have a good philosophy.

28

In the words of John Wesley: "Do all the good you can, by all the means you can, in all the ways you can, in all the places you can, at all the times you can, to all the people you can, as long as ever you can."

A Christian has been defined as a mind through which Christ thinks; a heart through which Christ loves; a hand through which Christ helps; a voice through which Christ speaks. What a worthy goal toward which to strive!

A youth leader must be sympathetic to the problems of children; he must have a knowledge of basic values of activity, and a skill in the activity. He must be alive with enthusiasm, and animated; yet he must be natural, relaxed, and pleasant. He may best exhibit these characteristics by adhering to certain principles of youth leadership:

1. Do more than your job. Leadership begins where the job ends.
2. Exercise power with people; don't try to force.
3. Don't be satisfied with the status quo. Meet people where they are, then raise them up.
4. Learn from failures and defeat. Don't rationalize, analyze.
5. A leader is his brother's keeper; he cares about the individual.
6. Advance your field of work; make a contribution.
7. Achieve. The best answer to all criticism is a going program.
8. Deserve and earn cooperation.
9. Develop leaders while leading.
10. Have ideals; fight for them. Don't be impatient, but don't abandon the ideals.
11. Radiate confidence and faith; don't show discouragement. Enthusiasm is contagious; a choir will be a reflection of its director.
12. Never have hidden motives; that turns leaders into dictators.
13. Rise above your own interests.
14. Always have time to listen and consult.

In order to achieve leadership qualities, observe at least some of these techniques:

1. Dare to be a pioneer; experiment.
2. Make decisions. Let people know where you stand.
3. Have definite goals; keep working toward them.
4. Be a spark plug; start good things going.
5. Start with people where they are.

6. Use gang leaders; sell individuals on an idea and the rest will follow.
7. Close the culture gap. Talk about things the children know.
8. Use community leaders.
9. Use children's heroes.
10. Use children's rules; give them a chance to experience success.
11. Play is their world. Keep interest and fun in your rehearsals.
12. Use children's questions; they are open doors.
13. Give credit liberally; the more you divide it, the more it multiples.
14. Remember that anticipation is often greater than realization.
15. Don't give them all the answers; let them find some themselves.
16. Solve problems by thinking, not by losing control.
17. Remember that you are teaching children, not music!
18. Find a niche for everyone.
19. See that everyone experiences the thrill of success.
20. Use spare moments to get better acquainted.
21. Feel the pulse of the group. Ask leading questions. What do they like?
22. Strike while the iron is hot.
23. Speak constructively; say nice things, or nothing.
24. Never show shock.
25. Keep a twinkle in your eye.
26. Remember that monotony is never in the task; it is always in the person.

It is a humbling thing to be an instrument in the hands of God. Let us strive to make of whatever knowledge may be ours a real dedication.

NORMA LOWDER

CHOIR MEMBERSHIP—WHO MAY ENTER?

"A choir is a dedicated group of people who have joyfully accepted the opportunities provided by their church for advancing the kingdom of God. Ultimate happiness probably results from creating something worthwhile, serving something besides one's self, and believing in something bigger than one's self. Singing in a church choir is an adventure in human service." (*Music and Worship in the Church,* Lovelace-Rice; Abingdon Press, 1960)

Herein lies the justification of any church choir. If our choirs, be they composed of adults or children, exist only as an art expression, we cannot conscientiously say that they belong in the church. For church music is not an expression of vocal or instrumental artistry and proficiency; it is rather a means of Christian service.

Music of the church must be available to all. In no other area of Christian service is the field a selective one. We do not limit membership in our church schools, no matter how crowded or inadequate we may consider the facilities; we may have double sessions, we may have crowded classrooms, but we deny no child his rightful place in the church school.

In our denomination, as no doubt in yours, we do not specify the number of persons who may serve with our Methodist Men and Women's Society of Christian Service. We may recommend a maximum number for our circles, thus giving more opportunity for service and expression to each member, but we do not thereby limit the total membership—we only form more circles.

How, then, can we as church musicians ever look upon the music of the church as anything other than Christian service? How can we fail to give immediate expression to all who wish to do service to God through church music? How dare we ask that one wait in order to serve his God? Such service knows no time nor season. When we speak of the "singing church" we surely must be speaking of its total membership!

Within the Methodist Youth Fellowship there are four areas of service: that to (1) the Church; (2) the Church School; (3) the Evening Fellowship; (4) the Youth Choir. Obviously music is not intended to be something which only the very talented can do. "But," you ask, "what about the ones who can't carry a tune? Surely you do not let them in your choir!"

We maintain that any person who is normal, physically and mentally, can be taught to sing. Only once have we had a teen-ager come to us who could not seem to hear or to match tones. It seemed as though his voice would not move in any direction, nor his ear hear any sound. Yet after a year and a half of patient work on his part and ours, and after infinite patience and encouragement from members of the choir, this boy has come to the place where he can sing nearly anything we put before him. His parents vow and declare that this is responsible for his regular attendance at church and church school. Before joining the choir, he came very seldom; yet he has missed only one Sunday and no rehearsal since joining the group. How could we

31

live with ourselves had we been responsible for denying this boy the means of Christian service that will probably tie him closer to the church throughout his entire lifetime? You have probably heard it said that volunteers often sing better than they can; professionals never do. Here is one who regularly sings "better than he can."

"The 9-to-12-year-old brings to a peak of perfection all of the physical, mental and emotional potentialities he showed when he entered the first grade. He is on the verge of the sometimes awkward, oftentimes painful period called adolescence. For a short time he is master of all he surveys. He is an affectionate extrovert, capable of magnificent accomplishments in his own mind and actually able to succeed at many complicated tasks." (*op. cit.*) I am convinced that we who work with children sell our children short; their only limitations are those that we put upon them.

(Children have astute and penetrating minds. We should never try to restrict our repertoire, for example, to what little minds can comprehend. They need music which, as Dr. Whittlesey has said, is "music they can grow into, not out of." Billy Graham has said, "The gospel is so simple a child can understand it and so complicated that theologians cannot." Children can sing anything but oratorios and the vast choruses of church music literature; at that, they are capable of doing many solo passages from the great oratorios in a manner that far surpasses the ability of the average soloist. In any event, we must use the most challenging texts and music available. Ruth Jacobs said, "Juniors like to feel that they are doing something worthwhile. You gain their allegiance by expecting the best they have to give.")

I once saw a sign posted in a quiet church hall which read: "Who dares to teach must never cease to learn." Certainly our earnest prayer should be that we who dare to direct a children's choir, who hold in our hands the future of our churches, and indeed of our very existence, must never stop searching for truths and for learning.

NORMA LOWDER

ON BEING A DIRECTOR OF MUSIC

(From an address by WARREN MARTIN to the graduating class
of Westminster Choir College. Used by permission.)

Eating an ice cream cone provides one kind of satisfaction. Reading *Hamlet* provides another kind. Nothing is wrong with either kind of satisfaction—they are just very different. There is much to be said for eating ice cream, in fact there are many times when ice cream is definitely more satisfying than Shakespeare; but the person who can enjoy Shakespeare as sincerely as he enjoys ice cream is better off than the person who lives his life on the ice cream level. Civilized, mature, educated people (this can mean you!) find happiness far above the ice cream level. They find happiness not only in things which please themselves but also in things they do with other people and for other people.

Take music. It almost goes without saying that a great deal of personal gratification is to be gotten from listening to music and knowing music and performing music. But discerning and ambitious people find a higher quality of gratification in leading other people in understanding, performing, and enjoying music. This satisfaction becomes real fulfillment when that leadership is exercised in places where music meets an honest need, places where music does an honest good, places such as churches.

A minister of music is not just a musician who happens to work in a church. Being a good musician is a splendid thing, but being a minister of music involves more than musical excellence. Nor is a minister of music a devout and active church worker who happens to dabble in music. Religion is poorly served by casual or inferior music. In the context of the phrase "minister of the gospel" a minister of music can well be said to reveal the word of God in his own appropriate way—by using the expressive power of music to enhance sacred words. The very function of singing in a service of worship is to set forth words in a different and more beautiful way than speaking can—not a better way, but a special and appealing way.

The word "minister" in the context of the phrase "ministering to people" may be used to describe the process by which a minister of music works to help the people who are involved in his program in a tremendous number of big and little ways—from bringing them together to find simple enjoyment and self-expression in music-making to giving them insights into greatness of thought and beauty of feeling to which they could never aspire as individuals. Music can comfort, music can combat loneliness, music can uplift the spirit, music can help people to love each other better. The minister of music is truly in a position to "minister to the people."

Making decisions is something we are all faced with daily, unless we are children or privates in the army. Any position of leadership brings with it large doses of decision-making. Some of the hardest decisions in a new church position are those arising from honest differences of opinion between you and the minister, you and the music committee, or you and the more strong-minded of your choir members. Shall you meekly give in? Shall you insist on "your way"? Shall we compromise, and rely on tact and persuasion to gain what you feel is best, later on? Percentage-wise, the latter course is the one to follow 90% of the time.

No matter how strong your convictions may be, or how confident you are that your background and training support your opinion, you must consider that harmonious personal relationships are of the greatest importance in your line of work. In a new church position, start by fitting in as gracefully as possible with the prevailing policies. Gradually, as you get to know the people and the situation, you can begin working to change the things you are sure need changing. Adaptability is not spinelessness. The fact that you work slowly and carefully toward a goal may make it more secure when you finally reach it.

Music is a magnificent language, but a minister of music will still find a great deal of use for English. You must be able to talk. You may be an excellent musician, you may love people, you may be strong in your personal religious faith, you may have a keen mind, and determination, and ambition, and patience and a dozen other praiseworthy qualities, but if you can't express yourself in words with a serviceable degree of clearness and fluency, you may as well resign your job and take up bird-watching. You don't need elegance or eloquence; what you do need is the ability to gather your ideas together in an orderly way and present them in plain words, whenever and wherever it may be helpful in your work.

It would be wonderful if, in your church job, you could always use the finest music and sing in the finest way, and work with everyone in an exclusively harmonious and mutually appreciative atmosphere. But most voices are just average, and the people with whom you work in churches are as human as anyone else, sometimes more so. You should have clearly in your mind various ideals—ideals of musical quality, of organizational effectiveness, of personal achievement. But these ideals must bow to common sense. Bow, not grovel! From your ideals you must derive objectives. For such objectives you will work out plans. And to each plan you will apply as much skill, enthusiasm, and patience as you can muster. To formulate your ideals you must dream—the kind of dreaming you do with your eyes and ears wide open. To reach objectives you must work, and keep on working, and not give up.

34

"IF I WERE A CHOIR DIRECTOR"

(Remarks by Methodist Bishop Northcott)

If I were a choir director, I'd buy a book. I would feel, no matter how good I might think myself to be, that I still had a lot to learn. No amount of natural talent or loving praise from my friends should blind me to the fact that a broad appreciation of the history and significance of music in the life of the church is essential to my greatest success. I'd buy a book, and I'd find some fresh appreciation of the place of music in human life.

I'd take a trip. Even a choir director needs to get away from his task once in a while. Being at the job a long time without a break is not always a sign of efficiency and greatest service.

When a choir director takes a trip, I mean that he should see what others are doing. As he hears other choirs and soloists sing in Bachville, he may come home more grateful than ever for what he has to work with in Wesleyana.

While visitation may teach the choir director some things that he should strive to avoid, it is more often true that he can learn something that will be helpful and worth striving for back home. Some of the finest improvements in certain churches I have known have come because someone has taken a trip and brought some good new ideas back home with him.

Yes, if I were a choir director, every once in a while I would like to see what others are doing. Maybe I'd learn that often the most effective directors are the least conspicuous ones.

If I were a choir director, I'd make a friend. A person does his best work when there are harmonious relationships and an understanding of problems and opportunities involved. This suggests to me that if I were a choir director, I would surely want to be on good terms with the minister. It helps, too, if the minister understands something of the real significance of music.

The director of music has an opportunity for friendly cooperation with the music committee of the church, where frequent and frank conferences may be held in order to maintain and improve the musical phase of the church's work.

Personally, I cannot see how a helpful service of worship can be carried on consistently without a sense of respect and friendship existing between the minister of the church and the choir director.

If I were a choir director, I'd belong to the team. I would ever keep in mind that I am working with others. The purpose is not to feature myself or any other star performers, but rather to utilize available talent to best serve the cause. When you are on the team, you will do some things that you would not otherwise do. There are some things likewise that you will find you cannot do.

Selfish star players cannot be used effectively in the service of the church. Pastors who talk through a solo or the anthem are not exhibiting team play, to say the least. Soloists or others who sneak out after the anthem has been sung are not doing teamwork. I doubt whether their presence in the choir offsets the psychological harm they do to the worshiping congregation as attentive eyes watch their cautious exit.

If I were a choir director, I'd glorify my faith. I would realize that basic to all as a leader in sacred music is sound Christian character. People everywhere are so constituted that they do not appreciate efforts of a spiritual leader, as a minister of music ought to be, if they do not have confidence in him as a person. If I were a choir director, I would like to demonstrate what the Christian faith can do through me as I strive to follow the example of Christ.

Yes, if I were a choir director, I'd buy a book, I'd take a trip, I'd make a friend, I'd belong to the team, I'd glorify my faith.

To this Norma Lowder comments: It is, then, up to each of us to turn to our local churches, renewed in strength and spirit, as we work toward building Christian character through children's choirs. The children with whom we work are as fragile as a bubble and as powerful as atomic energy. Let us strive unceasingly to make of this energy so powerful a force that when we meet our Master, our books may truly balance. This is the immortality which Ruth Jacobs has achieved and toward which each of us must yet work.

MINISTRY OF MUSIC CHART
designed by
WILLIAM CARNCROSS, Trinity Methodist Church
El Paso, Texas to help the church visualize the
scope of the Music Ministry.

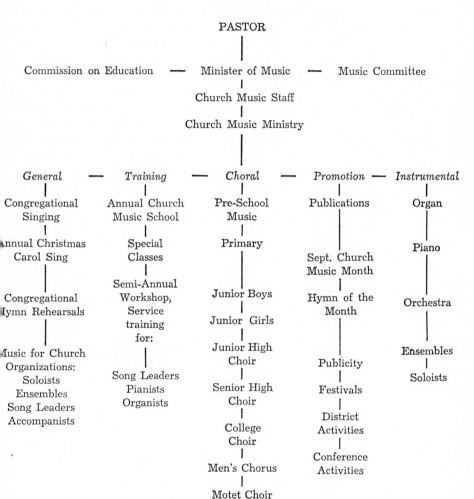

PASTOR

Commission on Education — Minister of Music — Music Committee

Church Music Staff

Church Music Ministry

General	*Training*	*Choral*	*Promotion*	*Instrumental*
Congregational Singing	Annual Church Music School	Pre-School Music	Publications	Organ
Annual Christmas Carol Sing	Special Classes	Primary		Piano
	Semi-Annual		Sept. Church Music Month	
Congregational Hymn Rehearsals	Workshop, Service training for:	Junior Boys	Hymn of the Month	Orchestra
		Junior Girls		
Music for Church Organizations:		Junior High Choir		Ensembles
Soloists	Song Leaders		Publicity	
Ensembles	Pianists	Senior High Choir	Festivals	Soloists
Song Leaders	Organists			
Accompanists		College Choir	District Activities	
		Men's Chorus	Conference Activities	
		Motet Choir		

DIAGNOSIS FOR AN AILING CHOIR PROGRAM

(as given by "Doctor" RUTH JACOBS)

THE PROBLEM

Dear Mrs. Jacobs:

We have the music, the physical facilities, the trained personnel. In fact, we have all but the most important thing: the enthusiastic support and participation of the congregation. We have six choirs going at the present time. Perhaps I should say that they are meeting at the prescribed times, but they are not being attended by the children or supported by the parents as they should be. This is also true of the chancel choir. There are approximately 30 members in a church of more than 1800 members. What is wrong? Where have I failed?

DIAGNOSIS

1. Are the people as indifferent in other areas of the church life?
2. Did you follow a much-loved director?
3. Does the minister give the program his active support?
4. Have you put the music committee to work on the problem?
5. Is the total church program well integrated?
6. Is there a serious transportation problem?
7. Is the school system strong, with many outside activities?
8. Is there an overabundance of activities for the children?
9. Are the choir quarters attractive?
10. Have you made use of the musically trained people in the church?
11. What have you done to gain and maintain interest?
12. Is your own training adequate to gain the respect of the people?
13. Is there something in your personality that repels people?

TRIAL REMEDIES (Numbers correspond to the diagnosis numbers)

1. Make a friend of the religious education director. Perhaps you can plan some attack on the irregularity together. Learn to know the parents; visit them in their homes; learn to state the values of the choir experience convincingly. Ask for their help in some *specific* way. Get your Choir Guild to work on the problem of wider interest. Use your church paper to spark interest. Is there a trained advertising man in the church who could help you?

2. If so, follow the established pattern, and make changes slowly. Never belittle your predecessor. Be patient, but persistent.

3. Find some good reason to have the pastor visit rehearsals frequently. Plan the major musical events of the year together. Make sure that the choirs are an asset whenever they appear.

4. Read Chapter XI in Vivian Morsch's *The Use of Music in Christian Education* (Westminster Press) for ideas on making the music committee a functioning unit.

5. Find ways to make the music department helpful to the other organizations. Do you know what music is being used in the church school? Could you help with the music there? This would be a good way to learn to know the children, and let them learn to know you.

6. Divide the city into school areas and find a responsible transportation chairman for each area. Car pools will help. Perhaps rehearsals should be changed to a more convenient time. With some assistance several choirs can meet at the same time. Or perhaps you could hold area rehearsals in area homes, a different school area every afternoon.

7. Don't try to compete. Set your dates so as not to conflict. Attend the school affairs. Show your interest.

8. Can you give the parents convincing arguments for the value of the choir experience? Incorporate the children's other interests in your choir program. Instrumental accompaniments, operettas, field trips, camping, etc.

9. If drab, give choir quarters a face-lifting. Let the children help plan and execute the project. Do you make good use of your bulletin board? Interesting charts and pictures about? Seasonal decorations?

10. Use musically trained members and give them responsibility. Let them take some of the choirs if they are capable of doing so. Let them lead the singing in the church school, and plan a hymn-learning program for them to follow. If there are no trained leaders, select promising young people, train them and use them. Don't try to do everything yourself.

11. Find someone who can advise you on effective publicity. Keep the church reminded of choir values. Have a competition within the choirs or between choirs for the greatest growth in attendance average. Get better acquainted with the church as a whole. Find something interesting for the choirs to do. Create

some real incentive for regularity—maybe a choir camp. Do you use the choristers' pin and the requirements that apply to it? Or the service cross?

12. Read the teachers' aid published by your denomination. Glean ideas from church music publications. Take notes on ideas that pop into your head; take time to work them out carefully before inaugurating them. Keep in touch with other music directors in your city. Set yourself a program of reading and study, and stick to it. Get yourself "recharged" regularly at some special conference.

13. When it comes right down to the root of a situation, the success or failure of a choir program is in proportion to the leader's ability to win and hold the respect and affection of the people with whom he works. Get the advice of some impartial person. Uncover your weaknesses and make it a point to conquer them.

RELAX!

No amount of musicianship and know-how will make a good children's choir director. Children may *respect* knowledge, but they *respond* to attitude.

Last summer in a seminar in Portland, Oregon, the members of the class were required to sing a simple hymn as they would sing it for their Primary Choir. By the end of the week everyone had improved in simplicity of tone and naturalness of manner, but the class found themselves responding more happily to some leaders than to others, exactly as they might expect the children to do. A vote at the end of the session showed that there were three members to whom everyone responded more happily than to any of the others. It was an interesting revelation to all of us, the teacher included, to discover that all three had a large share of three qualities: (1) They were natural and simple with no affectation; (2) they were friendly; (3) they created an atmosphere of togetherness. Those three qualities may be the clue to successful work with children.

DAY KAMMEYER, of El Segundo (California) Methodist Church, must have made the same discovery, judging from an article in the Choral Conductors Guild publication. "The relaxed attitude in training a junior choir cannot be over-emphasized. Children are keenly aware of existing tensions within their teachers and will reflect them. We who direct junior choirs must not develop habits of leadership which block the flow of their natural creative expression, but plan our

40

work to avoid a too-little-too-late situation. A child learns rapidly if he feels that he is not obliged to do so. Is your jaw set tightly, lips thrust forward in unnatural grimaces? Are wrists and fingers held stiffly, and your beat angular and brittle? Around the waist line, are you taut like a drum? Often adults sing in spite of such tensions, but children will not."

Actual conducting is of very minor importance with children. If the motion of the hand interferes with natural singing, it is better not to use the hands at all. For keeping an even tempo and a smooth continuous line I have found that a weight on a string, used as a pendulum, is vastly more effective than the smoothest hand-motion. The very fact that the eyes are following the up-swing of the pendulum encourages a lift to the singing. And the impersonal, unaccented, noiseless movement of the pendulum makes for the same kind of singing, which is a marvelous antidote to the series of vocal bumps and jolts that are so generally accepted as singing.

Obviously not even the most uninhibited among us would consider swinging a pendulum before his choir on a Sunday morning. But if, in rehearsal, the children have experienced the even movement of phrases and have sung them in that fashion week after week, they are likely to sing in the same manner on Sunday morning, regardless of whatever motions their director may consider necessary. In fact, once a number is learned, the children will sing according to habit. All they need is the rhythmic support of the organ, and there is no need for the director to become hot and bothered.

So, if you would enjoy your children's choir, and if you would make it enjoyable for the children too—relax!

RUTH KREHBIEL JACOBS

"LORD, KEEP ME GROWING!"

LORD, KEEP ME GROWING!
I give thee thanks for the divine laws of growth that I see in the lives and minds of my children.
Wilt thou grant that I may find them always working out their will in myself.
Save me from stagnation of spirit.
Spare me, O God, the lethargy of mind that comes at middle age.
Keep me free from the indolence of interest that would draw back from the new and the untried.
Keep me from the sameness of purpose that flinches at a new task.

41

Give me the spirit that seeks new ideas, and welcomes them when
they are found.
Grant me the courage to face without prejudice any challenge to my
long-accepted views.
May I have patience to live with new books, insight to enjoy new
friends, vigor of mind to push out into the unexplored.
Keep me aware, O Lord, aware of my time, of its moods, of its powers,
of its dangers.
Thus in body, mind, and spirit may I forget the things that are behind
and stretch forward to all that lies before.
Thus, Lord, keep me growing. Amen.

ANON.

* * * * *

If you succeed without sacrifice,
Someone has sacrified before you.
If you sacrifice without success,
Someone will succeed after you.

EDWARD JUDSON

UNDERSTANDING

(A paraphrase of 1 Corinthians 13:1-13 by ELOUISE RIVINIUS, as
found in a Sunday Bulletin of the Episcopal Church of St. John the
Divine, Houston, Texas)

"Though I teach with the skill of the finest teachers, and have not
understanding, I am become only a clever speaker and charming en-
tertainer. And though I understand all techniques and all methods,
and though I have much training, so that I feel quite competent, but
have no understanding of the way my pupils think, it is not enough.

"And if I spend many hours in lesson preparation, and become
tense and nervous with the strain, but have no understanding of the
personal problems of my pupils, it still is not enough.

"The understanding teacher is very patient, very kind; is not
shocked when young people bring him their confidences; does not gos-
sip; is not easily discouraged; does not behave himself in ways that are
unworthy, but is at all times a living example to his students of the
good Way of Life of which he speaks. Understanding never fails. But
whether there be materials, they shall become obsolete; whether there
be techniques, they shall be abandoned; for we know only a little, and
can pass on to our children only a little; but when we have under-

42

standing, then all our efforts will become creative, and our influence will live forever in the lives of our pupils.

"When I was a child, I spoke with immaturity, my emotions were uncontrolled and I behaved childishly; but now that I am an adult, I must face life as it is, with courage and understanding. And now abideth skill, devotion, understanding, these three, and the greatest of these is understanding."

A TEACHER'S PRAYER

Lord, I thank thee for the chance to work at a task that makes the hours so full. Let me use those hours to guide the precious lives entrusted to my care in ways of goodness. Help me to be calm in the face of disturbance, kind to all regardless of circumstances, tolerant when understanding is lacking, and faithful in duties great and small. I pray for the strength of mind and body to do what is expected of me without losing my willing spirit. Forgive the mistakes I made this day, and give me wisdom to correct them. In the name of the Great Teacher I pray. Amen.

FRANCES H. BUTLER

MY CODE

I have to live with myself, and so
I want to be fit for myself to know.

I want to be able, as days go by,
Always to look myself straight in the eye.
I don't want to stand, with the setting sun,
And hate myself for the things I've done.

I want to go out with my head erect;
I want to deserve all men's respect;
But here in the struggle for fame and pelf,
I want to be able to like myself.

I don't want to look at myself and know
That I'm bluster and bluff and empty show.

I never can fool myself, and so
Whatever happens, I want to be
Self-respecting and conscience-free.

ANON.

43

EDUCATORS—NOT SOLOISTS!

The successful director of children's choirs derives his greatest reward from noting and realizing the developmental progress and process of the children with whom he works. The individual who is interested primarily in his own performance should think twice about his own ideas regarding the children's choir and his own attitudes toward them.

Today the trend in music for music educators is primarily to training a very large body of people who are genuinely interested in making music a definite part of their lives, and of every-day lives at that, rather than in high-grade professional performance. The performance level of persons who make their living in performing only is at such a high level that most of us can never attain fully to it, or even begin to get there. Thus we must put our talents to work in helping other people.

It seems to me that the greatest desire must be to help others, and in your case, youngsters. The slogan of our organization is "The Development of Christian Character Through Children's Choirs." There can be no greater purpose or aim than such a one as the Guild suggests. For the level of perfection of a children's choir is not the perfection of an older group, nor even of an adult group, nor certainly of yourself. We must always realize that there exist degrees of perfection. What may be perfectly wonderful and fine at the youngster's level of performance is way down the ladder for an adult.

It seems to me, further, that we must recognize that children will be wiggly, and that a certain amount of inattention will happen in any rehearsal, even in the very best. Children are not little angels and cannot be expected to be such. The only time that they may ever be considered so is by their papas and mamas when they walk down the aisle to the chancel or choir loft in a service of worship. They are human beings in their own right, subject to all the foibles, weaknesses and problems that all the rest of us possess.

MARGARET KENDRICK

(The article above was sent in by that well-known educator, MARGARET KENDRICK, of Atlanta, Georgia, in answer to a letter from a choir director asking for suggestions about disciplinary problems. This director, an accomplished organist and pianist, wrote: "I am debating whether to keep on or not. I feel inadequate; I can't control the somewhat constant talking of the children. I sent a few home. . . . In a way, I would rather interpret music via my own playing than struggle with ways and means of keeping up children's interest. It seems as though the bulk of the time is spent in learning words and music, and that interpretation tends to become secondary.")

"ARE YOU A LEADER?"

How many young choirs are there in your town? Do you personally know their directors? Do you ever meet together to discuss mutual problems? Or is each choir maintained in its own little church-island?

A local Choristers Guild chapter is the answer to many problems and a source of inspiration to all directors. The discovery that all of us have many of the same problems, or that one of us has found a gimmick that works for her and may work for us, is worth the energy and time it takes to go to a meeting.

The Guild should be composed of all directors of children's and youth choirs, any interested potential choir directors, and all others who are concerned with the children's choir movement.

Meetings may be held at the discretion of the group, but once a month seems highly desirable for getting together. The Lynchburg (Virginia) chapter—the first to organize—finds that Saturday afternoons are best for its meetings. Held in churches, the chapter meetings have several hosts for each gathering. A brief fellowship hour over simple refreshments is held before business actually begins. Officers are elected for one year only, and care is taken to have all denominations in the Guild represented on committees.

Meetings should provide opportunities for attention to business matters, sharing of ideas, inspirational talks, and the cultivation of friendships. A local chapter can provide for seminars or workshops which will further animate the group. Here are a few suggested topics for use in such meetings:

1. Panel discussions on matters of mutual interest.
2. Talks by one or more ministers.
3. A dinner meeting for our ministers.
4. A demonstration by a public school music teacher.
5. A talk by a director of Christian education.
6. A visiting lecturer from a nearby town.
7. Planning for festivals.
8. A session on the selection, care, and use of vestments.
9. A study of new music.

10. A demonstration of musical instruments suitable for use with children's voices.
11. And one meeting "just for fun"!

Madeline Ingram

"GREAT EXPECTATIONS"

Ours is a large church situated on the edge of the downtown area. It has a membership of 6,050—mostly family groups who travel three to six miles to attend church.

Our two rehearsal rooms, one for children and one for adults, are shaped as half-circles, joined with seldom-used folding doors. The two rooms together form a huge circle. These rooms are used only by the music department, so that we can leave our set-up from day to day and week to week.

The Carol Choir (4th through 6th grades) is a mixed group. They use the adult choir room for rehearsal, for it is built with risers. This makes it easier to see and be seen, as well as making for better sound. Our Sunday church school has two sessions running simultaneously with the church services. In planning for the Carol Choir it is necessary to know which session the child attends. Approximately 60% of the children attend the 9:30 A.M. session, and 40% the 10:50 session. Thus we have a natural division.

The two groups rehearse everything together, but at the final rehearsal before they are to sing in the morning service (third Sunday of each month) each group works alone for a short time to familiarize themselves with the feel of the smaller group. Since the second session church school group sings for the 9:30 service when the Junior High and Senior High choirs are responsible for the service, we try to select music that will adapt itself to these groups and allow the use of the Carol Choir as a solo group, either alone or with the Junior High Choir. We try always to use music which will be sung at both services. The group which sings at the 10:50 service has as its accompanying choir the adult Sanctuary Choir.

Each children's choir has a one-hour rehearsal. Children under twelve are requested and expected to work on a notebook. This is part of our regular choir work. As the children come, I check their notebooks and give them any new pages. To keep a record of the notebook, and whether each child brings his regularly or not, the first page has a hymn with the staff, the stems of the notes, the bar-line and key signature—everything except notes and words! The notes are added, one each week, with a special rubber stamp I had made. The child

46

must decide by the end of the year, as his notes accumulate, what the hymn is, and write in the first stanza, give the composer, the author, and other data that he can find about it. To make it a bit harder, I usually change the key from the one in the hymnal. All this helps in the use of the hymnal, which nearly all the children have earned through their notebook credits and attendance credits each year.

Remember Dickens' book *Great Expectations?* Those two words are the key words in children's choir work. I *expect* to have no disciplinary problems; consequently we don't! I *expect* high standards, musically and spiritually; so we get them! We never have resorted to any kind of social "come-on." I just can't find time to teach "fun songs." I have a deep-seated conviction that children and young people have all the play and recreation that they need in their many school activities. When they join our choirs, they join to attain something spiritual, for youth is deeply spiritual; to find means of self-expression, for youth needs to express itself; to feel that they are serving instead of getting, for youth wants to give of itself, not always have things done for it.

As to techniques, I try to have a far-range goal, and many shorter-range goals, and then proceed with every means I can to reach those goals. If there is one thought that is paramount in our work with children, it is that we must not sell our children short. They are capable of wonderful things. They are limited only by the vision of their director. If that sounds like Ruth Jacobs—that is where I learned it!

Cecil Lapo, *Director of Music*
St. Luke Methodist Church
Oklahoma City, Oklahoma

PREPARING CHILDREN'S CHOIRS FOR PUBLIC APPEARANCE

Children's choirs can get stage fright just as devastating as that of the individual singer. Their voices disappear into nothing but a breathy murmur; they invariably flat or sing sharp in shrill, unlovely voices; they look blank when a new stanza comes along and stumble over the first words; they fail to start singing at the proper time; or, worse still, they fail to *stop* singing at the proper time. It can be a ghastly experience for performers and congregation too—not to mention the poor director! But there are certain steps their director can take well in advance of public appearance, which will greatly reduce the chance of catastrophe.

One step is to be sure to rehearse several times in the place where the public appearance is to take place—usually the choir loft. Try to make the circumstances of the rehearsal conform as nearly as possible to the circumstances of the performance: use organ accompaniment, have some choir mothers sitting in the pews, have the minister present, and even have the children wear their vestments. Try to keep the reverent attitude which will make for quiet worship.

Another step is to have every detail of the performance well-planned in advance and explained to the children. Elementary school children will easily panic in the face of the unknown or unexpected. Don't try any new interpretations or procedures at the last minute. Acquaint them in advance, and thoroughly, with every contingency. Of course the unexpected is bound to occur, but try to make it a minor event, through your thorough advance planning. A well-disciplined choir (using "disciplined" in a broader sense than mere behavior) has far less chance for stage fright than the one governed by happenstance.

A third step is to accustom your choir to public performance by degrees. This may sound impossible, but it can be done easily by having them sing before their own Sunday school department several times before attempting to sing for a formal church service. This singing may be the anthem soon to be sung in church, or it may be merely a special hymn or even just a stanza of the regular Sunday school hymn. But have them stand before the group in proper formation and follow the standard choir discipline. Singing before their friends may make them feel silly, but it will not give them stage fright.

ROSEMARY HADLER

(Adapted from *The Younger Choirs,* Lorenz Pub. Co., 1960. Used by permission.)

VARIETY AND FRESH APPROACHES IN REHEARSAL

The church is located in the center of a rapidly growing residential area of Tulsa. The membership is 1,050. Our choir program consists of eleven groups in five categories:

PRIMARY—First Grade Choir of 40; Second and Third Grade Choirs of 40 each.

JUNIOR—Boys Junior Choir of 30; Girls Junior Choir of 30.

JUNIOR HIGH—Junior High Choir of 50; two Handbell Choirs of 10 each.

SENIOR HIGH—Senior High Choir of 50.

ADULT—two Adult Choirs of 40 each.

There is no duplication of membership.

The choir rehearsal room is a large L-shaped, dual-purpose room with a wooden folding-door divider. Thus we can arrange several different set-ups. When combined groups are at work, the room can easily be arranged to accommodate 100 choristers. The minister of music's office, the music library, and robing facilities are in adjoining rooms.

All choirs up through Senior High rehearse one hour per week. A choir book is given to each of the children at the beginning of the choir year. The theme of work in the choir is the same as that in the "Faith and Life Curriculum" of the church school. Hymns are learned that parallel this theme, and related projects are studied or used. Rehearsals begin and close with prayers led by selected members of the choirs. A period of vocalization and ear-training follows.

All choirs (including adults) memorize their music. With children we often write the words on the board, then erase parts of the text to check their memory.

The choir book contains materials dealing with the study projects: how the indexes of the hymnal are used; the church year; the meaning of and parts of the services of worship; church and seasonal symbols; and so on.

Our approach to music theory is that we are learning to read a musical road map. When we can read and understand the signs on a page of music, we can make a good trip without accidents or wrong turns. It is great fun and very interesting to see how easily map symbols align themselves with musical symbols.

Musical baseball (or football or basketball) with competition between teams is an excellent way for us to check the growth and progress of each voice. Teams are appointed in many different ways to avoid loading any side. Behavior in rehearsals must be as dignified as in church; we must never forget how to act when "in uniform."

The First Grade Choir does not sing in services. The Second and Third Graders sing twice a year and present a musical play for a fellowship supper. The Junior Choirs appear in services of worship every five weeks. The Junior High and Senior High Choirs lead the entire service once every five weeks and give the two adult choirs a day off.

Changing patterns and ways of presenting materials seem to keep the youngsters alert and ready for new things, rather than throwing them off balance. Even though I use a written lesson plan for each rehearsal, I try to make sure that we have a new touch and approach each week. As long as I am eager for what will happen next week, I can count on the children being the same.

Does it work? Last year only two of our choirs averaged below 50% in attendance!

JAMES STEWART BOLES, *Director of Music*
John Knox Presbyterian Church
Tulsa, Oklahoma

SUGGESTIONS FOR MEMORIZATION

No one seems to have discovered a foolproof method for checking memory work, but here are some ideas that have worked for others:

Divide the choir into teams, have one choir mother responsible for each team, and encourage competition between the teams. The checking can easily be done before rehearsal. Keep a chart in the choir room recording the progress of each team. Let the children do as they prefer: say or sing the words. And finally, there are no normal children who cannot memorize, but many of them may need help in learning *how* to memorize. Other suggestions:

1. Say the words rhythmically.
2. Learn the first word of each line as a guide.
3. Learn only one stanza at a time.
4. Study the words the first thing in the morning.
5. Just before going to sleep, repeat them.
6. Keep a record of the time it takes to learn the first stanza, and try to learn each stanza a little faster than the one before.
7. Learn one *well,* before tackling the next.

(R. K. J.)

CLUES TO CHOIR DISCIPLINE

1. The *interested* child is seldom a problem.
2. "Whoso would kindle others must first himself glow."
3. To work successfully with children one must *enjoy* them.
4. The better we *understand* children, the easier it is to guide them.
5. Children need to feel important to *you.*
6. The better you know a child's *background,* the better you can deal with him.
7. The children must be *ready* for what they are to learn.
8. If we choose music beyond their experience and comprehension, and are not able to bring it into *their range of understanding,* we are inviting trouble.
9. Make the choir *important* to the children.
10. Let the children *help* set up choir standards and rules.

50

11. A long-range plan helps; children need *objectives.*
12. Activity is *natural;* plan your rehearsal to allow for it.
13. Make the rehearsal room as interesting and *attractive* as possible.
14. Plan your rehearsals *carefully.*
15. *Know your music.*
16. No matter what happens, *don't lose your temper.*
17. It *helps* to look cheerful and attractive.
18. Have a few *tricks* up your sleeve, in case things don't go as planned.
19. Don't stop the *whole choir* to discipline one offender.
20. Give them reason for *wanting to behave.*
21. Good discipline is *self-control,* not teacher-control.
22. It takes *time and practice* to acquire self-control.
23. Choir discipline begins with the *director's self-discipline.*
24. Each director must develop *his own* disciplinary methods.
25. There are no magic tricks, no foolproof formula.

(R. K. J.)

MONOTONES OR MERELY UNCOORDINATED EARS?

Most children's choir directors feel that no child should be refused membership in a choir. Special arrangements can be made for the handicapped child—the lame, the blind—to meet his particular problem. Soon he settles in comfortably and is accepted by the children, after their initial curiosity, without further ado. Often such a child tries so hard and succeeds so well beyond all expectation that by example he contributes immeasurably to the atmosphere of devotion and accomplishment, joy and loving-kindness found in all truly dedicated children's choirs.

In every group of children, however, there are usually one or more would-be choristers who cannot match tones, i.e., sing on pitch. These children are often embarrassed; they are shunned by the others, and they become a problem unless the alert director has spotted those who have pitch difficulty at private or group auditions and made arrangements for special guidance.

But *never* tell a child that he is a monotone. Call him a "listener" until he catches up with the other children. To postpone training until a later age may increase the difficulty in learning, and his desire to sing as others sing may be lost forever. Some youngsters learn faster than others, but no child is hopeless unless proven defects of ear, palate, or tongue exist. Children having uncertain or wavering pitch

51

can be seated among strong singers and with practice will show immediate improvement. Those who have difficulty rising above one tone need individual attention and no distraction before rehearsals or scheduled singing and ear-training lessons. Listeners must attend all rehearsals and services, but not sing until "promoted."

With infinite patience on the part of both teacher and child, monotones can be taught to *sing*. Each student may present a different problem and there are no pat solutions. Experienced teachers have developed a variety of activities, exercises, short-cuts, and quick-tricks that have had remedial results in a number of cases. Muriel Alford suggests that pitch-training can also be helped by a discussion with the parents so that they will encourage the child to match pitches at home, and also enlist the cooperation of older brothers and sisters or play-mates in helpful singing games.

ELIZABETH JANE ANDERSON in "The Junior Choir" (Bulletin XII, Church and Choral Series, Northwestern University) suggests the following exercises to promote higher tone-singing:

First find the tone the child can sing, and start from there.

1. Take child by hand and walk up a set of steps.
    a. Place foot on first step and say "one," next step, "two," etc.
    b. When relation between numbers and steps is firmly fixed, the child steps 1, 2, 3, etc. with teacher, singing up 8 tones.
    c. After numbers, sing syllables. Let child sing with you, then by himself.
2. Sing intervals 5 to 3 (*sol to mi*) on "pa-pa," "ma-ma," and "sis-ter." This is called the "natural, instinctive interval."
3. Imitate a train-whistle "toot-toot" on pitch given by child, then coax up higher.
4. Pull an imaginary bell-rope and sing "ding-dong" on ascending and descending tones.
5. Skip on "ho-ho" with the use of arpeggios up and down.
6. Try barking like a dog, or imitating a cat. Play high and low tones.
7. Whistle bird and insect calls: bobwhite is 5 to 8 (*sol to do*); katydid is 5, 5, 8 (*sol, sol, do*).
8. Tap a tone softly on piano three times before the children try to imitate.

MURIEL ALFORD in "Pitch Problems" in *The Younger Choirs* (Lorenz Pub. Co.) suggests praise whenever possible, encouraging the children to "smile with the eyes" on high notes and relax the throat. She uses pitch-games such as the elevator that goes up 8 floors; the train tooting on 1, 3, 2, 1 of every key; imitating animal sounds; singing questions and answers; enacting the fire siren.

A teacher who has helped one child to recognize pitches and then to sing will never forget the joy of discovery and the gratitude reflected in his eyes. He may never become a great singer, but he will probably love music and listen with appreciation and understanding all his life. How can we, as teachers, refuse to open doors, to unlatch ears and enlighten minds? Let us pray for patience, sympathy, and wider vision in helping children whose pitch-sense is undeveloped or uncoordinated.

NANCY POORE TUFTS

I AM THE CHILD

You hold in your hand my destiny.
You determine largely whether I shall succeed or fail.
Give me, I pray you, those things that make for happiness.
Train me, I beg you, that I may be a blessing to the world.

MAMIE GENE COLE

ANTIDOTE FOR "SLUMP-MONTH"

Happy New Year to my children's choir director friends! I'm sure most of you and your choirs are still bathing in the reflected glow of the beauty and excitement of the Christmas music. Yes, a glance backward is often a satisfying and almost nostalgic one, but that backward glance must be quickly followed by a long hard look forward.

January is usually the month for "slump symptoms" which, if recognized early and dealt with promptly, may be dispelled before the plight strikes. The first symptoms are usually found in the director! It may be the way he (or she) enters the rehearsal room a little late with an expression that says: "What shall I do with them today?" Keen on expression, children are aware of this as said director thumbs through the hymnal, searching for material, or as he looks over previously sung anthems.

The attendance card can also be an indication of a slump. Have you allowed several unexcused absences to slip by without checking for a reason? What about the degree of interest during rehearsals? Have you allowed routine to stifle your creative urge? Are you presenting new songs in the same old way? And what about the rehearsal room? Have you checked the lighting and ventilation or have you become used to a dull, stuffy, unattractive room?

Without exception all of the above conditions can be changed by the director. January is a good month to take inventory of yourself as a leader. One of the most difficult things for a children's choir director to do is to keep before him the *high purpose* of his work. Organizational details, church staff relations, discipline problems, personal pressures, all seem to pull us away from our central purpose, that of developing Christian character through children's choirs.

Why not make January a month of practical "choir resolutions"— things which you felt should be done, but just haven't got around to? This would be your immunization "shot" to prevent the mid-winter slump!

Start with your *rehearsal room*:

1. Is it as attractive as you can make it by arrangement of chairs, lighting, pictures, charts?
2. Are the chairs facing the entrance door? Can you change that arrangement so late-comers do not distract children who are working?
3. Do you have a blackboard or an easel available for teaching?
4. Are there interesting things for children in the room: an A-440 chime, good prints of fine religious paintings, pictures of composers, etc.?
5. Are your attendance records being kept accurately?

Vestments:

1. Are they clean? Are they stored carefully? Are they properly fitted and assigned?
2. Do the parents understand about regulations governing hairbows, shoes, socks?

Music:

1. Do you have children learn at least part of their anthems from the music? Having the children learn to read music is a real responsibility of the Junior Choir.
2. Do you have sight-reading phrases, melodic and rhythmic, written on the blackboard before the children arrive? These may lead into something you plan to teach.

Enthusiasm:

It's contagious! Children respond to it and I think it is a must for a number of reasons also. A dull, passive teacher can never expect to get a bright and floating singing tone from children. Have you

54

worked on your own singing lately? Try directing in front of a mirror and see if you would inspire a bright and shining response from your children.

Have you something to anticipate? Recent scientific experiments with children have proven that anticipation is far more enjoyable than actual fulfillment. Are your plans made far enough in advance so that your children can experience the creative joy of anticipation?

Are you using materials to their fullest? Have you read over past issues of the *Choristers Guild Letters* lately? They are a never-ending source of ideas. Even "way-back-when" copies will open up new and forgotten possibilities for you.

Have you had a good talk with your minister lately? Or with your Christian Education director? Communication is important. Talk over plans and future needs. Coordination of efforts is sure to pay off.

This is just a starting point. No one can evaluate *your* work as well as you can, and no one can determine *your* course of action better than you can.

A slump-less New Year to you all!

HELEN KEMP

A GREAT AWAKENING

Another evidence of the growing respect of the church for the influence of music is the position of Music Supervisor created by the Reorganized Church of Jesus Christ of Latter Day Saints for FRANK HUNTER. Numerically the denomination is small; most of its congregations have only 40 or 50 members; congregations as large as 400 are encouraged to divide into smaller units. The church is not a wealthy one, nor influential, but it has shown exceptional foresight in recognizing the need of trained leadership for healthy and uniform growth through music.

Although Mr. Hunter took over his new duties only this fall (1958) he has already made almost phenomenal strides, checking up the following projects:

1. A list of carefully selected anthems to meet the specific needs of the small church.

2. A list of suitable sacred solos. Both lists were published in the denominational journal which has reached 45,000 circulation.

3. A six-weeks' course (one evening a week) on church music, attended by 300 directors, organists, pastors, and lay leaders.

Topics of the six meetings were:
1. A lecture on worship.
2. Music for worship (for which a syllabus was provided).
3. Congregational participation in worship.
4. Choir organization and administration.
5. Playing the service.
6. Panel discussion of questions submitted.

4. A Radio Choir of 38 selected voices who will make recordings of the anthems in the selected list. These will be loaned to directors.
5. Training the Messiah Choir (300 singers) which will give its 42nd annual performance. This is also to be recorded and will be available for broadcasting to some 600 stations.
6. Organizing a Children's Choir Festival, for which almost a thousand children have been registered. Mr. Hunter has studied the festival anthems with 22 of the local directors.

These projects are already in operation. Others in the planning stage are:
1. A clinic on "Music for Living" from the standpoint of Christian Education, to be under the leadership of some recognized church leader.
2. A night school for choir directors, offering a certificate of proficiency in church music for 50 credit-hours over a period of four years at two quarters a year.

At headquarters for this denomination in Independence, Missouri, an acoustically perfect auditorium with a four-manual Aeolian-Skinner organ is being completed. The auditorium will provide for a choir of 1200 with proportionate room for audience.

"I JUST WANT TO BE NORMAL"

(A true story by VIRGINIA LOVELOCK MITCHELL)

Suddenly your thoughts race, tumbling and searching for a solution. What do you say? What can you do? Here you are in the warmth and security of your own home giving a piano lesson to a handsome lad of eight years—a boy who has perfect pitch and a voice that is clear, soft and whole as a flute. His mind is like a sponge, absorbing the mechanics of music notation. For a moment you have digressed from the high concentration of the lesson just to chat. And you said, "What do you want to do when you grow up?" Raising his head, which was bent low, he said, "I just want to be normal." This charming, bubbling, smiling little boy has been blind since shortly after birth!

You shuffle in your chair, and your mind flashes to the chain of events that led to this situation. About six years ago, at a meeting of the music fraternity Sigma Alpha Iota, one of the members told of the lack of Braille music transcribers; that no volunteers were available in this area, and that requests for music to be brailled had to be sent to New York, where there was a long waiting list. This sounded quite inconvenient and frustrating.

A few months later a feature article appearing in the local paper described the activities of a Braille transcriber of books, and the story went on to say that this lady taught literary Braille transcribing. You phoned her to say you'd like to learn music Braille. This is a special code, she informed you, which she doesn't know, but will get a printed music code book for you.

We decided that since music has considerable literary notations, it would help to learn the Braille literary code. During the time of studying the 12 weekly lessons you thumbed through the music code book. This is an ink-print edition of the same book in Braille which was designed for the blind. It contains exercises in learning touch reading of elementary music notation and is called *Primer of Braille Music*. As a sighted transcriber, you had to separate the wheat from the chaff.

After you had a working knowledge of the music code and had brailled many pieces of music for people you'd never seen, one afternoon a lady called to say that she had a six-year-old blind boy who wanted to play the clarinet. A clarinet teacher was willing to teach him, but neither the boy nor the teacher knew Braille music code, nor did they have any music in Braille for the clarinet. We used an ink-print copy of the elementary method in use in the public schools, and dictated to the boy the Braille signs for music, which he learned to recognize and play. It was necessary, in addition, to decode the Braille back to writing, above the Braille line, for the clarinet teacher. Months later everybody was happy that the boy knew the music code. The teacher became so interested in Braille that he is now proficient in brailling special numbers for his bright student.

Then we began the piano lessons. That was not enough. Private lessons do not meet the basic need for group activity.

Choir! Yes, that would be the answer—the joy of singing in a group and belonging to something splendid. Right here in our area we have a fine Boys' Choir. Would the director bother with him because of the extra time involved? The director would have to plan future music in detail further ahead than usual, so that it would give the volunteer transcribers time to get it done. We'd have to search for a hymnal in Braille. Anthems and responses would have to be transcribed. Problems, but not insurmountable!

"Yes," the director said, "I will be glad to interview him, and if his parents are willing to see that he is present for all rehearsals and services, we will accept him as a probationer." He is now a full-fledged member of the choir. To participate in this group is the most important activity in his life. Furthermore, he does the processionals down that long aisle straight as can be, up the steps to the chancel and into the pew as every chorister has been taught to do in a dignified manner. His participation has served as a real inspiration to the other choristers and to the congregation.

Perhaps you know of a blind child who musically could meet the requirements of your choir? If not now, at some future date you can be sure that one of these little people will cross your path. If you inquire around, there is probably a blind child, or several, who could benefit by the wonderful activity of being in a Children's Choir. You would find it a privilege and pleasure to work with them.

* * * * *

When Virginia Mitchell (Mrs. Richard Mitchell, Los Alamitos, California) first proposed some stories on her music work with blind children, we were a bit hesitant. The pages of the *Letters* are limited, and must be filled with matters useful to the greatest number of members. How wrong we were in this instance was evidenced by the many letters received. A sample: Mrs. E. A. Kammerling, Presbyterian Church, Bellwood, Ill., wrote: "A family in our church has two daughters, both born without sight . . . I must confess that I had misgivings when the first girl became old enough to join the Junior Choir, but now I feel that the experience of having both girls in the choir has been of great value to the other youngsters. They have learned to help during the processionals, and consider it an honor. . . . The girls' mother writes Braille and makes copies of the words for them. They memorize everything, though as a general rule our Junior Choir uses music copies for each service since we are responsible for services each week in a dual program. It never really occurred to me that there were others experiencing the opportunity to help blind children enjoy the church choir program, and I want to thank you for the many interesting things brought to light."

A blind child is God's child entrusted to our care and nurture. If even one child only is helped to become a member of one of our choirs, the efforts will have been worthwhile.

(R. K. J.)

"DO RIGHT BY THE COPYRIGHT"

As a prelude to the following article about the copyright law, a comment on the moral implications of the subject is quoted from the "Cantate Domino" articles in CGL written by Eleanor Fossick: "Concerning the matter of the copyright law, (choir directors and) good Sisters and noble lay teachers who wouldn't dream of pilfering from pupils' pocketbooks, or of cheating when grading papers, will blithely run off stacks of copyrighted material on a duplicator, thereby cheating both composer and publisher of the returns due them for their labors and investments. So, let our first revision of policy for the new school year be: 'Do right by the copyright.' "

COPYRIGHT AND THE CHILDREN'S CHOIR

By Ellen Jane Lorenz

A copyright gives its owner just what the words say: the exclusive right to make *copies*. Without this protection an author or composer would get no remuneration for his creation, and a publisher could not afford the costly process of printing and marketing a composition.

The provisions of the copyright law are necessarily strict and penalties for infringement are severe.

Since many people break the law innocently, publishers are now putting on a campaign to acquaint the musical public with the restrictions of the law.

Words—I. May legally be copied (by any means whatsoever: blackboard, hand-written, typed, mimeographed) *only if*

    a) In public domain

        1. Published more than 56 years ago.
           (scripture, standard hymns, etc.)

        2. Published for sale, without copyright notice either on inside title or on first music page of that musical setting.

59

b) Written permission to copy a published, copyrighted work is secured from copyright owner (usually the publisher).

c) Written permission to copy an unpublished manuscript is secured from the composer or author, whether copyrighted or not.

II. May legally be taught by rote.

III. Probably morally acceptable to:

a) Copy words for temporary use only, if a copy has been purchased for each singer.

b) To print in church bulletin, if a copy has been purchased for each singer.

IV. If copying of protected works is necessary, the publisher will usually give permission upon payment of a fee.

Music—Same rules and restrictions as for words, with following additions:

I. It is illegal to make an arrangement of a copyrighted work.

II. It is illegal to copy a copyrighted arrangement of a public domain work.

Recordings (tapes or dics) of copyrighted works may be made as follows:

I. If the number has already been recorded, you may make a new recording without permission.

II. If the number has not been recorded, you must secure written permission from the copyright owner or his agent.

III. A royalty of 2c per copyright selection per recording made must be paid to the copyright owner or his agent, whether or not they are placed on sale.

IV. Most of the standard publishers have appointed as their agent Harry J. Fox, Music Publishers Protective Assn., 460 Park Ave., New York, N. Y. 10022.

60

The Primary Choir

TWO REHEARSAL PLANS FOR THE PRIMARY CHOIR
Lesson I

1. *Registration*: Mother to take names; secure address and telephone number later. Most of the registration will be done in advance by calling the home, either personally or by telephone.
2. *What do you remember from last year?*
3. *Tune detective*:
   Using songs your children have learned, play the first phrase on the piano; ask who knows it; sing it.
4. *What will we learn this year?*
   A. What our Bible says about music: Psalm 100.
   B. What our Bible says about instruments from Bible times. Shall we make a scrap-book, a notebook? Story from Bible of David and his harp.
   C. Songs of worship and devotion. Songs that make us feel that God is always near us.
   D. Songs about Jesus, his birth, his boyhood, Jesus our Saviour and King.
5. *Do you remember?*
   UP and DOWN (Kitty and Doggie game): The cat is UP in the trees, the dog is DOWN on the ground. Every time the child hears a cluster of very high notes on the piano, he touches the kitty; low notes, the doggie. Have a large drawing of kitty in tree and doggie on ground, drawn on poster paper, large size, so that child will have to reach UP to kitty and DOWN for doggie.

SAD and HAPPY (Pumpkin faces): Child points to the one for major music, the other for minor.

FAST and SLOW (Raindrops in the house or umbrella): Draw a house or an umbrella on the board. Play light staccato music suggestive of raindrops. With free arm movement the children make chalk raindrops on the roof in time with the music. With a large blackboard several children can play this game at the same time.

6. *How quickly* can you learn a new closing prayer song? "Day by day"—No. 157 in *Hymnal for Boys and Girls* (Appleton-Century).

7. *Rhythmic Response* to music (either piano or recording): Walking, running, tiptoe, hopping, high-stepping horses, sleeping.

8. *Closing prayer* and quiet dismissal.

Lesson II

1. *Telephone Game* (for matching tones): Teacher sings into toy telephone to a child, "Hello," or "Hello, who are you?" Child answers on same tone, "Hello, I am John."

2. *Review Songs*: "Day by day"—No. 157 in *Hymnal for Boys and Girls*. Have children tell the meaning of text in their own words. "God is my helper"—No. 16 in *When the Little Child Wants to Sing* (Westminster Press).

3. *Story of David* (God was David's helper): page 89 in *Music in the Religious Growth of Children* (Shields; Abingdon-Cokesbury). Have children imitate sounds. What does a harp look like today? In David's time? Use pictures, large, mounted on poster board, or drawn. Suggestions for ancient instruments used in the Temple can be found in *And So the Wall Was Built* (Westminster Press). This is an excellent book to use with primary age children.

4. *Psalm 100:* Make a joyful noise unto the Lord all ye lands. Serve the Lord with gladness, come before his presence with singing. (This part to be memorized this week). Announce that next week each one will be given a chance to earn his colored star on his Psalm 100 sheet. Arrange for a choir mother to hear each child before rehearsal.

5. *Response to music*: Walking, running, tiptoe, high-stepping horses.

6. *New Song*: "Saviour, teach me, day by day"—No. 452 in *The Hymnal* (Presbyterian). Use the phrase "day by day" to tell how God wants boys and girls to grow and know more about his love *each* day.

62

7. *Closing Prayer Song*: "Day by day."

Helen Kemp

(*Editor's Note*: These are samples from a course of 26 Lessons for Primary Choir. The complete series may be found in *Choristers Guild Letters,* volumes X, XI, and XII. A full-page illustration of typical chart for the Kitty and Doggie game occurs as page 103 in the first volume of *The Children's Choir.*)

REHEARSAL TECHNIQUES FOR PRIMARY CHOIRS

1. *Count in rhythm*: Whisper the words; follow the director. All children can count. By whispering the numbers and following the director in tempo changes we are off to a quiet, attentive rehearsal.

2. *Major and minor chords* (all references here are to broken chords): Listen to various chords. Stand if they are happy, sit if sad. Sing a happy chord, then a sad one (start each chord on same note). Listen to the story of *Crybaby Calf* (a Rand-McNally Elf Book by Helen and Alf Evers). At the end of each page (really only a sentence or two) tell whether it was a happy page or a sad one by singing a happy or sad chord.

3. *Games*: Rhythm rumpus. Clap the rhythms of the flash cards. We have a "Clapping Band." Incidentally, we call notes by their correct names from the beginning: i.e., quarter note, half note, etc. (See the Carl Vandre books in note-reading and sight-singing published by Mills Music, Inc.)

4. *Matching tones*: What time is it? Set the hands on a cardboard clock to various times and then sing the question. Child sings the response.

5. *Interval study*: Sing the intervals you see on the chart. This starts with a physical correlation to the distance between notes: 1—stomach; 2—chest; 3—chin; 4—nose; 5—forehead; 6—top of head; 7—above head; 8—as high as you can reach. With this correlation, primaries quickly grasp the difference in pitches and are able readily to transfer this to the sight of the various intervals.

6. *Place-a-note*: The left hand is on the staff. The right-hand index finger is the note. We place the note on any designated line or space.

7. *The Angelus Bell Song from Anthems for Junior Choir, Book 2* (Westminster Press): Listen while I sing the beginning of this song (p. 18). Now show with your hands the direction the notes are going. Show me with your entire body. Sing it. Next there comes a simple pattern which I want you to hear ("ding, dong,"

etc., p. 19). What have we in church that sounds like "ding, dong"? Let's pull the rope as we sing "ding" and let it up as we sing "dong." Now let's do it again while I sing the melody. Could some of you ring the bell while others sing the melody? Thus in a very few minutes they know the entire song (omitting the optional second soprano part).

8. *Happy Birthday*: To any who have birthdays before next rehearsal.
9. *Benediction Prayer*: Always a song.

NORMA LOWDER (MRS. EARL LOWDER)
Bellaire Methodist Church
Bellaire, Texas

OUR PRIMARY CHOIR REHEARSALS

This group of 6-to-8-year-olds rehearses on Sunday morning during the sermon time. They come into church for the first part of the service, then leave on the hymn after the offertory. This makes the rehearsal time about 35 minutes and takes in the entire department. Our rehearsal procedure is as follows:

1. Singing-games and rhythm exercises.
2. Matching tones and listening for pitch (using small xylophone). Sing "Little Sir Echo" (one child is echo and answers back). "Bag of Songs" (small articles placed in bag; with eyes closed each child takes out an article. Leader sings, asking who has a certain article; child with article sings same tune). "Go on a Trip" (Leader sings or says directions which children repeat while patting hands on knees in rhythm. With a good imagination you can have a wonderful time, climbing mountains, stalking animals, seeing a pair of eyes in a cave, etc.).
3. Talk about the beauty of God's world. Sing "nature" songs, using autoharp. Have children take turns playing autoharp while leader presses the chords.
4. Have the children learn the scale, using magnetic staff. Have them place the notes on staff as you dictate them.
5. Dramatize a Bible song, using only simple headpieces for costumes.
6. End rehearsal with prayer.

This procedure is not held to strictly but is varied, according to the children, the day, and the weather. This group sings only at Christmas and Children's Day.

MRS. EARL F. SPENCER
University Baptist Church
State College, Pennsylvania

64

A SPECIAL PROGRAM FOR PRIMARIES

Since we move out of our church building to hold Easter services in the high school auditorium, it is impossible to include the Primary Choir in our Easter services. To keep these youngsters from feeling completely left out we planned an afternoon program before Easter for the youngsters and their families and friends. Two senior girls from our High School Choir assist me with this group. They help in teaching theory, playing games, telling stories, doing secretarial chores. The work has given them valuable training. I find them much more satisfactory to work with than mothers.

Following is a copy of the mimeographed program outline:

I. WE SING ROUNDS
"Sing! Sing!"   Jane Marshall
"All Praise to Thee"   Tallis' Canon
      (To train our ears to sing in parts)

II. WE LEARN ABOUT JESUS
Review stories about Jesus
      (To help us become good followers of Jesus)

III. WE PLAY GAMES
"Bounce, Catch"
"The Cow Jumped Over the Moon"
Making Notes
"Which Is a Step? Which Is a Skip?"
"Mr. Pumpkin."
(To train our ears, and muscles, and to learn music theory)

IV. WE PLAY RHYTHM INSTRUMENTS
"Three Frogs"
"The Grasshopper"
"Laugh a Little Every Day"
"Six Little Ducks"
      (To teach our bodies rhythmic coordination)

V. WE SING ABOUT GOD'S WORLD
"The Sun. The Rain"   Crowninshield
"The Snow Is Falling Softly Down"   Crowninshield

VI. WE SING ABOUT EASTER
"Step Softly, Little Donkey"
"Little Crocus"
"Christ the Lord Is Risen Today"

VII. WE COMPOSE
"Be with Me, Lord" (Written by the Bethlehem Choir)

Sources of material for the above program:
I.   *We Go to Church,* by Jane Marshall (Carl Fischer); Tallis' Canon from *Choristers Little Hymnal.*
II. This review was shown through the pictures we had used throughout January, February, and March.
III. Songs used by Mrs. Jacobs in many of her workshops.
IV. The "Frogs" and "Grasshopper" songs from *A Child's World* by Grant and Crowninshield (Belwin, Inc.); the laugh song from *Walk the World Together;* the duck song from any children's fun-song collection.
V.   "Sun" song and "Snow" song from *Walk the World Together* by Crowninshield (Boston Music Co.).
VI. The "Step Softly" song from *A Child's World;* the "Crocus" song from *New Songs and Carols for Children* by the Rev. William R. Grime.
VII. We took the following words down the *do re mi's;* added two more lines, setting them to music, for we do a lot of composing.

Be with us Lord, today, I pray,
In all I do and all I say;
Help me learn, and help me love,
O dear Lord in heaven above.

Almost all songs were sung unaccompanied, and an informal atmosphere was encouraged. Refreshments were served afterwards. The comment we heard over and over from proud parents was: "I had no idea you did so much in a choir rehearsal."

MRS. ROBERT ANSCHICKS
First Presbyterian Church
Littleton, Colorado

A REHEARSAL PLAN FOR PRIMARIES

Church membership—850; number of choirs—7.

The group: Second and Third Grades Choir; 35-minute rehearsal; semi-circle seating.

The rehearsal setting: Of necessity a church-school classroom is used, with a choir-corner full of teaching charts, games, puppets, records, and an assortment of "peculiar items," such as a feather to demonstrate floating quality, etc.

Planning procedure: The basic year's program and materials are worked out during the summer months, with weekly planning to meet individual needs of the children and to incorporate into the rehearsal songs and activities based on the week's concurrent church-school lessons from Bethany Graded Materials.

Rehearsal Plan One:

1. As children enter, I sing:
   "Friends, friends, all around, all around me I see;
   They're the boys and girls of the Chapel Choir,
   And they are friends to me."
2. Followed by: "Who's this friend?" using different intervals; children answering with the same intervals "I am Mary," etc.
3. *Discussion*: What a choir is. Why we have church choirs. (And here the emphasis for all future work is laid: "We sing because we love God, and we want others through our singing to love God more too.")
4. Pictures of church workers to identify. Game song: "I'm a worker in the church. Can you guess who I am?" as different workers are pantomimed. The last worker to be guessed is a choir boy or girl. This establishes another basic concept, introducing the child to a definite responsibility in the church.
5. Introduction of Charlie, the choir boy puppet, who teaches children the secret choir signals; high-low symbols; "how-many" game preparatory to note-reading, a "copy-cat" tone-matching game; and a call to worship: "I was glad when they said unto me."
6. Charlie teaches the children to *move quietly* in church. Rhythmic movement is used here to relax children, to study their rhythmic response, and to let them express themselves. The movement is based on things that move quietly: flags, flowers, trees, etc.
7. *Song*: "Quietly we walk into the church." (This basic tune will also be used later whenever the children process into the church.)
8. How well can you read? Choral speech is used in psalms from preceding week's church-school lessons, from charts printed in red and black ink for light and dark voices.
9. Now that you're real church workers, here is a calendar showing some of the work we'll be doing together. Chart shows Children's Book Week Party in November; Thanks-

giving Service; Christmas Activities; African Mission Adventure in January; Symphony Field Trip in February, etc.

10. "Shut your eyes and listen." Introduce monthly study project "Sounds in God's World," covering sounds from singers, instruments, Africa, nature, etc. Next week, tell me of the sounds you have heard around you.

11. *Closing Prayer*: sung by me this week, by children hereafter, using original words and tunes. "Quietly we walk into the church" is played as they leave the choir room.

Worship Service Participation: While this is a preparatory choir, it will share in special Christmas and Easter services, and special Family Week services in May.

Mrs. Christine Kallstrom
Lakeview Christian Church
Dallas, Texas

KEYSTONE OF THE CHURCH'S MUSICAL PROGRAM

Ours is a suburban church in a lovely setting. Our children attend ten different schools and must come to the church by car. Fortunately the music program is well established (my eighth year), and parents are convinced of the value of the whole Youth Choir program, giving enthusiastic cooperation and support.

Seven choral groups rehearse regularly, the Youth Choirs meeting in a large room under the sanctuary. This room is of sufficient size for an arrangement of semi-circular rows of chairs around a grand piano; I play for my own rehearsals. In addition, there is plenty of space for the most active of games, for a worship area, and a well-equipped kitchenette.

The Primary Choir meets for two ten-week units. One is timed to end the Sunday before Christmas, and the second ends this year with Palm Sunday. Very specific aims are planned and announced for this choir. We bluntly state that we do not consider it a "performing" choir, preferring instead to stress:

(1) Learning to sing in a natural, unforced voice.
(2) Learning to match pitches and sing with accurate intonation.
(3) Learning the basic items of musical notation.
(4) Learning what happens in a service of worship, and how the choristers contribute.

The musical material is drawn from a great wealth of sources, including our own denomination's graded hymnals and church-school

68

curriculum; other hymnals and song collections are used. The composition of songs is frequently included: last year, the children set the 100th Psalm to music, and sang it in church.

The reader may at this point say, "You don't consider this a performing choir, and yet the choir does perform." Everything that the choir does leads to smoothness in performance, but only incidentally. When the children sing in church, they do so early in the service, and with flocks of choir mothers surrounding them. They return to their church-school classes after singing. Our congregation understands, too, that the children only sing if they can do so in a worshipful manner. They do not have choir robes, but wear white blouses or shirts and dark trousers or skirts.

Many people would consider that the size of the group is impossible; we have had as many as 90 children, and this year the choir numbers about 70. Every minute of rehearsal is planned, and the various forms of activity change rapidly, so that even the shortest attention-span is accommodated; but I must handle the entire group myself, finding that in this way a real unity of purpose and achievement is attained. A group of mothers is present at each rehearsal, and parents understand when their child is enrolled that they will be called upon to work.

Attendance is taken by means of name-tags which the children wear for a few weeks; after their names are known, the choir mothers simply note the date on the back of the tag (a 3" x 5" card) when the children arrive. The parents are requested to inform the music office in advance if a child is ill or has an unavoidable conflict.

The Primary Choir Program is, in many ways, the keystone of the church's musical program, since 96% of the children who sing in Primary Choir go on to the Melody Choir (4th to 6th grade girls) and the Crusaders (4th to 7th grade boys). In the eighth year of the program, we are really beginning to feel its effects all the way through the church's musical life, and know that while we have come a long way, the horizons are ever expanding, ever exciting in their possibilities.

WILLIAM GILES, *Director of Music*
First Presbyterian Church
Middletown, Ohio

INSTRUMENTS OF THE ORCHESTRA FOR PRIMARIES

If one of your Primary Choir projects is to familiarize the children with the instruments of the orchestra, you could have no better material than that provided by Keyboard Jr. Publications, 1346 Chapel Street, New Haven, Conn. . . . A set of *14 orchestral instrument pictures* (6½x9½) in playing position, posed by members of the Firestone Orchestra sells for $1.30. . . . *Build Your Own Orchestra* provides perforated cardboard figures of symphony-orchestra players in correct playing position, and a complete floor-plan, with directions for setting up the orchestra. The price is $1.50.

(R. K. J.)

PRIMARIES ENJOY "FISH-POND" GAME

VIVIAN BLUM of Monroe, Wisconsin, plays an interesting game called "Fish Pond" with her Primary Choir. Each child draws a symbol out of the fish pond. Then Mrs. Blum calls, "Who has the clef? the time signature? whole note?" and so on. As she calls, each places his symbol on the flannel-board, and it makes a tune.

Mrs. Blum also has an original approach to creative writing. The most interesting news of the week is made into a song. It might be "Terry has a new baby brother." The children choose the tune they like the best, and then Mrs. Blum writes it on the board for them to see and sing. Sometimes, too, the children are encouraged to draw illustrations of hymns or songs as the choir sings them. This often reveals what the children are thinking.

Those of you who are concerned about your non-singers, take heart! Mrs. Blum says that at the beginning of the year 25 out of 28 of her little ones could not carry a tune. By the end of the year there was only one who could not carry a tune through to the end alone.

Last year Mrs. Blum had 76 in the Primary Choir (1st to 3rd grades). Each grade sat in a separate row. At the beginning of rehearsal one child from each grade went to the board and wrote down the number of absences in his grade, then all applauded the winning grade. So simple, but it made all 76 very attendance-conscious!

✕ FOR YOUR PRIMARIES

MRS. DONA M. HOFFMAN sent in recently the following idea for helping primary youngsters to open their mouths for singing. It is very clever. She wrote:

"Another idea:

"I'm enclosing a little bird, "Henry." Henry has not learned to sing with his mouth more open; our Primary Choir must encourage him to open w-i-d-e! Closed mouths make mumbling

70

sounds. Poor Henry. Can you, John, illustrate how to sing with your head up and mouth open?

"This psychology (if you will) worked wonders for two shy little angels in a recent rehearsal."

INSTRUCTIONS for making a paper bird:

1. Use construction paper for best results.
2. Cut and fold an 8" square four ways, as illustrated in Figure 1, red or other color.
3. Cut and fold (white paper) a 4" square once, diagonally; draw bird-face.
4. Place bird-head on 8" square with beak pointing toward center as in Figure 2.
5. Refold 8" square on the diagonal, bringing point under head.
6. Tape wings as in Figure 3.

To make bird open and close mouth, push wings toward center and back.

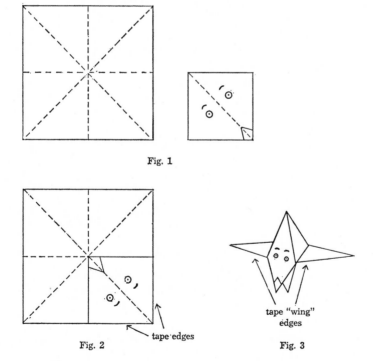

Fig. 1

Fig. 2   tape edges

tape "wing"
edges

Fig. 3

The Junior Choir

PURPOSEFUL VARIETY IN JUNIOR CHOIR REHEARSAL

GETTING ACQUAINTED WITH A NEW CHOIR

1. *Start with something very easy to learn, having*:
   Comfortable range;
   Easy intervals (mostly stepwise);
   No accidentals;
   Repetition (melodic, rhythmic, or both);
   Simple rhythmic patterns.

2. *Why simple?*
   To eliminate strain from their voices.
   To give them confidence in their learning ability.

3. *Use it to estimate their*:
   Tone quality;
   Melodic memory;
   Sight-singing ability;
   Power of concentration.

4. *How to teach it*:
   Rote (sing it for them once, whole or part, and have them repeat after you).
   Have them read it from a large copy on blackboard.
   Do not give them the music; you want their attention focused on one spot.

Preparation

1. Study the number in detail, observing:
   Structural pattern;
   Repeated phrases;
   Rhythmic patterns;
   Difficult phrases;
   Intervals that occur with unusual frequency;
   Relationship between accompaniment and voices: imitation; contrast; unusual entrances.

2. Sing it often, imitating as nearly as possible the child-voice.

3. Memorize it.

4. Find a clue to simplify difficult spots.

Introducing the new number

1. The first approach should establish a foundation that will make the learning of the whole easier.

2. The dominant character of the anthem: rhythmic complexity, melodic repetition, rhythmic repetition, unusual intervals, etc., will be determining factors in selecting the way to introduce it.

3. Ways to introduce a new anthem:
   a) Write the basic rhythmic patterns on the board, then discover them in the music.
   b) Memorize the several melodic phrases that appear most frequently.
   c) Review meaning of time-signatures and note-values, then clap a new number at sight (if it is within the ability of the choir).
   d) Write the octave scale on the board (in the key of the anthem); have the choir sing as you point out (first) scale progressions, up and down; (second) stepwise progressions and larger intervals; (third) the melody of the number. Point it out in the *rhythm* of the number.
   e) Find the most frequently used interval, sing it in many keys. Play melody of the number and have choir watch for and sing that interval whenever it occurs.
   f) Read the text, discuss its meaning, and the type of music it should have.

74

Carrying on

1. At second rehearsal check their memory of what they have learned.

   Examples: (letters correspond to those in "Ways to introduce a new anthem" above)

   a) Place rhythmic patterns on the board and ask:
      "What is the name of the song in which these occur?"
   b) Write the melodic phrase on the board, then let choir sing without any help.
   c) See if you can clap without any mistakes.
   d) Place music in their hands and ask:
      "Do you recognize this? Can you sing it at sight?"
   e) Play the melody through. Give the choir copies of the music and have them count the number of times the interval occurs.
   f) Play the melody (or the accompaniment) and ask:
      "What sort of words do you think should go with this music? sad? happy? praise? prayer? quiet? festive?"

2. Develop a different phase of each anthem each week. Don't do the same thing with all of them at the same rehearsal.

3. Correct tune and pronunciation as you go along. Don't leave that until after melody and rhythm are learned.

4. Whenever possible, use what they have learned as a basis for what they are about to learn.

5. Whenever possible, use phrases from anthems for vocal exercises.

6. Keep a careful record of the stage of development of each anthem.

Ruth Krehbiel Jacobs

CHARACTERISTICS OF THE JUNIOR CHILD

1. Spontaneous reactions; unpremeditated.
2. Full of energy; must be guided or it will take over rehearsal.
3. Strong sense of competition.
4. Group-loyalty developing.
5. Hero worship.
6. Habits not settled.
7. Visual-minded.
8. Strong imagination.

WORKING WITH THESE CHARACTERISTICS

1. You can't expect a completely calm rehearsal.
   If there is no *evident* response to the music, there *is* none.
   Learn to relax; not every issue is a crisis.

2. Vary the rehearsal to let off steam: clapping; moving into sanctuary; show picture of angelic choir boy with black eye.
   Provide for pre-rehearsal activities.
   Establish area habits: playroom, rehearsal room, sanctuary.

3. Within the choir-teams: best attendance record; most hymns learned.
   With other choirs: baseball game; festivals (each choir to sing); exchange churches.
   Through the Choristers' Guild: compare their achievements with others.

4. Requirements that they understand and accept.
   Loyalty *through* the director *to* the church and what it stands for.
   Place responsibility for decisions on *them.*
   Don't make decisions for exceptions yourself.
   Bring some issues to them for decisions.
   Keep in touch with parents; their support is essential.
   Follow up immediately on absence or misbehavior.

5. The director must be emotionally mature.
   Show no favoritism.
   Don't curry their favor.
   Acquaint them with the great heroes of church history: Jesus; Luther; Grenfell; Laubach; Mellon.

6. Review standards occasionally.
   Keep the rehearsal room orderly.
   Establish order in the rehearsal pattern: roll call, seating, dismissal, care of vestments.
   Director must be free to observe and correct.
   Rehearsal reflects the order or disorganization of the director.
   Rehearse *details* of performance.
   Honor sustained effort: Choristers' pin; Service Cross.

7. Use their eyes: blackboard; learning procedures; room interest.
   Attendance records; hymn-learning chart.
   Parents night; interesting display; children act as guides and hosts.

8. Let your own imagination develop: use it in your interpretation of music.

(R. K. J.)

76

JUNIOR CHOIR REHEARSAL TECHNIQUES
1. Critique of First Rehearsal

First impressions and first experiences are important to children, and I try to keep this in mind in planning the new start for any group. There are always a number of children who are *made* to come to choir at the start of fall by Mama. Now I believe that in most cases Mama is right in insisting that a start be made. At that initial encounter the choir director has quite a battle to win in the effort to capture enough interest so that those few who are "made to come" will want to come. Through the years I have come to realize that thorough planning and imaginative teaching are a great deal more important than the qualities of personal magnetism upon which we sometimes rely.

Having taught in a number of seminar courses, I am more than ordinarily aware of the value of evaluation, that cool-sounding word which means: "Did I do what I planned, and was what I planned worthy of the endeavor?"

We should ask ourselves this question after every rehearsal and in so doing get up our plan for the next rehearsal. Since we learn by facing our failures as well as by our successes, this constant process of trial and error can work wonders for you.

Take for instance our registration and first rehearsal yesterday. Here is how it was set up:

1. *Plan*: Last Sunday I visited all the church school classes of the 4th through 6th grades (with advance notice to teachers), at which time registration cards and "Let's Get Acquainted" sheets were distributed. We asked that the latter sheet be done entirely by the children, not the parents. They liked the idea! (*For sample sheet see below*).

Evaluation: Children forgot or lost cards and sheets but the visit to the church school got them to come to choirs. The extra sheets and cards were a good investment.

2. *Plan*: Card tables were set up in the large hallway for children to fill in the information necessary before they could come into the rehearsal room.

Evaluation: Slightly "chaotic" but psychologically successful. We needed more helpers for this.

3. *Plan*: Different colored 3"x5" cards used as name-tags (printed with a felt pen); one color for each grade (white—4th, yellow—5th, and blue—6th).

Evaluation: Helped me a great deal to get to recognize 4th graders and new children whom I had not known before; helped me realize that this particular combination of 6th-grade boys cannot be together on the back row. Work out semi-permanent seating plans for next week.

4. *Plan*: Have a choir-rehearsal schedule printed on large colored poster and displayed on easel.

5:00	Chime	Special Solo or Guest Musician
	Prayer	Hymns for Church School
	New Anthem	Review of New Anthem
	Theory	Closing Prayer
	Hymn of the Month	"God be in my head"

Evaluation: They liked the idea of a working plan. Made rehearsal go by quickly. Interest was good. I had to be careful to get to everything. We may adjust this.

5. *Plan*: Get an "earful" of the singing sound they are making to see where the biggest vocal need is.

Evaluation: Heavens! Doug is now a fourth-grader. He is the one I have heard about from church-school teachers, school teachers, and choir directors. He *loves* to sing—*loud* and one or two octaves *low!* Everybody is chuckling, waiting to see what I do with him. I didn't do a thing today but wince inside and think: "This I'll have to work out."

6. *Plan*: Stimulate interest for the year by explaining the importance of our participation in the worship service each month. Boys challenge girls on best percentage of attendance each week. Festival possibilities. Christmas caroling for shut-ins.

Evaluation: Greatest interest stimulated by actual "doings" of rehearsal. They don't go for long announcements too far in advance. This is a lively, large (70) group. I must choose two more high-school aides—one a boy, interested in sports and singing. I'd have it made if I could tell my boys that Micky Mantle or Roger Maris were star singers in their Junior Choirs!

HELEN KEMP

(For any Children's Choir)

LET'S GET ACQUAINTED

NAME _____ AGE _____

Name I am called, if different from above _____

Address _____ Telephone _____

Date of Birth _____ School Grade this Fall _____

Mother's Name _____ Father's Name _____

Mother's Occupation _____ Father's Occupation _____

Names and ages of other children in my family:

_____   _____

_____   _____

_____   _____

_____   _____

_____   _____

_____   _____

My hobbies are: _____

My favorite subject in school is: _____

One of my favorite Bible verses is: _____

My favorite hymn is: _____

(Please paste a snapshot
or school picture here)

Three things I like best to do:
1.
2.
3.

Three things I like least to do:
1.
2.
3.

My favorite people in the Bible are: _____

My favorite people *not* in the Bible are: _____

As a special Chapel Choir project, I would like *best* to:
1. Give a play.
2. Join with several other Junior Choirs for a Children's Choir Festival.
3. Go caroling at Christmas time for some of the shut-ins of our church.

79

2. Evaluation and Changes

Last month I attempted to give you the plan, and then the evaluation of the first rehearsal of our own Junior Choir, with the idea that such an analysis might be of some value to you. I should like to follow through with this idea one step further.

Usually I find that not *everything* needs alteration. After several rehearsals, here is a list of things which are working very well as a weekly procedure.

1. The children enjoy the "count-down" just before the opening chime; they seem to like order and a certain uniformity of procedure.

2. They are most enthusiastic about the contest of attendance between boys and girls (%) who are seated, ready to sing at precisely 5:00 o'clock. The banner-winners do not applaud *themselves* if they win. (Losers congratulate the winners with what turns out to be a rather mild response!)

3. *Permanent seating arrangements*: This one item has solved more problems for me than any other gimmick or procedure I have used. The group is rather large (76 enrolled) and as many as I feel I can teach effectively, so the entrance into the rehearsal room could be and has been rather hectic at times, when two or three boys aim for the same chair. This problem, I believe, we have solved. The exact number of chairs is arranged in advance as follows:

5th and 6th Grade Girls

5th Girls		5th Girls
4th Girls	Boys	4th Girls
4th Girls	Boys	4th Girls
	Boys	

On each chair is the 3" x 5" name-cards designating each one's place. Notice the arrangement of boys—separated by *space* from the girls, and planned to dilute the esprit-de-corps of the 6th-grade boys as a unit. This way I am trying to encourage them to feel responsible as leaders for the younger boys who sit next to them. So far it has worked wonders.

This may seem very time-taking to you. Most of it is "thinking-through" time, though, since choir mothers and young assistants are perfectly capable of setting up physical arrangements one-half hour in advance, if instructions are clear and a chart has been worked out.

4. The children have been most responsive in volunteering for the "share-your-music" time. When a youngster has a solo memorized in piano, violin, cello, drum, flute—anything he is studying—he may volunteer to share it with us at rehearsal. This is limited to one person each week; time-limit is three minutes. This is checked through the choir mother in charge. She has quite a list in advance and usually calls the child to remind him. The respectful attention of the listeners is as important as the efforts of the performer. This we *teach,* and I believe it is taking hold.

5. This list could not be complete without mentioning the effectiveness of an opening and closing prayer. I like to pray the opening prayer myself so that I can direct the thoughts of the children toward the high purpose of their choir work and ask God's help in all our efforts. A short, direct prayer for guidance helps both children and teacher. I prefer to have a child lead the closing prayer which all of us pray in unison: "Bless, O Lord, us thy servants who minister in thy house; grant that what we sing with our lips we may believe in our hearts, and what we believe in our hearts we may show forth in our lives; through Jesus Christ our Lord. Amen."

HELEN KEMP

3. Planning and Practice

Somehow these articles have taken on the character of a Junior Choir Director's diary! Let me hasten to say that the main idea is to stress the importance of long-term planning, individual-rehearsal planning, then evaluation and contemplation in an attempt to solve each problem as it arises and to build a store of successful creative teaching ideas which work for you. Techniques which grow out of such constant searching can be used as seemingly spontaneous ways to achieve the desired results.

Do you remember Doug, our fourth-grader, enthusiastic, loud and low? Well, he has finally "discovered" how to sing with a head-tone! Of course we haven't gone into technical terms with him, but he reacted successfully to certain phrases such as "Sing through your eyes" or "Pretend there is a little hole in the very top of your head and sing through it." We found that Doug's was not an ear problem. He sang correct intervals, but an octave or two below the given pitch in a big chest voice which strained all of his throat muscles and caused him to stretch his chin out and up. This is very harmful to a child's voice and can cause a chronic hoarseness. Any child who sings like this in Junior Choir needs your personal help.

1. Get him to do the fire-siren "whoo-oo" going into the upper range.
2. If his jow is rigid, tell him to keep his lower jaw the same but raise his *upper* jaw. (This usually results in dropping the lower jaw—try it!)
3. Stress a *small* sound. Tell him that a dart or an arrow will fly straighter and surer than a big heavy handball!
4. Use a lifting motion or a jabbing upward-pointing finger to help him get the idea.
5. Talk about launching a rocket—straight up!

Never allow a child to continue to sing an octave lower than your unison treble choir. I suggest that all the above methods be used *outside* the choir hour. If you do not know the child and his personal reactions, don't make the mistake of embarrassing him in front of the other children. If you have taken ten minutes with him alone and know he can demonstrate his improvement for the other children— that's fine; it can give the child a feeling of success and the desire to keep trying.

This chest-singing happens in junior-age girls as well as boys. Although you are never safe in teaching by sensation alone, there is the discovery of a certain "feeling" by a child when he catches on to singing with his head-voice instead of a strained and coarse chest-voice. Keep listening to fine boy-choir recordings to establish within yourself the tone you want to hear. It helps considerably if you can model for the children, or if you can have a capable high-school girl do this.

Several other wrinkles have been ironed out since the first rehearsal. After the Junior Choir had sung for its first service of worship this season, the choir helpers met with me to solve several problems. These remedial plans were made:

1. Junior Department Church School Coordinator was called about dismissal of Junior classes at five-minute intervals so that all children do not arrive to vest at the same time. The youngest come first. Coordinator cooperative!
2. Two card-tables set up in dressing room (boys and girls) for

82

orderly placement of Bibles, church-school papers and things to be taken home.

3. Extra hangers provided for children to hang coats and jackets *before getting vestments* (to avoid jackets on floor, etc.).
4. A *father and mother team* in charge of vesting boys.
5. Chairs arranged in rehearsal room to duplicate seating in sanctuary.
6. Instructions clearly given concerning the *return of hymnals* to proper bookcases before vestment is removed after the service.
7. A meeting scheduled for mothers of all Junior choristers. Plans made for coffee, rolls, and a "communicative" talk concerning purposes, requirements, responsibilities, benefits, and desired "high hopes." Schedule for the rest of the year announced.
8. A personal call to be made to the five (of the 78 enrolled) children who have missed three times.
9. A postcard sent out to *all parents* with schedule of rehearsals, services, and special events, listing dates, times, and places for all of the December holiday season—and including the first rehearsal of the New Year.

Helen Kemp

4. More Than Music

The teaching of musicianship is an important choir responsibility. To foster musical growth in our children is essential. Much of our time with Primary and Junior choirs is taken up with the study of musical symbols. Sharps, flats, clefs and notes are all part of a visual communication which directs our musical thinking.

Since our children's choirs are planned to be church-centered, *Christian symbols* can also be effective aids to your teaching. These too are visual communications developed in the early centuries of the Christian church to be reminders and signs of Christian truths.

According to our calendar February is a month of secular symbols: hearts for St. Valentine's Day, logs for Lincoln's Birthday, and cherries for George Washington's Birthday. Perhaps this would be a good time to look at certain Christian symbols and allow them to communicate their meaning to us as Christian leaders.

The season of Lent will soon be with us. I have always felt that this was the time for real contemplation, study, and—hopefully—spiritual growth. Why not make this whole period culminating with the festival of Easter one of strengthening the roots of our faith to insure the fruits of our labor? We in the church are certainly committed to teach more than music! With the current strong feeling, politically, of the importance of the separation of church and state, the church must take on complete responsibility for the Christian education of its children. As Christian leaders must, we regard every moment of the time allotted to us as a singular opportunity to teach Christian truths through music. Music must be the servant, not the sovereign!

During the holidays one of the returning college students said to me: "Mrs. Kemp, I realized at school this year that most of the Biblical passages I have retained in memory have come from texts of anthems and songs I learned in the Junior Choir or through the Youth Chorale." That did more to convince me of the power of recall in music than any speech I had ever heard on the subject. This is Christian education through music!

I do not want to give the impression that the quality of the music we sing is not important. Children especially should be taught that an anthem presented in a service of worship to the glory of God should be the finest offering they can bring. Help children to understand that their prime objective is not to please you or the minister or the congregation, but to lead worshipers to a closer relationship with God. They respond to an earnest prayer that their offering in song be used to this end.

Recently our church was privileged to sponsor the Korean Orphan Choir, a touching and heart-stirring group of 34 children, 8-to-12 years of age, who were selected from the 13,000 children in Korean orphanages. Talk about an outreach through the common bond of music! This was a living mission-experience for our children in the Junior Choir. These Korean youngsters sang beautifully, and certainly shared with us *more than music!* As a result our Chapel Choir has "adopted" a Korean orphan, a little choir singer whom we shall support for a year. The children will take turns writing letters, sending pictures, and perhaps sending copies of the music we are learning. A most moving experience was hearing the Korean children and our own children's choir sing a hymn together during the morning service of worship, one group in English and one in Korean. Though neither could understand the other's language, their singing opened a wonderful door of communication. If you and your children's choir have a chance to hear this group, you should. There is a recording available, and I recommend it to you for lovely singing and—yes, more than music!   HELEN KEMP

84

5. Click Like Clockwork

"The rehearsal must click like clockwork, and singers kept so occupied that there is never a chance for their attention to wander." The haunting refrain of that phrase keeps running through my head and I cannot forget it. But the second half of that statement is the real story, especially for the great number of us who have only one hour a week with our volunteer groups. Sixty short minutes a week is a very meager time in which to accomplish the things we dream about. It is true that we must use every minute of time allotted to us if we are to make real our claim: "Christian Character Through Children's Choirs."

For every single high hope or ideal we strive to reach as choir directors, we must have a whole host of practical ideas ready to call on. We cannot tell children: "We are attempting to develop your Christian character." Their growth, spiritual, mental and physical, comes through *action*. They need to have standards and goals set up for them. They need to be directed, spurred on, encouraged. Sometimes they need to be chastised, sometimes praised. They need to work hard on the ability to be completely attentive, and they need to know also the joy of a spontaneous burst of laughter.

Now to be practical, how do you get your rehearsal with Juniors to "click like clockwork"? Here are some ideas based on personal experience.

Active Responsibility

Because our choir starts at 5: 00 P.M., we sometimes have children come as early as 4: 15 P.M., while I am getting the room in order. I believe they come to get the special job of washing the blackboard with the large sponge!

Definite Assignments

Children place hymnals on chairs exactly right, not just flung down. Anthem books are placed with equal care.

Visual Instructions

We have one blackboard hung permanently on the back wall of the room, visible to choristers as they come into the room, on which the general seating plan for the day is drawn. This is something new and is proving very valuable. The arrangements of chairs and rows is painted on permanently. We fill in with chalk.

4th Girls	6th Girls	5th Girls
4th Boys	4th and 5th Girls	5th Boys
4th Boys	6th Boys	5th Boys

Each week we change the arrangement of sections. At the Wednesday rehearsal before we are going to sing in church the seating is arranged for Sunday. The children look eagerly for their place by grades as soon as they enter the door.

Something to Anticipate

After I have written rhythmic phrases or melodies for sight-reading on the front blackboard, all are invited around the piano for a *preview* of rehearsal music. (Choir mothers check non-participants so I can be free to concentrate.)

Prompt Start, Prayer, and Work

Five minutes before time to begin, the children take their seats, ready for the chime which is rung by an assigned child at exactly five o'clock. Immediately have an opening prayer asking for the power of concentration and the spirit of consecration. Have the accompanist introduce the anthem on which the most work is going to be done. During this first 25 minutes don't plan to do much talking. Have in mind what you want to achieve: memorization and musical finishing in tone, phrasing, articulation, and projection of thought and sound. Try to encourage an attitude of "working toward a goal much bigger than ourselves." Make necessary repetition interesting by a little competition between boys and girls, or among the three school grades as groups—4th, 5th, 6th—or by rows. Change groupings often so that you do not encourage permanent group rivalry. There is a big difference between healthy and spirited competition and harmful rivalry.

Change of Pace

I allow the children to remind me when 5:30 arrives. This is solo time, and also time for the attendance banner to be brought in. This provides a change of pace and puts a logical limit on the length of time I should expect complete concentration from these children. After this planned break (about 4 minutes), we are all ready for Hymn of the Month study and coordinated efforts with church-school materials.

86

Group Self-Analysis

This week we are having a short semi-spontaneous play, "You Were There," by the children to dramatize several distracting things which happened during the morning service of worship last Sunday. The choir will be the congregation. One of the children will be the minister reading the Bible as the Junior Choir (several children prepared ahead of time) does the things which distracted on Sunday. Then a discussion: "Were you, the congregation, able to think about the Bible message?" Second Act: corrected situation. (Time: five minutes.)

Keep Singing and End on Time

By this time hands will be raised to ask: "May we please sing our favorite, now?"—which currently is "O Lord, our Governor" by Marcello. (What makes them love this so?) Last year six boys sang the solo part. This year I have been besieged by the girls: "Please, give us a chance!" So we are having two solo groups—one of boys and one of girls. We plan to sing at both services (the choir's idea). This decision was made after a lively discussion of "Won't you be too tired?" "bored with two sermons?" "hungry?"

The rest of the hour is singing time again. Fill your rehearsals with singing. Allow no time for choir-jabbering between anthems, hymns, or special projects. Save your own words whenever you can by listing rehearsal agenda on the blackboard. And end on time!

HELEN KEMP

6. Purposeful Activity

In a 40-page booklet entitled *Help Your Child Succeed in School* educator Leslie J. Nason has many constructive and practical suggestions concerning the child's attitude toward the learning process. Although this booklet is directed to parents of children, its contents are tremendously valuable to anyone responsible for teaching children.

One point Professor Nason makes is that of our obligation to help children develop *purposeful activity.* He states: "Some children go to school, do their work, play their games and take charge of their other activities in ways that show they know *what* they are expected do, *how* they intend to go about it, and *why* they are doing it. Teachers say that such children are demonstrating *purposeful activity.*

"Such children grow into secure students who are able to handle the problems they meet along the way. The children who lack this sense of purpose, however, usually just drift along."

87

Of course we see them in choir, the "drifters" with eyes, ears, and minds "tuned out." This always concerns me greatly, for if I allow it to continue, I am contributing to the development of poor learning attitudes in many areas of their lives. One of the best remedies known for the drifter is to put him to work with purposeful activity. The children's choir plan offers unique opportunities of Christian service for every child we name on our swelling choir rolls. Let us not allow the large numbers in our choirs to be a contributing factor in the development of drifters who miss out on the purpose of this activity. Are we really making a spiritual as well as musical impact on our children? Are goals set up for children, and are these goals *understood* by them? Do they know the *why* of choir? Do you make the *what* and the *how* interesting and inspiring? Are their parents aware of these same things?

By May most of our regular choir activities are coming to a close, and we are torn between reflection upon the past year and anticipation of the possibilities ahead.

Often the inspiration for future plans comes through an awareness of the successful ideas of co-workers in the field. Active awareness often sets up a chain reaction of creative thinking on your own. I feel that one of the prime purposes of the annual Choristers Guild Seminar is the exchange of successful ideas among directors. "Talking shop" should be the most stimulating experience during these sessions.

(To revitalize your planning for the next Junior Choir season, Mrs. Kemp here makes reference to two lists from the lecture notes of two outstanding leaders in the children's choir field—Madeline Ingram and Ruth Jacobs.)

"An Evaluation of the Concept of Your Work" by Madeline Ingram

1. What are my deficiencies and what am I doing to correct them?
2. Do I take advantage of every opportunity to hear good music?
3. Do I try to hear music of other faiths?
4. Am I keeping up with *modern* educational methods?
5. Am I continuing my study of music?
6. Do I continually seek for new materials and ideas?
7. Am I improving my teaching ability?
8. Am I daily striving to become a better Christian?
9. Do I have a set of rules that is worth transmission to children?

10. What reasons have I for believing that I am contributing to the Christian education program in my church?

"Points for Effective Teaching" by Ruth Jacobs

1. See teaching as important. The attitude will be reflected.
2. Start with a vital *faith*.
3. Get advanced training.
4. Learn the best methods. Learn by experience.
5. Know what makes Tommy tick.
6. Study the *whole* course. See years ahead.
7. Find out what Betty *knows*. Don't let your only contact be music.
8. Plan a whole unit.
9. Use supplementary material.
10. Draw the parents in.
11. Be a member of a team.
12. Plan each session carefully.
13. Encourage the pupils to prepare.
14. Bring about *active* learning.
15. Lift learning to the level of worship.
16. Help children to *live* what they learn.
17. Evaluate and plan again.
18. Find joy in teaching.
19. Interpret your work to the church.
20. Accept your responsibility as a teacher no matter what the results.

It was not a choir director who said, "Nothing great was ever accomplished without enthusiasm." It was Ralph Waldo Emerson, and truer words were never spoken concerning our labors as ministers of music and directors of choirs. I should like to add that enthusiasm plus a constant endeavor to increase our knowledge and skill is a combination that is sure to culminate in purposeful activity and rewarding results.

HELEN KEMP

7. Summer Plan Suggestions for the Junior Choir Director

School is over! Swimming pools are open! Parents and children are adjusting to the "freedom" of summer schedules. For any household responsible for a number of children, or even one, this freedom can mean a number of things. It can mean bedlam—a constant racing from one amusement to another. It can mean aimless drifting by shrugging off any responsibility smacking of the winter routine. Or it can mean the freedom to choose a course of action which will pay great dividends throughout the year. According to the need, this plan can be geared to instruct, inspire, strengthen, relax, renew, and reward those who decide upon such an approach to summer.

For children's choir directors the summer months can be the springboard to a successful choir year. It can be a time for unhurried creative thinking and constructive planning which will allow you to meet September with enthusiasm, poise, and an eagerness to begin.

There are several ways to initiate such a summer. First on my list is to attend the Choristers Guild Seminar where your association with others in your field is sure to fire your imagination, strengthen your abilities, and fill you with practical ideas.

If you cannot attend a school, outline a *reading* schedule for yourself. How about those books which were recommended during the year in the *Letters*? If you have not read *Boys* by Roscoe Gilmore Stott (Standard Publishing Foundation, Cincinnati, Ohio), you are allowing one of the most practical and philosophical, informative and enjoyable manuals on the subject of dealing with boys (and girls) to pass you by. What about those books on special subjects: diction, the child's voice, worship, hymnody?

Summer is the time also for listening to recordings of good children's choirs, allowing your mind to absorb the sounds you will want to strive for in your own groups.

Then there is opportunity to play over, sing over, and study the texts of new anthems or of older ones which you have never used. Make those lists of repertoire suggestions come alive by ordering a single copy of each for your own files.

Why not aim at accomplishing one or two organizational details each week through the summer? This can be done at a more relaxed tempo. Here is a suggested outline:

JUNE—1st week—Evaluate carefully the past season's program. What needs special attention for improvement? attendance? worship attitudes? rehearsal procedures?

June—2nd week—Contact choir mothers for definite assignments during next year.

June—3rd week—CHORISTERS GUILD SEMINAR or another good workshop (shifting your schedule to meet the date.)

June—4th week—Full of new ideas! Plan program for coming year. Select music. Decide on projects.

JULY—1st week—Arrange for conferences with minister. Discuss *total* program. Check details, dates choirs will sing, special services, etc.

July—2nd week &
3rd week—Vacation. Include with shorts and fishing pole at least one book for personal growth.

July—4th week—Get lists of children attending Vacation Church School. Make note of those who were not in Junior Choir. (Prospects?)

AUGUST—1st week—Get mimeographed materials ready for stencils: registration letters and cards.

August—2nd week—General check on condition of vestments. (Do this with a choir mother.) These should be ready for measurements during first rehearsal.

August—3rd week—Make attendance charts. Get advance registration mailing out.

August—4th week—Check teaching aids: charts, autoharps, easels, pictures. Decide on general seating arrangement.

HELEN KEMP

8. You Need Boys? The Boys Need You!

From many directors come these questions:

How do I get enough tenors and basses in my adult choir to balance the large number of sopranos?

How do I get and keep high-school boys interested in the Youth Choir? How do I work with their voices?

What do I do with junior-high boys?

How can I keep the boys in the Junior Choir interested, and what about discipline with them?

Now it is true that in many church choirs across the nation (perhaps in most of them) the women far outnumber and many times outsing the men. Architecturally speaking, these choirs are based on the steeple instead of the foundation!

In working with any age group of people the psychological impact of surrounding conditions cannot be ignored. If children and young people attending church always see the choir-loft jammed with women and in the back row one line of men, if they always hear the choir dominated by sopranos, the boys and young men aren't going to be very enthusiastic about joining the forces of the minority group!

Now where do we begin with ideas which may help? Since we in the Choristers Guild are bound together by our interest in the development of Christian character through children's choirs, I propose that we start with the Junior Choir.

I have often been accused of being partial to boys. This is true only to the extent that I like to have as many boys as girls in my Junior Choir. In establishing this ratio, I am also looking ahead toward feeding the Youth Choir with interested and capable tenors and basses, and eventually supplying the need for adult male singers who have come through the younger choirs. These singers will be prepared to change the usual architectural choir balance with the basses providing the foundation and women's voices singing in proportion to that foundation.

This is "Cloud 9" thinking, but if you will get down to the "brass tacks" of endeavor, you can start this year blazing the trail toward a better balance of boys and girls, men and women in your choirs.

Of one thing I am sure. No matter how good a musician you are, if you have not learned to *communicate* effectively, especially with boys, you stand a good chance of losing them. Learn *about boys*—not just about vocal technique and repertoire. Discover their current interests, their hobbies, abilities, courses in school, their serious thoughts, their normal behavior patterns, their dreams and ambitions, their individual backgrounds, strengths and weaknesses.

This year, go after them! Enlist the help of one or two Dads with whom you have discussed this problem and your plan to interest more boys. Persuade Dads to be counselors, choir fathers, helpers on Sunday mornings when the boys sing.

Put the boys to work! Invent responsible jobs for them. Actually make a list of things to assign. Be business-like in your approach—no "nice little boy" tactics. Give honest praise for work well done. Give personal suggestions where improvement is needed. Regard assignments as important work.

Discipline problems always arise. Don't let them throw you. Decide what you want from your group and work toward achieving what you expect.

Don't be discouraged by failure. Often by the system of "after-rehearsal evaluations" and a "What can I do next week to correct it?" attitude, your weakness can become your strength.

Behavior problems are mostly centered in a few ring leaders, usually boys! Recognize this fact. Try personal contact as your first approach—not in choir, but with the boy alone, after the rehearsal. Make this a rule: follow up on disciplinary measures immediately after rehearsal. "An ounce of prevention is worth a pound of cure."

Discipline, of course, is not a club! I like to think of it as orderly growth—an act of becoming. It is an attitude, the quality of which can be greatly enriched by the creative teacher.

HELEN KEMP

9. Expressive Singing by Children

By spring most of our choirs are ready to do the best work of the year, since they now have had months of foundation training. This is the time to go beyond earlier goals instead of coasting along until the end of the choir season.

I have read many times Lotte Lehman's inspiring book for singers entitled *More Than Singing*. The central thought of this artist is that the learning of notes and words, plus the continuous effort and self-discipline necessary to develop good tone-quality are only the foundations for music-making.

Can this principle be applied to the singing of our children's choirs? I believe it can and should be applied. Children are capable of going far beyond memorization of words and tunes, but the degree to which they can communicate the content of the text and create living music in a melody is determined by the director. What is this magic that can be breathed into notes on a page and make these notes become a joyful expression of gratitude or a prayer for forgiveness?

Imagination is the magic. It is the creative expression of thoughts through the mind and that which we call the soul or the spirit.

Now there are practical ways to encourage children to reach out with their minds in order to communicate with their singing voices. It has to do with vocal method, yes, but much more with imaginative teaching. Though this subject could be an exhaustive one, we shall suggest only several practical ideas for directors.

1. The phrase starts with the *intake of breath*—not with the sound of the voice. To start on a phrase expressively, then, the right mood must prompt the intake of breath.

By the power of suggestion (empathy) the director should establish the desired mood with sensitive facial aliveness, and in the mood and method of his own breathing. To make children aware of the

93

necessity to prepare thoughts before singing, have them sing "Joyful, joyful, we adore thee," but ask them to breathe and sing as though the song were "O sacred head, now wounded." It is very difficult, perhaps impossible, to breathe sorrow and sing joy!

Another interest-catcher to stress this point is to have written on the board something like the following:

| (breathe) | I hope | I hate | I love |
| | I fear | I laugh | I mourn |

Sing through these phrases, trying to capture the mood of the words hope, hate, love, etc., by breathing in according to the thought. Listen for their natural differences in tone-color.

2. *Loud* and *soft* are often wrongly thought of as interpreting. Thinking in only two degrees of volume certainly does not leave much room for imaginative and sensitive phrasing. We can train our children to be aware of at least five degrees of volume: pp, p, mf, f, ff. (This is, of course geared to the child-voice, not to the adult-voice.) Perhaps the following would be fun to try:

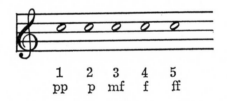

| 1 | 2 | 3 | 4 | 5 |
| pp | p | mf | f | ff |

a. Using the vowel "aw," sing each tone for 2 or 4 counts, breathing between each tone, striving for gradual increase.

b. Repeat, starting from ff, gradually diminishing.

c. Repeat, sustaining the notes, increasing gradually from note to note (but without breathing).

d. Repeat above, starting with ff and gradually diminishing. It is a good idea to be aware of the impression made by the word "louder." Loudness carries with it a suggestion of harshness.

3. Dynamic markings "a—a" are often observed by a sudden

94

bulging of tone or a disappearing whisper. To correct this fault the teacher should study the text and music to see where the *climax* of the phrase really is. He should then encourage the children to be able to build in tone gradually until this point is reached, then just as gradually diminish, so that the phrase is rounded but not weakened. Such careful regard for dynamic scaling can do much to increase your choir's ability to sing with those magic ingredients of imagination and communication.

Whenever one speaks of mood, emotion, expression or interpretation, he must make clear that these words do not imply taking great liberty with tempo, nor allowing romantic embellishments nor anything that would destroy the simplicity of children's singing.

HELEN KEMP

10. Vocal Methods

The right way of singing, to my ears, includes three things:

1. Head tone—floating and alive;
2. Uniform pronunciation of vowels;
3. A prepared consciousness of phrasing (which controls posture and breathing).

I am convinced that all children need help and encouragement in order to learn the right way of singing. The average young child does not sing correctly by instinct. By the time they are seven years old, average children have picked up singing habits that seem to be in the direction of two extremes. One is the whispery, breathy, puny voice, usually the result of not knowing the text or the music, and lack of initiative. The other is a loud, boisterous, neck-swelling sound. The latter is usually heard in what we call fun-songs, pitched too low and sung with great physical and mental abandon.

It is amazing, though, how quickly this latter type of singing can be changed by a director who knows what he should hear. Unharnessed enthusiasm can be disciplined and directed tonally without eliminating the joy of musical expression. The children also should share in knowing the sound you are working for. Good children's choir recordings and your own tape recorder for use during rehearsal can serve you and the children well.

I find the wispy voice more difficult to work with. The best results have been secured by making the children conscious of the *projection* of sound (aiming at a target), and establishing in the children the desire to communicate through text and tune.

Alertness is a necessary ingredient. Keen attention achieved through the captured interest of the children by imaginative teaching is far superior to the "big stick" approach to discipline.

Alertness has much to do with posture, correct breathing, projection of tone and thought. Teach children to be stingy with breath as they sing. Encourage them to think in long phrases. Breathing in the middle of every phrase is an undesirable singing habit, entirely unnecessary for junior-age children. Sing phrases instead of notes. Sing thoughts instead of words.

To achieve accuracy of pitch, and avoid the breathing attack, teach children to *think* before singing. "Breathe—*think*—sing" or "breathe—*pause*—sing" is good advice.

For increased volume stress projection (distance) rather than loudness.

Use many media for focusing eye-attention: blackboard work, pictures, note-charts.

The better routine matters are organized (perhaps simplified) and carried out, the more energy and time left for creative teaching.

Don't be so busy *doing* that you lose the ability to listen as your choir rehearses. The dullest rehearsals I can remember were ones marked by statements such as: "Let's sing it through again from the beginning." Aimless repetition is boring. Constructive and *inventive* repetition is a valuable teaching technique. Help children to recognize honest improvement.

You have perhaps heard of the diamond-cutter who, while he was working and evaluating gems, kept a perfect diamond in his pocket. Occasionally he would take this perfect gem from his pocket and take a long look at it so that he would not become insensitive to the imperfections of the other stones.

Listening to fine recordings and going to concerts of great choirs is like this. We cannot and do not expect perfection from our unselective children's choirs, but our ears must continually hear and absorb the beauty and aliveness of the vocal sounds for which we should strive.

As Father Finn says: "An extra-ordinary choir is usually made up of ordinary voices."

HELEN KEMP

TONE-QUALITY IN CHILDREN'S CHOIRS

Many volumes and chapters have been written on the child-voice. Yet every director must have a concept of his or her ideal tone to which all sounds must be compared, and towards which all groups must strive. Somewhere between a lifeless, thin, apathetic tone and the ugly, throaty tone that is all too common (on familiar material) is that kind of tone which a conscientious director wants.

There are times, especially in rehearsals, when we get anything but the ideal tone. When children know their material, and like it a little too well, you know what happens. They shout! On the other hand, when they are learning something new, and they are a bit lazy mentally and physically, that lazy, lifeless tone comes forth which is quite lacking in every good positive quality.

I like to start any new group vocalizing on a familiar melody. Since we are speaking of church choirs, let it be a good hymn tune. I like to use the vowel "ah" first, insisting on a wide-open mouth with a completely relaxed jaw. The old trick of putting two fingers vertically between the teeth helps to keep the mouth open, and after the novelty has worn off most children can keep their fingers in this position and at the same time relax. There is always a joker in the choir who tries to use a fist, but even this novelty passes. If the director is in front of the children, showing the proper mouth-position, and the attention of the children is focused, one can get a semblance of correct sound the third or fourth time through.

Experimenting with different keys stimulates the interest. Even the uninitiated child can hit those high F's and G's the first day, given the right mouth-position and a little energy. After trying "ah" I like to use "oh" the same way—different keys, open mouth, relaxed jaw, energy! After this I settle for "oo."

When I took my first course in vocal work for children, the emphasis was on the vowel "oo" and head tones. I have come to realize that it is not necessary to restrict the child-voice to "head tone." The sound has more character if there is some "body" in the tone; it has been called "undertone" by some. This has nothing that resembles the ugly shouting tone we get from the average group on "Onward, Christian soldiers" or "My Country 'tis of thee."

We have all discovered that it is one thing to get a good sound on an exercise (arpeggio or melody) and another to get it on words. Two things I have found helpful, and both of these must be thought of continually to keep good tone flowing through the choir. First, always have on hand something quite slow and sustained that demands a fine legato. It is amazing how fast an inexperienced choir can learn the tricks of a good legato by rote, if the director insists on the children watching and holding those "vowel moulds." This is accomplished more easily on a piece which has few words and moves slowly from note to note. A few phrases of Handel's "Thanks be to thee" or Bach's "Come, dearest Lord" illustrate this. Second, on hymns and other pieces which have more words and move along more rapidly, reading aloud with active lips before singing is surely very helpful. Those second and third stanzas of familiar hymns tax the reading ability of Junior-age children, and often it is laziness in reading words that produces the ineffective tone we hear on unfamiliar material. If they get the habit of speaking the words firmly with crisp consonants, it begins to carry over into the singing a little faster.

Assuming that we have induced some "body" into the tone, and some enthusiasm into the words, when do we have to start worrying about the "over-eager" tone? The answer is—the minute it starts! My children know I will not permit even one phrase of that offensive quality; I will stop any phrase the instant I hear it. I will ask for a showing of hands: "How many know the difference between singing and screaming?" I may even demonstrate how bad their screaming sounded to me. I threaten to stop them right in the middle of church if they do it (of course, I have never done that!)* I will try to find new ways to tell the children I want it as solid, and even as loud, as it can be without sounding like shouting. In order to sing with confidence they must know the material. And in order to know the material much repetition must take place, especially of difficult phrases.

To sum up: What sounds do I want from my children's choirs? A natural sound that has vitality, using the full power of the voice without shouting for fortissimos, and the same kind of sound with vitality, but less volume, for softer passages. I want them to know that music is more interesting if it has contrast where called for, and that a choir is a really good choir where everyone watches the director, and remembers that everyone must try for the same thing at the same time.

ROBERTA BITGOOD

*EDITORS' NOTE:

We know a cooperative, musically appreciative clergyman who, when the children's choir has sung too timidly or too boisterously in a service of worship, may say quietly something like this: "The children's choir is perfectly capable of making a more beautiful offering. I have heard them in rehearsal. This is splendid music and an inspiring text. (Here he may repeat a portion of the text.) The ushers will please wait while the choir repeats the anthem." Then the children always sing like angels with stars in their eyes! The congregation must feel a quickened interest too, for the hymn-singing is noticeably hearty after such an occurrence.

SEVEN CHOIR DIRECTORS PRESENT THEIR VIEWS ON JUNIOR CHOIR TECHNIQUES

No. 1

By STEPHEN ORTLIP

Presbyterian Church, Lookout Mountain, Tennessee

The plan for a rehearsal, complete as it may appear of itself, is really adequate only as it is executed as part of a broader scheme. Long-range planning provides the "sighting points" which affect a generally forward-moving direction. Two immediate considerations of a musical nature come to mind. These will be taken into account in setting up rehearsal plans each week:

1. Obtaining good singing of forthcoming anthems and service music.
2. Teaching of the basic skills (pitch-consciousness, tone, enunciation, chord-sense, reading, rhythm, etc.) with a view to musical foundation and future growth. Attention to this will determine ultimate progress over an extended period of time.

Our Junior Choir consists of 40 auditioned boys and girls including 4—6th graders. (There are also a few 7th and 8th grade boys, since to date we have no choir for boys in Junior High.) This group, now in its third season, practices 55 minutes per week, right after school. Most of the members attend school directly across the street. The 12 boys of the choir are seated separately from the girls.

The choir assembles in one room where they place wraps and books, answer roll call, and have a brief devotional. Then they line up in their regular order (each has a number, according to height, for the year) and proceed to the rehearsal room. A typical rehearsal may be as follows:

1. Vocalize on "woo" downward, starting on 4th line D.
2. Sing an already-learned song through. Check back on details needing attention (tone, diction, rhythm, pitch, etc.).
3. Drill on word memorization of new song. (All anthems must be individually memorized.) Test individuals on words, several at a time. Those who hesitate can be singled out. The choir mother checks names of those who pass. This can be real sport to the children when handled with strict fairness and some degree of humor and lightness.
4. Rhythm drill or notation study. Some physical activity such as clapping is desirable.
5. Singing of chord and scale patterns.

99

6. New song, learned from words on board. Certain songs are easily learned by this process.
7. Practice of service music and anthem in chancel. Over-rehearsing of Juniors on all cues, entrances, etc., is good insurance.
8. Short game out of doors, if time permits. Choir is divided into two teams for the year. The team accumulating most points by end of year is in some way rewarded over (or by) the losing team.

A balance of fun, work, dignity and achievement seem to answer the need of any choir, young or old. Details for this prescription, of necessity, vary according to the age and temperament of every group. No pattern is the final answer, for our choral salvation lies in a keen sense of empathy, and in our ability to adjust our activities to the needs of the hour.

No. 2

By Mrs. Aaron Epp
First Mennonite Church, Reedley, California

Our church is located in a rural town having a population of about 5,000. The church membership is 584. Our choir membership totals 150 for four choirs: Adult, Young People's, Junior, and Carol Choir.

Our Junior Choir has functioned for four years and includes children from the 5th—8th grades. The enrollment is 43 at present. Parents may enroll the children either in September or in January. All children are accepted, including monotones, in the hope that even if they don't all learn to sing well, they will at least learn to appreciate good music. Several who were unable to produce any melody whatsoever several years ago can now carry simple tunes.

Many of our people live in the country and have to make a special trip to town to get their children to rehearsals. Therefore our rehearsal time is scheduled for Saturday from 4-5 P.M., allowing the parents to do some shopping while the children are at rehearsal. We stress perfect attendance. If a choir member misses the rehearsal previous to the service at which they are to sing, he cannot sing with us at the service.

The choir is expected to sing for a Sunday morning service of worship once a month. Two special programs are worked on during the year: a Christmas program, and a Spring program at the close of the season in conjunction with a Promotion Service, at which time our 8th graders are promoted to the Young People's Choir. This schedule keeps the choir busy and on its toes, since everything is sung from memory.

The facilities are nothing to boast of. There is no rehearsal room, and the choirs must meet in the choir loft. As a rule the children are given no music to handle except hymnals. Since there is no blackboard, I write out melodies to be learned on large sheets of paper and tack them on a frame. This teaches the children to keep their eyes up, and it helps memorization, since I take the notes and words from them as soon as possible.

Rehearsal is usually begun with prayer, followed by several warming-up exercises. The hour is a busy one. A new song, often two-part, is introduced at almost every rehearsal. Some theory is taught but is brought in incidentally. Hymns with descants are learned easily and are especially enjoyed. Rounds are popular.

A group of choir mothers helps with robes when the children sing in the service of worship; they also help with occasional social functions and treats.

Interest and enthusiasm as well as regular attendance in our choir are very much dependent on the parents' attitude. We have been pleased with the cooperation and encouragement coming from our homes.

No. 3

By DOROTHEA HEISLER

Grace Lutheran Church, Westchester, Illinois

Grace Lutheran Church is located in a flourishing new suburb of greater Chicago. The church membership is 450. The church school membership is 325. All children in the four choirs must be members of the church school. The four divisions of our youth choirs are the following:

Cherub Choir: 24 members. 2nd and 3rd graders who sing the fourth Sunday of the month at 11 A.M. service. Rehearsal time is Saturday mornings 10:45—11:15 A.M.

Junior Choir: 75 members. 4th—8th graders who sing every Sunday at the 8:30 A.M. service. Rehearsal time is Saturday mornings 11:15—12:15.

Choristers: 14 members. High-school girls who sing the third Sunday of the month at the 11 A.M. service. (Only a year old, this is our weakest group. It will build up as the Juniors graduate into it.) Rehearsal time is Tuesday evenings 6:30—7:30 P.M.

Crusaders: 8 members. Handbell Choir of 8 high-school boys. No regular schedule, but they play at all special occasions and have many invitations from organizations outside the church. Rehearsal time is Tuesday evenings 7:30—8:30 P.M.

In June, when the public schools have been dismissed, I send a personal letter to mothers of the new second and fourth graders in our church school who are not members of our choirs inviting them to enroll their children. Rehearsal times are stipulated as well as some of the things that are expected of the children and the parents. At this time I also invite the children who were confirmed on Palm Sunday (they still belong to the Junior Choir) to a barbecue at my home as the guests of the Choristers and Crusaders. This is their formal dismissal from the Junior Choir and admission to the high school choirs.

We carry all choir rehearsals along through the summer as well as possible (although I do not care for this procedure) since our pastor has asked me to have a choir prepared for each service except the three week-ends I have for my vacation. Summer rehearsals are earlier and shorter.

In September we begin full rehearsals with full choirs. A letter goes out to every mother the day before Labor Day giving the fall schedule plus dates for future special programs. Usually two or three of these letters are sent to parents during the year, making it their responsibility to have the children prepared and informed. Choir Dedication Service is held in September. Our Christmas program rehearsals start at the first rehearsal in September for all four choirs. This year we are giving an Advent concert featuring the story of Advent and a large Advent wreath.

During Lent the choirs present a Lenten concert followed by a Silver Tea (referring to the extra plate on the table for silver offerings) for all guests. The choirs are served in a separate room to avoid confusion and so that they can unwind after the service.

The choirs are sponsored by the Choir Guild with a membership made up of persons interested in furthering the monetary efforts of the choirs. These women robe the children and help with transportation and robe repair. It is the Guild that serves the Silver Tea and in October holds an Open House to which all mothers of choir children are invited. An interesting program is planned and invitations extended to join the Choir Guild.

102

Rehearsals follow much the same pattern in all choirs. Music is laid out, each anthem on a separate pile. As the children come into the church they pick up one copy of each anthem and take it to their places which have been assigned for the year. Unfortunately we must rehearse in the church pews; however, the assigned seats in two divided lofts simplify the division of voices for two-part singing and also processional arrangements.

We begin rehearsals with vocal exercises, then go right into the various numbers being studied. When we have finished practicing a piece, it is passed to the center aisle. One assigned child from each side picks up the copies and quietly puts them back in the folder, then returns to his seat. We go quickly from one number to another, allowing no time for disorder to begin. We rehearse sometimes eight to ten numbers, each in a different stage of perfection. Difficult phrases are worked on and pronunciation is emphasized. The last step in the rehearsal is singing the next Sunday's music while standing in position in the chancel.

Strict adherence to all rules is the secret of good rehearsals and performances. Once the members know you mean what you say, success is on the way. Attention during rehearsals is required. During services choristers must watch the director and maintain good posture. No misbehavior is tolerated during services: any violator is spoken to immediately afterward. Repeated offenses warrant dismissal from the choir. No child is allowed to sing on Sunday if he has not attended the previous rehearsal. This rule stands for any performance, including special programs, regardless of the excuse: dancing lessons, football games, Scouts, etc.

After Christmas and again after Easter awards are given to children who have had perfect attendance. During my summer vacation I assigned the choristers a psalm to memorize.

Perfection does not come immediately, for a child is a peculiar creature and you will receive from him only what you expect of him. Set your goals high!

No. 4

By ELDO NEUFELD

Indianola Presbyterian Church, Columbus, Ohio

Church membership—1500; located in a fraternity-sorority area two blocks from the campus of Ohio State University; greatest problem—parking!

The youth choirs of the church are divided into three-year group-ings: Melody Choir (Grades 1—3); Junior Choir (Grades 4—6); Junior High (Grades 7 and 8); Chapel Choir (Grades 9—12).

The rehearsal room is long and rather narrow, with hard floor and walls but acoustical tile ceiling, creating a rather "dead" feeling that is not too good for singing.

Most of the Junior Choir children come on foot from neighboring schools, with a few coming by bus and more distant car pools. The early arrivals work on notebooks, or are tested for memory work, or play games in the Youth Center next door to the Choir Room.

Rehearsal begins with simple vocal exercises, either the usual vocalises or melodic excerpts from a piece that the choir is working on. The effort here is to create a listening atmosphere, as well as to foster clear, head-voice production.

The rehearsal is as varied as possible. We alternate 10 or 15 minutes of steady work on an anthem with the A B C's or the *do re mi's,* sight-singing, or listening to something on the piano or tape. Rarely do more than two anthems appear in a rehearsal.

New pieces of music are introduced with a story, a discussion, clapping the rhythm, memorizing short snatches of melody—anything to make them *wish* to see the music, which is then handed out. Copies are used only as long as they are absolutely necessary. The children are encouraged to learn to read, but also to realize that their "memorizers" tend to become lazy through lack of use.

The rehearsal ends with an Amen, Evening Hymn, or Benediction.

The largest share of our time throughout the year is consumed by preparation for the Columbus Presbytery Junior Choir Festival, which is held in March each year. Last year it grew to 600 children; this year we are dividing it into two parts. The program is carefully planned around the Church Year and so facilitates our programing.

We experimented last year with an operetta ("Tom Sawyer" by Jonathan Elkus). Although it provided a tremendous stimulus and interest, it made the choir too rushed in getting its service of worship responsibilities fulfilled.

The Junior Choir is responsible for the first Service (9:30 A.M.) one Sunday a month, with introit, anthem, responses, etc. Additional activities include caroling in December in connection with the local Heart Association, the Carol Service of Christmas Eve, and three parties during the year.

104

No. 5

By ELLEN JANE LORENZ PORTER

Fairmont Presbyterian Church, Dayton, Ohio

Our church (2,000 members in a small building) is in a mushrooming suburb; because the community and the church are young, we have two capacity sessions of all Sunday School departments through Junior.

I direct the Primary Choir of 30 (Grades 2-3), the Junior Choir of 60 (Grades 4-5-6), and the Handbell Choir of 12 (from the Junior Choir). Our Minister of Music has the Adult Choir of 25 and the Junior High Choir of 20, and Herbert Huffman has a Boy Choir of about 18.

The Junior Choir has, until this year, rehearsed only during the half-hour between Sunday School sessions. This was far too little; yet, perhaps because of the pressure, they learned and behaved amazingly well. This year, because the Sunday School classes were out of proportion and overcrowded, we are experimenting with a Junior Choir rehearsal of a full hour during the 9:30 session of Sunday School.

Our rehearsal room? The chapel, seating 70, a beautiful room, but with hard pews, no space for movement, no stationary blackboards, no piano. I refuse to tell you what instrument we use for accompaniment except to say that it's puny! The seating plan? All boys in front pews, one side; 4th Grade girls in front pews, other side; 5th Grade girls in back, one side; 6th Grade girls in back, other side. I like this because I utilize the friendly rivalry between grades. We sing once a month in a church service and participate in the city-wide Junior Choir Festival sponsored by the Dayton Choirmasters Club and in the Festival of Faith of Kettering, a suburb. We have had other out-of-church appearances through the years. Special rehearsals for acquainting the children with singing in the sanctuary are essential, especially at the beginning of the year.

Special procedures? I enjoy writing little songs for certain uses: a Quieting Song, a Relaxing Song, a Prayer Before Singing in a Church Service, a Setting-up Song, etc. We do not sing in two formal parts, but enjoy "two-melody" effects which develop independence. My assistant coaches one melody, I the other, and the children learn fast. This past summer I taught a Hymn-Study Class of old and young; and in order to follow up this start, and also to foster better hymn singing in the Junior Department, we are having a hymn-learning project with 24 hymns as our year's goal. These hymns are ones appearing in both the Sunday school and the church hymnals. I hope the Junior Choir will be ready to demonstrate hymns at our Family Hymn Night later this year.

Besides our Secretary, Librarian, and Mother Helper, we have the Timekeeper who is authorized to keep me working on schedule: 1. Prayer song. 2. Voice-training period (3 minutes). 3. Hymn period (10 minutes). 4. Attendance report and announcements (5 minutes). 5. Anthem practice (10 minutes). 6. Relaxation (2 minutes). 7. Ear-training and theory (10 minutes). 8. Service-music practice and new anthems (10 minutes). 9. Final theme song.

I really have few problems, for the children are charming and intelligent, the mothers are helpful and appreciative, and the entire church staff cooperates willingly. Doubtless the weak link in our set-up is the director, but I have a wonderful time working with the children and count it as one of the heart-warming experiences of my life.

No. 6
By Mrs. Earl F. Spencer
University Baptist Church, State College, Pennsylvania

When we moved here three years ago, there was only one choir of adults with 8 to 12 members. Now we have a graded choir program for six age-groups which has proved most successful in spite of this being a "transient" congregation. The groups vary each year because of those earning degrees or being sent to foreign countries for a year or two. This problem is a real challenge.

Our church membership is 245. Last year there were 120 in the six choirs. This year (so far) we have 26 in the Primary Choir, 25 in the Junior Choir, 18 in the Junior High Choir, 12 in the Senior High Choir, and 25 in the Adult Choir, making a total of 106. A Student Choir gets started later in the season.

The Junior Choir (9-11) rehearses on Fridays at 3:50 P.M. Those arriving early enjoy supervised activities: folk-dancing, marching, and tag. At 3:50 punch and cookies are served. This is supplied by the mothers, taking turns each week. I, as director, do the telephoning for the refreshments, since it gives me contact with parents, which I feel is very valuable. The children help serve the refreshments and clean up, after which they line up with good posture and proceed quietly to the sanctuary. (We rehearse in the sanctuary so that they may learn respect and reverence for the House of God.) The fact is stressed that they are ministers of music and should conduct themselves in fitting manner.

Rehearsal Procedures
1. Deep-breathing exercises.
2. Vocalizing on "looh," trying for a bell-like tone.
3. Practicing songs already learned.
4. Learning a new song:
   Listening first with eyes closed;
   Clapping the rhythm;
   Singing it on "looh" until melody is learned;
   Reading words and discussing them;
   Singing words and melody.
5. In between serious rehearsing, break it up with a "fun song."
6. Learn the "hymn of the month" and its background.
7. Each child is given a sheet every week to put in a folder to make up a yearbook pertaining to religious education. At the end of the year each child makes his own cover and staples the book together. This is done at the final rehearsal, after which we have a supper that they plan, suggesting their own menu.
8. The rehearsal ends at 5 o'clock with a prayer, or singing the Navajo "Spirit of the Living God" with gestures:

SPIRIT OF THE LIVING GOD," (reach arms upwards, hands facing each other, and look up on the word "living"; wave right hand back and forth; on "God" point right hand upward) Repeat phrase and gestures.

"FALL AFRESH ON ME." (On "fall" bring hands down; on "me" place hands on chest) Repeat.

"BREAK ME," (Clench hands, place together with fingers down, and make a breaking motion)

"MOLD ME," (Clasp right hand over left hand, then left hand over right hand)

"MELT ME," (Make oval motions away from you, passing one hand over the other)

"FILL ME." (Make large oval motions with arms towards yourself)

"SPIRIT OF THE LIVING (Same motions as above)
GOD,"
"FALL AFRESH ON ME." (Same motions as above)
The tune of this Navajo song may be found in the booklet *In Harmony.*

The Junior Choir sings once a month in the church service on the 4th Sunday, in the Candlelight Service at Christmas, in a special service on "The Life of Christ in Scripture and Song" given on Passion Sunday, and in the Junior Choir Festival.

We do not use an award system, as we consider this unnecessary expense and record-keeping. The children are made to feel that choir work is a vital part of the church and a way in which they can serve. We have no attendance problem. Each year the children are encouraged to write a hymn; one is chosen to be sung on Children's Day. On Children's Day the Primary and Junior Choirs bring bouquets of flowers which are carried in the processional as they sing "For the Beauty of the Earth"; then the flowers are placed in foil-covered cans arranged across the pupit platform. Following the service the children take their bouquets to a shut-in, a sick person, or a friend. This has become an annual tradition, and is very beautiful.

No. 7
By Ruth Parkhurst
The American Church, Caracas, Venezuela

The American Church in Caracas is an interdenominational church whose members come from many of the major denominations and from more than twenty different countries. The church membership is 640, including members of small branches in the interior of Venezuela in the larger oil fields.

The church also serves a large "non-member" list—people who are active while they are here, but often do not join because of the brief span of their stay in the city. Length of contact with a family can vary from six months to an average of two years. Some few reside here for a longer length of time, but the congregation is accurately termed a "floating" one. In the adult Choir, which fluctuates between 25 and 60 voices, there are only ten voices who were here five years ago.

Oil is the economic center of the community, and everything eventually ties in with it. The families with whom we have contact are embassy and army families and technical personnel who have

108

lived everywhere from Bombay to Paris. The children of these families have been exposed to many varieties of education; but for the most part, music education is lacking, simply because time and energy did not permit it. Instability is the keynote of our congregation. The chief aim of this particular church is to be one of the few stable elements in the community.

We have the following choirs:

Treble Choir of Adult Women: 6 to 12 voices; sings regularly for the first of duplicate services.

Chancel Choir of Mixed Adults: 25-60 voices; sings regularly for the second of duplicate services and for special services.

(The Adult Choir season is year-round; the Youth Choirs, September—May)

Chapel Choir: 40 Intermediates, 12-15 years; sings once a month for 5:30 Vespers, youth-led services, and for special services—a total of 15 services.

Crusader Choir: 50 Juniors, 9-11 years; sings seven times during their season, for regular and special services.

Carol Choir: 28 Primaries, 7-8 years; sings five times during their season, for regular and special services.

Because much of our youth-choir work begins "at scratch" and there is a limited carry-over from year to year, the emphasis must be on training rather than performing. For this reason the two younger choirs appear in services less often than the Chapel Choir.

The main problems of youth-choir work are to fill in the lack of general music education (there is almost no supplementing from schools here); get voices on the right track; and combat the unmixed chest-tone which is widespread in Venezuela. This goes from child through adult, probably due to their Indian heritage, and applies to both speaking and singing voices. This is the tone which is heard in general—at school, on the radio, in the street—and carries its influence, in spite of good modulation which may be in use at home.

For the above reasons our youth-choir work carries a heavier training emphasis in basic things than in most churches, and our literature sticks to music which we hope the children will contact later when they move on. There is no room for branching out into new and different fields which might be exciting for a few. All elements are stressed which will make for solidity later on, regardless of the denomination they may move into.

When the children register in September, I listen to each voice individually, and make note of any individual problems. Those who need extra help come early for individual pre-rehearsal work each week until their specific problem is eliminated. In the beginning of the season the group for this work is a rather large one, but I find there is no substitute for the individual handling of the problems. The voices come onto the right track much quicker in this way. I have found that the best way to work at basic tone-matching is with the sounds of "yoo-hoo" on the fifth and third of the triad. When they can do this, they move into matching the whole triad, and then consecutive triads.

I work with the Primaries entirely by rote for song-learning and work with elements of sight-reading from the blackboard. The Juniors use the music until it is memorized; the Intermediates work from music for rehearsals and services. We do unison singing entirely with the Primary and Junior groups; we do not begin two-part work with the Intermediates until their unison singing is unanimous. The Intermediates have done some outstanding work in combination with the Adult Choir, such as Clokey's Easter cantata "For He Is Risen." (I recommend this highly for combined work with youth and adult choirs.)

Music for rehearsals of the youth choirs is placed on each chair beforehand. Seats are assigned for the year with a careful eye as to weak and strong voices and explosive mixtures of personality.

Many authorities claim that children think vocal exercises are either funny or boring. I have found their reaction to be one of interest and enthusiasm. I started exercises because of our unusual tone problem, and regard them as invaluable in establishing correct singing habits quickly. During the past five years I have worked out the following system which works for us, at least, like a charm:

1. All youth-choir rehearsals begin with a Choral Grace, spoken together; then with members in "singing position" (feet flat on floor, knees together, back straight, hands in lap) we do the following vocal exercises until the full choir is singing correctly. In the early part of the season it sometimes takes 15 minutes to eradicate the unmixed chest-tone which the children hear everywhere. As the season moves on they can go through the exercises perfectly, first time through.

2. Begin with the A-C-E triad and sing it on "moo" from top to bottom and back (5-3-1-3-5). This starts it in easy head-tone and helps to carry it down.

3. Once the right tone is established, sing consecutive triads in

110

this way, permitting no change, working down from the A-C-E triad to the middle C-E-G triad.

4. Turn the triad around and with no change sing it from bottom to top (1-3-5-3-1).

5. Sing consecutive triads, still on "moo," in this way—working up from middle C to: 2nd F for Primaries;
   2nd A for Juniors;
   High C for Intermediates.

6. Begin again with the A-C-E triad, and move from "moo" to "wah," permitting no flicker of change between the two vowels.

7. Cover the same range of consecutive triads with "wah-wah-wah-wah-wah."

8. Then move to sustained singing, using the five steps within the triad, working down from the 2nd E to middle C.

7. When the full choir is singing correctly, the "Dresden Amen" is sung in three keys: F, G, and A. This Amen is sung as a response to the prayer and benediction in services of worship. At least we can always count on a beautiful free tone at two points in the service!

We never move on to the next exercise until the whole choir is navigating the one in hand as well as they can for their particular phase. By the time we reach the final Amen everyone is doing the best he can at that moment. As the weeks go by, and they *can* achieve correct singing, then I demand it every step of the way. The youngest to the oldest children seem to love this challenge and feel real gratification when they achieve promotion to the next exercise. When the three Amens are right, we begin the hymns for the next service, and try to carry over into the words the same elements we have been working on.

We try to begin with music that is familiar, and then move on to new material. At frequent intervals, depending on the age group, the children are allowed to relax from the singing position. Periods of working on the processional and other mechanics are interspersed through the rehearsal for variety.

When the hymn work is acceptable, the other service music is rehearsed. Here the flowing line, phrasing, and diction are especially stressed.

With such techniques adapted to our special needs do we conduct the work of the several youth choirs of an interdenominational American church in a Latin-American setting.

REHEARSAL DISCIPLINE

Never do I see a list of problems that face a choir director but that the word *discipline* appears. I have read long and elaborate helps to better discipline. Yet I think the solution is really a simple one: the best time to solve your discipline problems is before you enter the rehearsal room. The best way to solve them is to "plan your work and then work your plan." This I cannot emphasize strongly enough. No matter how capable we may be, none of us can go to a rehearsal unprepared and expect to achieve results.

The rehearsal must be interesting; it must be varied in approach—varied in difficulty, key, style, and purpose. We dare not use left-overs for our rehearsals. Ideas must be new, fresh, challenging; they must be fast-moving. If all this is true, our children will have neither the time nor the desire to misbehave.

There must be a clear indication as to the starting time of a rehearsal. Dr. Whittlesey has a bell which he rings two minutes before rehearsal time. At the end of two minutes, when the bell rings again, each chorister is in his seat and ready to rehearse.

(I play a hymn tune in the form of a prelude. This is followed by a Biblical passage, read by choir members to whom the passage has been assigned a week in advance. Many times the selections are among the many in the Bible which have reference to the use of music in worship. Other selections may contain the text of a hymn or anthem to be studied during the rehearsal. The rehearsal ends with a prayer and benediction response. For those who are confronted with the problem of holding rehearsals in the sanctuary, this would be doubly desirable in helping to remind the children that this is God's house.)

The rehearsal room should be set up, if possible, in the same formation as that of the sanctuary. We have a divided chancel with about twenty feet between opposite sides. The necessity of rehearsing in such a formation is obvious.

Children need a minimum of formal directing, I believe. Through experimentation we have found that we get the best results when I play for the children. Over our altar hangs a long wooden cross. Each child is trained to center his visual attention at the foot of the cross. (Is this not truly the place where we need to center more of our attention?) This means that no child sees me during the singing of an anthem. But by careful rehearsing we find that the children will not miss an attack or release.

Another question concerns the division of authority between choir director and organist. The answer may be to have them one and the same person. But if this is not the case, then I (as the organist) will have to admit that the director is the final authority. It is unfortunately true that many of our organists are better musicians than many of our choir directors. Many problems may arise as a result of this situation. Yet again I feel that the answer is for the director to plan his work in such a way that he knows what he wants and that he can give valid reasons for wanting it. Nearly any organist will accept this, I believe. Certainly the relationship must be one of give and take on both sides; if this is impossible, all other things being equal, I feel that you need a new organist.

Children like recognition. We seldom forget to recognize birthdays. At the beginning of each month I write the cards for all who have birthdays during that month, dating each envelope. Cards are then mailed on the dates indicated.

This year our bulletin board held a separate card for each member of the children's choirs. On the right side was space for a picture of the child. Following each rehearsal and service, a colorful sticker was added to the card. This the children could watch grow and were easily reminded of their own stewardship level.

NORMA LOWDER

"PLAN YOUR WORK AND WORK YOUR PLAN"

Not only is it important that each rehearsal be planned well, it is also important that at the beginning of the choir year we have over-all plans made for the entire season. We mimeograph a brochure for each choir which lists:

1. The calendar for the year;
2. The hymns which will receive special emphasis;
3. The anthems to be sung in services;
4. Social activities;
5. Membership, addresses and telephones;
6. Standards.

It is seldom necessary to change our schedule once it has been planned in conjunction with the complete church program as drawn up by the staff in their annual retreat. Again we say, "Plan your work, then work your plan." The best-drawn plans are useless if the house is never built!

Social activities become increasingly important to the child of junior age, and some extra-choir activities are desirable. We schedule

113

four such occasions each year, among which are Christmas caroling to shut-ins and older members of the church, and the annual School of Choirs Banquet.

We are strong believers in warm-up rehearsals. Our choirs have never sung in a service without having had a vocal, emotional, and spiritual warm-up before that service. This is as important for children as for adults.

All of our choirs process; on occasion, the children process silently. We do not march. Ordinarily the congregation stands at the sound of the first notes of the organ and joins in the singing of all stanzas. The choirs never sing stanzas alone. Hymns belong to the entire congregation and should be sung by all. The choirs immediately begin to move forward when the hymn is announced, so that a goodly number of choristers will be inside the sanctuary for the opening verses of the hymn.

I am, perhaps, one of the few directors of children's choirs in the United States who does not have a Mothers' Guild, or Parents' Guild, as such. The children respond much better when their parents, or other adults, are not around. In fact, I believe *I* am more effective when other adults are not around! This does not mean that I do not call on parents for help when needed; they are always ready to do more than their part. The children bring their robes from home and keep them at home during the choir year, therefore I have no need of special help with robing. Ours is a community church, so transportation committees are not necessary. We do not serve refreshments at rehearsal, so no help is needed here. I prefer to call personally those who are unable to attend a service or a rehearsal; the list is never long enough to become a problem, even when schedules get tight.

On the other hand fortunately we seem always to have young people who are considering entering the ministry of music, and it is to these I turn for help. They do not have any of the personal prejudices that parents naturally feel toward their own children. They are most willing to do whatever I ask of them without question; additionally, I feel that it may in some small way help them along the road as they prepare to handle programs of their own. These young people check attendance, keep rolls, send cards to absentees, organize processionals, etc.

For us this seems the best solution. We must, however, be in the minority, for an active Mothers' Club seems to be the accepted thing in the organization and administration of children's choirs. Perhaps, like the Pentagon, there are five sides to *every* question!

114

The prime consideration is that each director must use the plan that for him works best. None of us wishes to be just like someone else; the carbon copy is never as clear as the original!

NORMA LOWDER

OUTLINE FOR A JUNIOR CHOIR REHEARSAL

Here is an outline of a typical Junior Choir rehearsal of the Bellaire Methodist Church, Bellaire, Texas. The hymns and responsive reading are all in *The Methodist Hymnal.* They are scheduled for use in the Worship Service for the following Sunday.

1. Hymn Number 505: "God the Omnipotent!"
   (This is to be Sunday's processional hymn for the morning service)
   What does it symbolize?
   In what ways does it describe God?
   > Discuss meaning of "omnipotent," "all-merciful" and "all-righteous One."
   What is our petition?
   What can we as individuals do to achieve this?
   Sing the hymn.
2. Responsive Reading, page 567 (4th Sunday, 2nd Reading)
   Do you know from what part of the Bible this Scripture comes?
   (They should, and will, for they have sung some of the text.)
   Let's check to be sure. (See Index)
3. Hymn Number 18: "For the beauty of the earth"
   Here is another hymn we sing many times.
   For what things do we thank God?
   > (Beauty of earth, glory of skies, day, night, hill, vale, tree, flower, sun, moon, stars, ear, eye, heart, mind, sense of sound and sight, human love, friends, gentle thoughts, the church, God himself.)
   When was this hymn written?
   What is the meaning of 7, 7, 7, 7, 7, 7, 7, 7?
   How did this hymn get its name?
   > (We have, earlier in the year, made quite a study of meter and of the various ways hymn tunes are named.)
   Where else can we find this tune in our Hymnal? (See Index)
4. Vocal calisthenics:
   Put two fingers in your mouth (up and down); sing 1-3-5-8-5-3-1 in various keys, gradually ascending the chromatic scale.

115

(This is one of my favorite exercises. The children think it is fun. They can reach almost no end of height in pitch. They relax the throat in doing so, and the tone begins to float.)

5. Anthem: "All Praise to Thee, Eternal Lord" 17th Century Melody. (Presser)

   Same melody as "Ye Watchers and Ye Holy Ones." (This has been read in previous rehearsals.)

   Sing all verses in unison.

   Sing antiphonally. (Everyone echo the first musical idea in the second.)

   Sing as dialogue. (Girls reply to boys.)

   Sing in parts. (This is more or less a canon.)

6. Anthem: "Saviour, Blessed Saviour" Carl Mueller. (C. Fischer)

   First reading. Detailed tuning work on "Amen."

   Altos sing the four-tone scale, starting on B-flat, with sopranos taking over and continuing up the scale another four notes.

   Add resolutions in both parts.

   Work for blend and beauty of tone and feeling.

   Read words of entire song, one person at a time, stopping at the end of a phrase, where the next reader continues. This will not only give a total picture of the text, but will give a basic concept of phrasing.

   All read first verse together, with particular attention to phrasing. Whisper words as melody is played.

   Sing (melody only).

7. Announcements and recognition of birthdays.

8. Closing Hymn, Number 171: "Rejoice, the Lord is King"

9. Benediction Prayer.

Even though this choir does not participate as such in the morning service, we feel the meaning of the service will be much greater to our children if they know in advance the music and reading to be used.

NORMA LOWDER

OUTLINE FOR TWO ANTHEM STUDIES

ANTHEM NO. 1: "O Lord Our Governor" Marcello. (Concordia CH 1045)

First Week

1. See how quickly the choir can learn the first tutti phrase and the last phrase just before the tutti on page 5. These are the two climax phrases.

116

2. Learn one of them well before introducing the second. Sing them on "fah" in progressive keys as a vocal exercise.

Second Week

1. Write the two phrases on the board with the words.
2. See if the children recognize them and can sing them.
3. Repeat until they can sing them well and easily.
4. Write on the board the short phrase "is thy great Name" that just precedes the second of these longer phrases. Learn to sing it.
5. Either sing or play the anthem (singing is preferable) and let the choir sing these three phrases whenever they appear. Point to the phrase on the board just before they are to sing it.
6. Do the same thing over again, and this time let some child make a record on the board of the number of times each phrase is repeated. (This is a good way to get active interest in repetition.)

Third Week

1. Let the choir discover the pattern of phrases in each section of the anthem.
   First section: first phrase ascends; next two are identical descending phrases; then three short phrases, each one a little lower.

Second section:

```
high \      / high \
       \  /         \
        low          low
```

Third section:

```
           / higher \
high     /            \
                      low-low
```

Fourth section: one long descending phrase, like coming downstairs.
Fifth section: (Omit.)

2. Sing again, the choir indicating by hand the shape of the sections.

Fourth Week

1. Review the pattern of the sections.
2. Sing the whole anthem with the choir, using the pattern outlines as reminders.
3. From this point on, it is a matter of repetition until the children can sing it with spirit and assurance. The more secure they are, the less you will sing, until you are not singing with them at all.

117

1. You must know this anthem from memory to teach it well.
2. The first impression must be one of enjoyable rhythmic vigor.
3. Be sure that each step is secure before you go to the next one, otherwise the children will be confused and lose interest.
4. Disregard the solo parts; use the full choir throughout.
5. This is an excellent number; it has vitality, is a challenge to flexibility and good diction, and has a comfortable range.

ANTHEM NO. 2: "Lord and Savior, True and Kind" Lovelace. (Flammer 86162)

First Week

1. Write these rhythmic phrases on the board:

2. Say: "Our new anthem is made up of two-measure phrases. If we can clap these five patterns without a mistake, we can sing this anthem very quickly."
3. Clap one of the rhythms; let the children call out the number.
4. When they recognize them quickly, call out a number and let choir clap it.
5. Let one child clap a pattern; whoever recognizes it first, claps another. (Be sure to count clearly throughout clapping.)
6. Pass out the music; play the melody, two measures at a time, and let the choir call out the number of the pattern.
7. Repeat; let one child mark on the board the number of times each pattern appears.
8. Repeat melody again; choir claps rhythm and sings melody on "fah."

118

9. Say: "The piano has many more notes to play than you have to sing. Sometimes it moves on while you stay on one note. Can you keep your part going clear and true while I play *all* of the piano part? (Be sure to play clearly and rhythmically.)

Second Week

1. Quick review.
2. Say: "In the Temple in Jerusalem, where Jesus went with his parents when he was twelve years old, they had a very large choir. The Book of Psalms was their hymnbook, and it was the custom to sing *antiphonally*. Antiphonal means responsive, like the responsive readings in our church. Perhaps the big choir sang one phrase, and a small choir at the other end of the big Temple answered. This anthem that Bach wrote is like that. Suppose you read the words to yourself while I play it through." (Be sure to observe the *mf* and *mp* markings). "What words does the answering choir sing? Now let's read together the words that the big choir sings . . . Now sing the whole anthem, but make it sound like a full choir and an answering choir far off . . . What do these marks mean: *mf* and *mp?*" (Write them on board.)
3. Give each child an attractive card with these words. Suggest that they use it as their daily prayer this week.

   "Lord and Savior, true and kind,
       be the master of my mind;
   Bless and guide and strengthen still
       all my powers of thought and will.
   Striving, thinking, learning still,
       let me follow thus thy will,
   Till my whole glad nature be
       trained for duty and for thee."

Third Week

1. Either open or close the rehearsal by repeating this prayer.
2. Sing through from memory, reminding them of the big choir and the small one.
3. Sing through again, this time having everyone sing the lower part where it is divided. (Play the alto part with them.) Tell them that next week you will have a contest, and those who can sing the alto part alone and without a mistake may sing that part when you sing in church. (If the choir is small and has difficulty in singing parts, let them all sing the melody throughout. Spend your time instead on clear diction; after some concentrated practice, invite

the minister or secretary or a choir mother in to test how well the words can be understood.)
4. Repeat until alto part is fairly secure. Then play soprano part, while the choir sings the alto part.

Fourth Week
1. Review step 4 of previous week.
2. Contest: Volunteer stands beside you and sings with choir on unison phrases, but sings alto part alone while choir continues on soprano. Close the contest when there are enough for a balance. If there are not enough, review whole choir on alto part, and continue contest next week.

RUTH KREHBIEL JACOBS

ACCOMPANYING THE JUNIOR CHOIR

How many organists have shared with me the realization that on certain occasions when a children's choir sang rather well the total musical effect was ruined by the inadequate organ accompaniment? And how often, when something is lacking in performance, we hear that unfortunate and uniformed remark: "Oh well, children need the piano to give them confidence!"

Children can sing with organ just as well as they can with piano, and children can sing with less visible direction than adults. Whether or not they hold word or music, children learn their choir music at least partially by note, and when they do, certain things come through reliably: ritards are always the same (don't try to change after they are learned); shading is always the same; also phrasing, diction, blend. If the director insists on certain correct procedures as the learning is begun, the final result will always be the same—barring sudden fright or unforeseen distractions. It is, of course, of great importance to have the children's attention focused on the director. But even with all this, poor accompanying can certainly spoil the finished product.

This does not mean that a lot of rehearsal time should be spent in the choir loft rehearsing with organ. Music should not be rehearsed with the organ until it is learned and practically ready for performance. A rehearsal of an hour is much more profitably spent with 40 or 50 minutes in a smaller rehearsal room with the piano. When my children beg to go into the church to practice, I tell them that they may when they are "ready." Often I will rehearse a few minutes in the church without instrument, just so they will focus their attention on the right person in the right spot. If they know their music and are

120

completely disciplined about watching, they will not depend on the organ sound to pull the tone out of them. If one of the unfortunate times occurs when they "freeze," nothing could have helped except possibly 15 minutes more practice time in the rehearsal room. The children need to feel at home in the choir loft and in whatever spot they occupy for singing. They need constant reminders about posture, mouth position, watching the director, and so on; but let's not blame the organ for situations that neither piano nor organ can help.

Now about the organ accompaniments themselves: In general the type of pieces that children sing in unison should have a certain ethereal quality in the accompaniment. The tone quality should be distinct, but not necessarily loud. It is impossible to suggest exactly what stops to use. Flutes are ideal on some organs; on others, too loud or tubby; on others, too soft and indistinct. Be sure that something can be heard at the 4' pitch, either by sound stop or coupler. If the accompaniment has right-hand chords that also include the melody, perhaps a swell gamba plus a 4' flute will do the trick. On some organs this might sound horrible. Perhaps you have a soft dulciana that can be played with a 4' coupler which will sound well. If the accompaniment has an independent melody in the right hand with chords in the left, try the dulciana at 8' and 4' for the left, with flutes 8' and 4' in the right, and a light pedal coupled with dulciana. On electronic organs, playing the whole piece an octave higher sometimes gives just the clarity needed.

The touch used must not be overlooked. Organists who play everything with an unphrased and muddy legato will not suddenly acquire the right touch for accompanying a children's choir. A command of the various touches used in the best organ-playing does not come by accident. It is the result of careful practice and the guidance of a skilled teacher. Without good technique an organist is bound to lack the qualities needed for accompanying certain kinds of music. Don't expect to make a wonderful organ accompanist out of a person who does not already possess keyboard facility.

Don't feel you must play the pedals *all* the time. (Do the double basses play every minute with the cellos in the orchestra?) There is no excuse for a staccato, thumpy pedal. The continuo type of bass is often better played with the left hand alone and a very occasional pedal note. These choices are suggested to an imaginative performer by the music itself, regardless of whether the choir sings in unison or parts. Sometimes there is a spot in an anthem where the organ should predominate and rise above the sound of the singing; however, this

121

seldom happens in the type of music used with children's voices alone. An exception is the massed type of composition for combined choirs where a thin accompaniment would give a pitiful lack of support for dynamic climaxes.

Let us remember that most organs are inadequate for *something*. Organists have to be resourceful when their instruments just do not have the right stops, the right pitches, the right volume, the right tone color. It is rather ridiculous to hear that certain directors will not allow their organists to use strings to accompany voices. A broad string that is not too loud is much better than a tubby flute. On the other hand I know another director, famous for work with children's choirs, who says: "Never use flutes." If I were limited by the piercing strings on some organs I know, I would be seriously hampered in accompanying children. Contrast flutes with strings, don't always mix them. Use each alone for sections. Try a diapason with a mixture for a solo line in the accompaniment. Don't close your mind to the possibilities of anything at all; an unorthodox idea sometimes produces the best ensemble sound. Use the tremulo sparingly, if at all, with accompaniments. In general, avoid the use of celestes. A stop that derives its character from off-pitch tuning should not be depended on to keep singing children on pitch. However, it is possible that a vox celeste or unda maris may be just the filler needed between the stop that is too soft and the one that is too loud.

A good accompanist on any instrument must learn the "feel" of a good vocal line. Listening to a fine singer who has perfect command of a real legato can teach an organist much about organ legato. An experienced accompanist learns that persons of strictly vocal background tend to take more liberties with rhythm and other musical factors than those trained entirely instrumentally. Somewhere between the two extremes the good accompanist fits into the picture—encouraging, helpful, and maintaining a level of good taste.

Phrasing is so important in vocal accompaniment of any kind. It is particularly true on the organ, since phrasing on that instrument is always a conscious effort which must never be forgotten. This need not mean a pause at every comma or catch-breath. Since children often can sing only rather short phrases, this could be deadly. Most music is clearer when the organist makes a complete but short break (½ to ¼ second) at the end of longer phrases, obviously at the places where the young singers breathe.

What are some of the principles we apply to good organ playing? When it should be legato, let it be a good legato. When passage work

122

demands a slightly detached touch, let this be even and clean-cut. Add to this a convincing rhythm that demands attention and logical phrasing that follows the vocal line. For accompanying use the swell pedal sparingly and slowly, but use it without pumping. Have a concept of the ideal tone-quality; approximate it as closely as you can on the instrument at hand. Don't fuss around too much with registrations in a short piece. Listen as you play and be ready to make minor adjustments at any moment your ear demands them. And let's get away from the idea that *anyone* can play for a Junior Choir. It takes quite a somebody to do it well!

ROBERTA BITGOOD

FOR JUNIOR HERO-WORSHIPERS

A Junior is a hero worshiper. Let's provide him with worthy heroes. *The Story of the Church* by Walter Russell Bowie (Abingdon Press) makes the heroes of the church come to glowing life. The telling of the church's long story from the time of Christ to the present is both vivid and scholarly. It is the ideal book to use with your Juniors as the basis for a study of the heroes of the church in 33 short chapters. Using one chapter at each rehearsal would provide dramatic and compelling material for a whole year of study. I got it from our church library, and until I had finished reading it, everything else was neglected.

(R. K. J.)

The Boy Choir

THE BOY CHOIR: FUN AND FUNDAMENTALS

To many a choral director the mere mention of the words "boy choir" causes a certain tremor of something less than joy to vibrate up and down the spinal cord. But with a stout heart and real desire to create a musical understanding in the growing spirit of boyhood much can be accomplished.

One basic problem which presents itself is a preoccupation with the job of making the choir "fun," often over the more important concern of musical fundamentals. This article does not purport to belittle its importance, only its origin and growth.

February is the time of year when most directors are at the midpoint between the seasons of Christmas and Easter. The choir program now rises or falls according to which direction the director has taken in terms of fun or fundamentals. My thesis is that a well-organized choir makes an atmosphere in which *both* fun and music flourish. This article deals with the two basic criteria for a well-organized group in church or school. These are the creation of a choir in which the boy feels real and personal identification, and one in which a musical spirit is encouraged and fostered.

In my experience I have found the Choir Handbook and Membership Card the means of helping the boy to identify himself with the choir and to make it an organization worthy of his interest and loyalty. How does this fit into the overall organization of the group?

Boys in the church community are informed of the first rehearsal through the special choir news sent into the homes early in September by our Department of Music. The first meeting is an important one both from the standpoint of the individual and the group. When the boys arrive they are interviewed by three older members of the group and certain information is recorded on a sheet which also contains coded data for at least two individual voice tests. In addition, the boy is also helped to address an envelope to himself. The boys in our group (third through eighth grade) are then interviewed at the piano in groups of four or five. This is the end of the first meeting.

During the following week each boy receives in the mail his self-addressed envelope containing a colorful mimeographed booklet entitled "PPC Boy Choir, Your Handbook." The cover contains these words: "Welcome upon becoming a member." This is followed by his name—written, not printed. (Boys of this age do not appreciate the typed signature.) This when received through the mail gives the boy a real sense of pride and worth in the choral program. The sense of personal identification is an important one in the beginning, as it is broadened to include a loyalty to the group as well. The cover of the booklet also contains his classification, which in our group would be one of the following three: Senior Member, Junior Member, or Trainee.

The Choir Handbook itself contains five parts for the information of the members:

What We Do as a Choir
Rehearsals
The Choir Year
On Your Good Behavior
Membership and Awards

After a few weeks of singing together, officers are elected. As a part of their assumption of duties a membership ceremony is held, usually in the chapel, with the minister of the church giving a short talk to the members of the choir reminding them of their responsibilities and opportunities for service. The membership card is simple and contains a short creed.

Fun now triumphs. But it is a different kind of fun from that of disorderly games or a constant party-like spirit. Choir is fun because each boy is involved in an activity of his liking: in planning roller-skating activities; in engaging in the total church program by singing in church; and, most of all, in having a personal stake in his own choir.

With diligence and thought on the part of the director the fundamentals of fine musicianship may be introduced from time to time while learning new selections. Even this becomes fun—the real fun which comes from learning and growing.

And our last point. The creation of musical spirit, our second criterion, does not have to compete with athletic activities. The job

126

of the director at this point is a two-lane highway. He must build a strong program while at the same time educating parents to realize that music and sports *can* go hand in hand. A boy can play football and sing in the boy choir. Too often we either try to convert our choir into a full-fledged football team or we reconcile ourselves to receiving and training the leftovers from various recreation programs. It is said that the middle ground often seems to be the safest ground. Through the wise interest of the choir director in the activities of the boys in his choir he can easily create a spirit of understanding which bridges the gap between the two activities. At this point many parents need to be gently reminded and helped to appreciate the value of the boy-choir program.

Most of the remarks in this article are equally true at church and school. Is it too much to expect these "angels" to come bounding into the rehearsal room even in February with the same excited enthusiasm which they exhibited in December? A most emphatic "No"! But it is a test of how well you have organized for fun and fundamentals. If the boy believes it to be a worthwhile outlet for his energies, loyalty, and interest, the church and school music programs will be the recipients of a most important rendering of service from the sincere devotion of the spirit of boyhood.

DARWIN R. RUSSELL

ON BOY CHOIRS

Last Sunday morning in our first service the minister had seven young men (Junior High and High School) line up at the chancel steps. They were commended for the winning of trophies for sportsmanship in the various city-wide church leagues for basketball, baseball, etc. I thought at the time how many of the youngsters in the various grades were impressed by this recognition. Most of the winners were selected by vote of their team-mates. I also know what the winning of a letter means to those in school—a tangible evidence to themselves and others of their loyalty, cooperation, spirit and contribution.

Too many times boys particularly think there is something sissy about choir membership. I wish there was some way to impress upon the youngsters themselves, their parents, and their friends, what loyalty, devotion, cooperation and contribution mean in the choir. How can it be pointed up? What could we do to impress this upon them? Are hoods for yearly attendance or crosses the answer? Or is there something more that can be done? A ceremony in the service? Or is there more significance in an individual rather than a group "blessing"?

DR. CHARLES LEE

A BOY NEEDS A MAN

Johnny's school teacher is a woman. Johnny's Sunday School teacher is in nine cases out of ten a woman. The librarian from whom he gets his books is undoubtedly a woman. The principal of his school is probably a woman. More likely than not it is his mother who disciplines him at home. About the only man in his daily life is his father who probably comes home late, and leaves early, and is too busy to spend any time with Johnny. That is, if Johnny is lucky enough to have a father. Some Johnnies don't!

And Johnny's choir director is very likely a woman too. What a pity that so many church musicians are afraid of Johnny and never discover the wonderfully exhilarating and humbling experience of earning a small boy's trust and devotion. Those occasional men who have had the courage and vitality to tackle a choir of boys have found the rewards well worth the scars of battle. A boy needs a man!

ANON.

ALEC WYTON AND A NEW GROUP OF BOYS

An observer writes of ALEC WYTON as he worked with a group of boys he had never seen before.

His first move, in a natural and friendly way, was to establish a feeling of ease and of pleasurable anticipation. Then in a comfortable and unhurried manner he took them through the following exercises, and as the rehearsal proceeded, the boys responded with increasing freedom and interest.

Mr. Wyton played for the rehearsal himself. Over the top of the spinet piano he could see the boys, who were seated around him in a semicircle.

1. All sang the first stanza of *America,* the piano giving substantial support.

2. "Now stand and sing as far as you can on one breath. When you have to take a new breath, sit down."

3. Played individual notes on the piano, asked boys to match it. Played two notes, asked boys to sing the bottom one. Played three together, asked boys to sing the middle one.

4. Played five notes in succession, asked boys to repeat them; then varied five notes in different ways, each variation somewhat more difficult and less obvious; boys had to listen intently to *do re mi fa sol; do mi re fa sol; do sol fa re mi.*

5. Had boys stand and showed them how to breathe, using diaphragm. Gave them a pitch, then had them breathe together, then hum.

128

Breathe—hum—ah; same using oh, then aye, oo, ee. (Mr. Wyton shaped the vowels with his lips, but did not sound them.)

Hum-oo-oh-ah-aye-ee (indicating with his lips when to change from one vowel to another); all on one pitch and one breath.

6. Showed them the *shape* of the vowels. Boys recognized vowels from mouth position only (no sound).

7. "Now sing *America* again, this time with mouth shaping the vowels."

8. Repeated several times the phrase "bella signora" (bel-la seen-yo-rah). "Do you know what that means?" Boys repeat it after him several times. Then (with a smile): It means "beautiful lady." Then the boys sing up and down the scale:

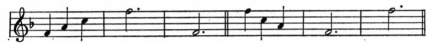

9. The next exercise was this, starting fairly slowly and increasing the speed with each new key (sounding "ha" on each note):

After the boys were dismissed, Mr. Wyton gave several valuable pointers to the directors. Two of them particularly every Guilder should remember: "If good habits of singing and breathing are established and insisted upon, one never bothers much with them afterwards." "Always give them the most challenging texts and music. They are much more grown up than we ever give them credit for."

THE BOY CHOIR IN THE PAROCHIAL SCHOOL

It is impossible for me to think of the parish church without a boy choir at Christmas. It is a very special group set apart from all other singing groups in the parochial school in that it is capable of functioning in every phase of the Catholic liturgy. As a director of multiple choirs in Catholic churches for thirty years, I have found the boy choir indispensable.

Boys are indefatigable workers. Once they become interested in their choir they will surrender their precious Saturday mornings to attend rehearsals. They can be depended upon throughout the school year and summer and Christmas vacations to sing the daily masses, funerals, weddings, and other services that are a continual part of the

129

parish pattern. There is no branch of the parochial-school musician's work that is so absolutely rewarding, so delightfully satisfying as the boy choir.

A boy has a keen sense of fairness; he will accept a reprimand and come back for more, provided the director understands him. He (or she) must hold the reins firmly but get inside the boy's mind to try to understand why he is "a joiner," for instance. Why must the chorister become a member of the Scouts, the Little League, the football and basketball teams? The smart director will not fight these activities, but rather find a way to effect a compromise now and then with the scoutmaster and the coach. It *can* be managed so that the conflict between choir responsibilities and the other activities is reduced to a minimum. However, the choir director should be seen occasionally at the games, contests, or Yo-Yo exhibitions in which his boys participate. Furthermore, he must "root" lustily no matter how "beat" the day's trials have left him!

A healthy, wide-awake boy will try every trick in the book at times to get the "mischief-ball" rolling at rehearsals, but he likes the director who like the lion-tamer is always in command; one who disciplines by teaching self-discipline (the only kind that is worth anything at all). Self-discipline such as that shown by Bob, age 10, who used to get up Saturday mornings, cook himself a farmhand breakfast, steal out of the house and walk seven blocks to sing at 8 o'clock Mass and then remain for rehearsal.

Or 12-year old Mike, who had little home supervision, but got to Mass at 7 A.M. on wintry mornings entirely on his own power, arriving in the assembly room ahead of everyone else, sleepy-eyed, with a clasp missing from his robe and his hands quite grimy. This handsome chap had the voice of an angel and it was no chore for the director to sew on the missing clasp while Mike "remembered" to wash his hands.

Treat the boy-voice gently. His natural impulse is to shout, but this must not be allowed. He should be taught to listen to his own tones and to those of the other choristers. Mlle. Nadia Boulanger once remarked despairingly to an American pupil in Paris: "American children have talent, intelligence and willingness to work, but they *cannot* hear."

Above all, treat all boys alike; boys are especially quick to detect favoritism. Make few rules, but enforce them! For a serious infraction of rules, a swift withdrawal of a privilege or a temporary suspension will quickly set a fellow straight. There was the time Chris, now married and a father, joined forces with Halloween pranksters who did a classic job of soaping up the schoolhouse windows. We did not consider this dignified behavior for a Cantor, so his rank was revoked for 30 days. His

130

great brown eyes filled and spilled over, but he admitted he understood and deserved the penalty.

And then there was Billy, who was seldom out of the well-known "dog-house," but who was as dependable as the rising sun. It was he who won the contest when the boys were asked one day to compose a choir-boy's prayer during rehearsal. This is what he wrote: "Dear God, in singing your praises I am far more honored than those who are called upon to appear before the leaders of the world. Accept the offering I make of my small voice, and grant that I may offer you always, in all things, only my best efforts. Amen."

Billy was 13 the day he wrote this prayer. Six years later his plane was shot down over the Black Sea in World War II.

The names have not been changed to protect the innocent. None was "innocent," but all were important. For two years now I have directed a choir of nuns. Surely this is a beautiful and serene experience, and self-discipline has already been mastered by the Sisters. Yet to recall the incidents of turbulent times fills me with nostalgia for the mischievous elves who came trooping toward me, down the long corridors of thirty years, to sing the ageless hymns of the liturgy as only boys can sing them.

ELEANOR DUBUISSON FOSSICK

TRAINING THE BOY CHOIR

1. Getting Started

The most enthusiastic of our seven choirs is the Boy Choir. Two years ago I was finding it difficult to interest boys in the Junior Choir which was composed of fifth and sixth grade boys and girls. Besides thinking that choir was mainly for girls, most of the boys were dropping out for seasonal sports that practiced each afternoon immediately after school. My Junior High Boys Choir was meeting on Sunday afternoons with semi-interest because most of the voices were changing and we seldom had any soprano voices.

In September 1957 I combined all my boys of grades five through nine into a Boy Choir, and membership more than doubled. This is a wide age-span with which to work, but I have found it to be successful. The older boys become buddies to the younger ones, and some deep friendships have been formed.

One of the big "selling points" of the choir was the way we worked out our rehearsal schedule. For those who have sports every afternoon, we set our rehearsal at 9 o'clock Saturday morning. Those who are out

131

of town on weekends can report to rehearsal on Thursday afternoons at 4:00 P.M. The two rehearsals are identical, and the choir members may attend either one, depending on the week's schedule.

Besides sending out publicity in mid-August I try to make a personal call on each of the boys in his home to explain some of the goals for the ensuing year. On Saturday morning every other week we have a Sports Hour at a nearby gymnasium. Occasionally we go on hikes, go bowling, or take a weekend camping trip. Although these special activities are a means to an end, I find now that many of the boys choose only to come to rehearsal, and seem to enjoy singing most of all.

After you have contacted all possible members for the Boy Choir, be prepared in those first rehearsals to prove to the boys that singing can be fun as well as inspirational. Choose a mixed list of fun, sacred, and familiar songs, and strive for a feeling of fellowship rather than quality.

Be frank with the boys. Tell them exactly what you plan to do. Explain briefly what is happening to their voices. You might start with the approach that Dr. Irwin Cooper uses:

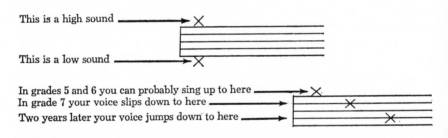

To classify the voices—unchanged, changing, and changed—have the boys sing a familiar song with an octave range, such as "Clementine" or "Old Folks at Home," in B-flat. Tap boys on the shoulder who are singing low, and tell them they are baritones. Some of the boys are not going to be near the tune at all. Don't bother about that for the time being.

The boys who have not been tapped are to sing the same song in the key of G on "ah" or "loo." This time tap the *sopranos* on the shoulder, since they are more easily recognizable.

The changing quality (alto-tenor or cambiata) will fool you time after time. Put in with this group the boys who are drifting around on no part at all. You should now have three voice groups: unchanged, changing, and changed; or soprano, cambiata, and baritone.

132

Your next problem is to find songs to begin the choir year that will fall in the following ranges . . .

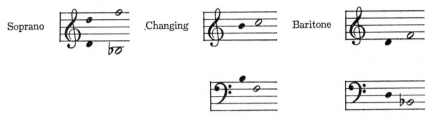

(Whole notes represent the vocalizing range; black ones the singing range.)

Warning: This group will not be ready to perform publicly very early in the choir season. Last year we started with a song appropriate for Thanksgiving: "Now Thank We All Our God." The sopranos sang the first stanza in the key of F major. The cambiatas sang the second stanza in B-flat major, and all joined in the last stanza in C major. Study carefully the above ranges and select those songs that can be sung in unison.

These two books have been a good source of anthems and fun songs:

Unison Songs for Teen Age Boys, by Irvin Cooper
(Gordon V. Thompson, Inc., Niagara Falls, N.Y.) 75c
Songs for Pre-Teentime, by Irvin Cooper
(Carl Fischer, 62 Cooper Square, New York, N.Y.) 85c

2. Matching the Voice

Matching the voice with a given pitch is an ever-present problem. We do not limit membership in the Boy Choir to those who can carry a tune. Consequently, at the beginning of the choir year, there may be as many as ten or twelve boys "floating around" in the changing-voice section, not knowing how to match their voices to a specific pitch. I have learned that with time, patience, and interest on the director's part, most boys can carry a tune. But this does take a considerable amount of individual work.

At the beginning of the choir year I explain what is happening to them physically as they approach the Junior High period of adolescence: each boy's voice will be getting lower, and we will have to change parts as the year progresses. "At times you may sound like a frog croaking," I tell them, "but at one time or another, we are all going to be in the same boat, so there is no point of making fun of anyone; and if we are going to have a good choir, we'll have to pull together like the players on a football team."

Always assure the boy that he may not be matching his voice at present, but if he'll work with you and give of his best, he'll be singing with the rest of the choir in time.

I have found it helpful to ask one or two of the boys who need special help to remain for five or ten minutes after choir. We work to match the voice to individual pitches, and sing over short passages of the anthems we are learning in choir. Don't try to flatter the boy by telling him that he sounds good if he doesn't. Always be frank, but at the same time encouraging. For instance: "George, your first two pitches were correct, but from then on, you missed the whole works. Let's try again." It may be of help to keep a notebook on each boy's present range and check throughout the year to see if progress is being made.

Be sure that the boy is listening to the desired pitch. One of my boys worked and worked to sing a short passage. Finally it was through the use of a tape-recorder that he could hear the desired pitches. The "before" and "after" results were amazing. Of course, he was immensely pleased when he heard his *new* voice!

Different words that have an inflection like "hello" or "good morning" often help the boy to raise his voice if you find that he is singing along on one pitch or a few low pitches. After speaking these words, have him sing on the same pitches. Another device that I have found helpful is to have the boy yell as though he were excited and calling a friend some distance away, such as "Hey, John, look!"

Many times we assume that a boy can't carry a tune, and yet when he is on a hike or alone, he can sing any of the popular songs in certain keys. This can be a good starting point for individual work. Ask him to sing his favorite song, then match the piano with his voice. Many boys can sing in a limited range. It's the director's duty to increase this range.

When we are performing in public, I often have the boy sopranos sing an anthem by themselves, then we include an anthem by the entire choir. This makes it possible to use the exceptionally good voices, and spare the feelings of the others.

Time, patience, and interest—these are the qualities that every director must have in working with boys who have pitch difficulties. I have found that when the boy can begin to sing with others it releases a new sense of freedom, and you have an enthusiastic choir member who for the first time is enjoying choir as much as, if not more than, any of his other activities.

134

3. Making the Choir Enjoyable

When we first began our rehearsals as a Boy Choir, I considered the many different approaches that I was going to have to use to interest the boys in choir work. Knowing that most boys are interested in instruments, I decided to use that as a starter.

The first Saturday we met I had several different instruments on the "interest table" such as bongos, claves, maracas, and a congo drum. I explained that along with our anthems and church-service work we would devote fifteen or twenty minutes of each rehearsal to various rhythms. Sooner or later every boy present would have his chance to learn to play the different instruments. I also suggested that they might want to make their own instruments and referred them to Gladys Andrews' *Creative Rhythmic Movement for Children*, pages 110-118.

That year we devoted our rhythm time to the learning of calypso rhythms. We used *Little Calypsos* by Krugman and Ludwig (published by Carl Van Roy Co.) and *Songs from South Africa* (published by G. Schirmer) for most of our songs. The boys became so enthusiastic over the songs that we decided to prepare a Calypso Night program for one of the family-night dinners.

Four of the boys painted a backdrop for the stage. On long sheets of white wrapping paper they painted a scene of a banana boat loading at a dock. The boys all wore black Ivy League trousers, bright colored shirts, red sashes, and large straw hats with fringe.

We used all the instruments mentioned above plus a guitar, which one of our boys plays. A couple of the boys thought up some action to the songs, and we sang: "Sugarbush," "Down by the River," "Little Boy Song," "Boy from Trinidad," and "Song of Damballah."

The boys were a big hit, even though the singing was not of concert caliber according to a musician's standards. The boys who couldn't carry a tune didn't carry one that night. They all had a good time just singing, and the crowd thought they were excellent.

In May we decided that for the first time the sopranos in our Boy Choir had worked hard enough to be the chosen choir to sing on Children's Day. They sang "Jesus, Blest Redeemer" (arranged by Black) and with the Chancel Choir, "Master, Speak to Me" (SATB with solo, arranged by Luvaas). The boys sang the solo part. All of the boys were used in our annual church-wide proportionate-giving program, singing and acting out a special song as a part of the entertainment.

There are many ways to make choir enjoyable. But it begins by capturing the boys' interest and imagination, and by helping them to realize their contribution to the church and its program of making this a better world in which to live.

4. Rehearsal Procedure

Here is a typical example of one of our rehearsals in the Boy Choir. We always begin promptly at 9:00 A.M. on Saturday morning. For our beginning prayer we repeat together the Choristers' Prayer.

1. "Praise to the Lord, the Almighty" by Bunjes (published by Concordia). One of the boys was asked to put the measure of difficult rhythm on the board that we had discussed the previous week (♩．♪ ♩); I then played *America,* and had all the boys close their eyes, and raise their hands when they heard the same pattern of notes.

After singing through all five verses, I had the boys close their music and tell me the notes that should follow G on the staff at the end of the first phrase. Then we did the same thing with the D at the end of the song.

2. Flash Cards. We start with a different row each week, and each boy has a turn at naming one card. If a mistake is made, we have to put the box of cards away until next week. Our goal is to see how quickly we can identify all the cards before one of the other choirs does. They love this spirit of competition.

3. "Supplication" (page 18 in *Unison Songs for Teen-Age Boys* by Irvin Cooper, published by Gordon V. Thompson, Inc., Niagara Falls, N.Y.). We discussed the meaning of this song and some of the difficult words, such as "supplication," "irksome," and "generation."

4. Breath Support. "Supplication" calls for long phrases, so we stood and worked on breathing. With hands on diaphragm they inhale while I count 1-2-3-4 slowly; hold while I count 1-2-3-4; exhale on 1-2-3-4. Our goal is to be able to do this to eight counts soon.

5. Rhythm Time. This year we are going to play several well-known songs with the beguine, rhumba, and bolero rhythms. A very helpful book is *Songs to Sing with Recreational Instruments* by Cheyette and Renna (published by Presser).

I put the beguine rhythms for "Jingle Bells" (pages 10 and 20 of the above book) on the blackboard. This was our first "go-around" with the beguine, so I didn't pass out the instruments. We clapped the rhythms and tapped our knees. We'll do this again next week until the rhythms are more thoroughly learned.

By now it was time for our closing prayer. I might add that, while working on our own songs, I found it necessary to stop and help some of the individual voices that were having difficulty. We were all pleased to find that one of our non-singing ninth grader's voice had shown a big change; he is to be moved to the baritone section. singing the correct pitches next week.

136

5. The Problem of Discipline

I have tried various approaches with the boys in our choir to keep them interested in the rehearsal. It has taken me three years to find out that the stricter I am, the more they enjoy the choir!

This fall I decided that I had been a bit too lenient, and that beginning with the first rehearsal in September we would start off on a new footing.

We have a standard rule that if any boy gets ten demerits within a choir year, he is no longer entitled to receive the Choristers Choir pin. At our first rehearsal I announced that each week I would play a hymn at the beginning of our rehearsal. When the hymn was finished, every boy was to be in his chair sitting quietly. We immediately repeat our Choristers' Prayer together, and if any boy speaks without raising his hand he gets a demerit.

The boys quickly got into the swing of this plan, and have since added additional rules that they think deserve demerits. The list now includes a demerit for elbowing your neighbor, whispering, sitting with your feet on the chair in front of you, etc. At times we will give demerits if any boy takes his eyes off the director while we are rehearsing an anthem that is soon to be sung in one of our worship services.

At first there were several "show me" show-offs in the group, and I had to list five or six names on the blackboard. It took two or three weeks before everyone knew that I would carry out this new plan. I'll have to admit it was hard for me to list some of the boys who were so innocent, and yet forgot and popped out with a question or comment before thinking to raise his hand.

Now that we are rehearsing in the sanctuary occasionally, we have added a demerit if anyone talks in the halls of the church going to or coming from the sanctuary.

With the exception of two of the younger boys who remind me of the Katzenjammer Kids, and who each had six demerits early in the choir year, no boy has over two demerits, and I am overwhelmed with the interest and attention evidenced at each rehearsal.

The boys themselves have seen how this has improved not only the singing but also the attitude of each individual, the team spirit, and the quality of work we are able to accomplish at each rehearsal.

Psychologists may call this a negative approach to learning, but I am more than pleased with the positive results that are taking place with our choir, now that ye old choir director has turned 30 and is becoming more strict!

6. Social Functions for the Choir

During our choir year we have three or four special social functions. Our most eagerly anticipated event is always the overnight camping trip to a nearby lake. Each spring we start gathering sleeping bags, cots, hammocks, tents, and all sorts of outdoor camping equipment. One of the most interesting things we do is to leave all knives, forks, and mess gear at home. We cook with no pots or pans, using only No. 10 tin cans. We wrap our steaks, potatoes, strips of carrot and bell peppers in a large piece of foil, and cook them for 45 minutes in hot coals. Each boy prepares his own food at each meal.

For recreation we play softball, volleyball, kick the can, etc. Facilities are available for swimming and fishing. One of the highlights is sitting around the campfire at night singing songs with a guitar and the autoharp, and ending the day with a period of prayer. Needless to say, the camping trip gives all of us the opportunity to become friends and to understand each other better in this new and different setting.

Another function that rates high on our list is an all-day hike, usually in the fall. The family of one of boys owns a large farm nearby. We take our own sack lunches and spend the day hiking and playing outdoor games.

At Christmas-time we divide our choir and join forces with the girls for a Christmas Caroling Party. The Junior boys and Junior girls go caroling, and the Junior High boys and Junior High girls have a caroling party.

Occasionally we will arrange for a bowling party immediately after our Saturday morning rehearsal. Many of the boys who had never bowled before have become quite interested in this wholesome sport.

Luckily we have two or three boys who have private swimming pools. We always end our last rehearsal of the season with a big splash at one of these homes.

This may look like all play and no work, but foremost on each boy's list is the weekly rehearsal and the importance of regular attendance. There is a sense of satisfaction, however, in knowing that there will be special occasions of "real good times" along with the choir work.

JAMES LAMBERTSON
First Methodist Church
Shreveport, Louisiana

BOY CHOIR REHEARSAL TECHNIQUES

Pre-rehearsal

Our "choir father" meets the boys for basketball immediately after school. They are ushered into the choir room on time with all the "wiggles" worked out on the basketball court.

Rehearsal

A. Music

  I. Hymn Study

  a) Use hymns being studied for prelude music.

  b) Hymn of the Month:

   1. Learned from memory during month.

   2. Page for notebook; discussion of pages in rehearsal.

   3. Discussion of meter, key, time-signatures, etc. of hymn.

   4. Hymn-memory contest.

  II. Review of Anthem Material

  a) Memorized material must be kept fresh in mind.

  b) Sing "favorites" for sheer enjoyment.

  III. New Anthems

  a) Introduce before choristers get too tired.

  b) Interesting presentation:

   1. Theory introduction.

   2. Story about composer.

   3. Visual aids: pictures, slides, etc.

B. Theory

  I. Flash cards (I find *Kenworthy Music Symbol Flash Cards* best.)

  II. Maestro games (*Maestro, the Musical Bingo,* Remick Music Corp.)

  III. Felt Board.

  IV. Discussion of notebook pages on theory.

  V. Games such as "Music Wheel of Fortune" use Spin-a-Test chalk-board spinner with music symbols around it. (Spin-a-Test, Hermosa Beach, California)

C. Music Appreciation

  I. Composers

  a) Pictures and books (recommend books in church library).

  b) Find name and works of composers in print in newspapers, church bulletins, magazines, etc.

  c) Identify composer of music played on piano or record.

  II. Music Instruments

  a) Orchestra (Mrs. Boyter's *My Musical Instrument Book*).

139

b) Organ structure and sound.

c) Instruments of foreign lands (we used this in connection with a mission emphasis).

III. Study of structure of oratorio, cantata, anthem and other church music forms.

D. Organization for rehearsal

    I. Use a rehearsal plan well worked out and developed.

    II. Helpers

a) Choir father (see "Pre-rehearsal" above).

b) Choir mother checks roll, inserts new pages in notebooks, and takes care of any emergencies.

c) Accompanist.

d) Director: with the above help, the director should be able to give his full time to the teaching.

These are some of the methods used with the *Singing Lads* in our church of 5,700 members. This boy choir is made up of 25 boys aged 9 to 11.

SAXE ADAMS

WHEN BOYS' VOICES CHANGE
An Experiment in Junior High School Music

Music teachers lose the boys in the eighth grade. Why? Because boys are not as musical as girls? Music is not for boys? Boys have no time for music? The public does not enjoy hearing boys sing? No, I'm afraid these answers are too glib, too shaky when analyzed. We lose our boys in the eighth grade because something is happening to our junior-high lads in their early teens that does not happen to their girl classmates, and we music teachers have not known what to do about that something.

At about the eighth grade our boys are going through that frustrating phenomenon called the voice change. All the habits and skills so carefully acquired in the earlier grades are suddenly thrown awry. What was easy and fun suddenly becomes difficult and thwarting. Just to make the situation more difficult, not all boys' voices change at the same time. Thus many a lad finds himself the *only* one at a given time whose voice is out of control! He gets no good explanation of what is occurring and very little training or attention to make things easier. Alas, boy-like, he wants to give up. (Well, can *you* imagine a teen-age boy who cannot swim well *choosing* to swim with a group of classmates who are good swimmers? Especially if some of them are girls?)

140

To put it bluntly, not many *teachers* know just what is going on in this voice-mutation process, so they don't know how to handle the situation. Try these questions on yourself:

1. Do you know just *how* a boy's voice changes?

2. Can you predict *when* his voice is about to make this radical shift?

3. Can you mention any study, based on many observed cases, that describes the vocal development patterns of adolescent boys?

4. Would you, as a vocal teacher, know what song material is suitable for a boy to sing while his voice is changing?

For over fifteen years now the writer has kept records of the vocal development of junior high school boys, month by month, season by season. He has listened to hear what tones are singable, what tones are hard to handle, what tones cannot be sung at all. And during the last several years, notations of physical development have accompanied these case histories. From these records, accompanied by research, a pattern has emerged and some workable hypotheses have been developed. Here are some that have appeared.

First of all, the voice change is directly related to sexual development. Voice mutation occurs because of the rapid growth in size and proportion of the larynx, resulting from certain hormones appearing in the body as the male sex organs begin to function. The writer had always assumed that this is common knowledge, but he has been sometimes amused, or more often dismayed, at the reaction of adults when this statement is made!

The best predictor of voice mutation is the development of pubic hair. Signs of voice mutation typically appear at about stage three on the Davenport Scale (see Note 1), rarely before stage two, always by the time stage four has been reached. Height and weight are only fairly dependable predictors: a fat boy may be quite immature, as may a tall one; while a short, thin boy may be quite mature sexually, hence well into the stages of voice mutation.

Another hypothesis asserts that the voice change, if not anticipated with special vocal training, may be characterized by a rather sudden and radical change. The lower tones of the bass clef emerge rather suddenly, while the higher tones of the boy-voice are still produceable. It is the range of tones immediately above and below middle C that are the troublesome ones. In some cases the tones near middle C cannot be produced at all; in other cases these tones can be sung only by great effort, with a tendency for the voice to "crack," to waver, or

141

to be off pitch and unpleasant in quality. If the voice change is anticipated and suitable vocal exercises are begun (e.g. while the boy is in stages one or two on the Davenport Scale), this awkward area need not get out of control and "breaks" can be kept at a minimum.

Hypotheses are not good for much unless they are tested and evaluated. So for one year an entire eighth-grade class in John Deere Junior High School, Moline, Illinois, was used to test the above hypotheses. The basic plan was to use homogeneous grouping. Boys with similar vocal problems were to be put in the same vocal classes, with no girls present; in other words, boys in stages four to six were in one class, boys in stages one to three in another class. We discovered that this was easy to do, since physical education classes alternated with music classes, and we simply worked out a deal with the boys' physical education teacher to group our classes according to maturity (see Note 2).

Our first hunch had proved right. Boys in stages four to six were all definitely in the changing stage, some quite drastically. Boys in stages one to three were not experiencing any loss of vocal control (except for one case). Class sizes balanced well, with about 30 singers per section.

Class grouping was of course only the preliminary. The urgent question was what to do with the boys now that they were organized. We wanted them to sing happily and successfully; we wanted them to get control of their new voices with a minimum of frustration. Reading skills acquired in the elementary schools were to be advanced to the bass-tenor idiom; part-singing was to be enjoyed (the girls down the hall would be expecting some tenors and basses to be developed for mixed chorus singing).

We started with motivation. The approach was something like this:

"Boys have a special problem in singing that girls do not. Boys' voices change; they get deeper, richer, stronger, and move into what we call the tenor and bass ranges. You are about to be given a new voice, maybe a more beautiful voice, and a whole new kind of singing will open up for you. But there is a price to pay, and all boys must pay it before they become men. For a while you will not be able to handle this new voice, and in some ways you may have to learn to sing all over again. That's why you are separated from the girls. This is strictly boys' business and the girls aren't even going to know what is going on until one day you will invite them in and they will be amazed at the new sounds they will hear."

This approach paid off handsomely. Immediately there was interest, curiosity, a spark of eagerness, plus some assurance, as the boys looked

142

about and saw a whole roomful of age-mates and friends all apparently facing the same problems.

Then we sang. In the less mature group this offered no difficulty, for voices were still under control. But in what sad estate were the boys in stages four to six! We literally went back to first-grade tone-matching for a while: no books and everything by rote as we tried to find those elusive pitches. We quickly discovered that anything from first-space A to fourth-space G (bass clef) could be handled by many of the class; beyond that voices cracked, ciphered, went off-key. So we transposed ("Caisson Song" and "Marine's Hymn," for instance, to the key of A-flat). And I learned to blow the pitch pipe six holes from the right one! When we could not find songs (it amazed me to discover how few men's songs lie within the range of less than an octave), we manufactured tunes—simple, trite, but singable. And soon there were enough voices under control to carry on; each day a few more boys found their new voices and assurance increased. By mid-October they were singing, happily, assuredly, with at least passable musical quality. Visitors began to pop in—the principal, dean of boys, classroom teachers—wondering where these new sounds were coming from in a junior high school. As visitors appeared, so did a sense of pride and esprit de corps among the boys.

Using the analogy of developing skills in sports, we sold the boys on the idea that "setting-up exercise" would develop control and increase ability. So it seemed appropriate to vocalize and to introduce other sports approaches.

Breathing exercises: "Any swimmer or runner needs good breathing habits to sustain him."

Relaxed, open throat: "Any batter needs a relaxed swing."

Scales and arpeggios to increase range: "Any golfer needs to increase his distance."

Vowel formations and focus of tone: "Any basketball player has to improve his aim for the basket."

Then cautiously we approached the problem of head-tones (falsetto) and working down across the break (see Note 3). Results were hilarious at first. Many fellows had already lost their boys' voices; with others, all that remained was a thin, quavering squeak. But there were interest and eagerness, and not very much self-consciousness. (Wasn't the next guy having the same trouble?) One by one a few of the boys found a falsetto tone somewhere in the treble-clef range. A few boys never did sing a passable falsetto tone; apparently we were too late. With the

143

class we slowly worked down, approaching the shaky middle C area. Voices thinned out to nothing or "cracked" into a full octave below. A few crossed the barrier, shifted (clumsily and noisily, it is true) into their bass voices and continued down the scale. Success and assurance increased this facility (progress was oh, so slow!). One by one some of the boys found they could "cross over" and the lost areas of their voices were being regained.

In the less mature groups, where there were no bass tones, we worked from the treble clef down into the bass clef gradually to a low G, then F, and soon to E and D. Here the intent was never to let a "break" develop, but to keep control of treble tones as the bass tones emerged. During the school year normal physical growth went on and boys became more mature, larynxes grew, and the lower tones began to be heard. It is noteworthy that only two boys actually developed a loss of tone around middle C. Many developed an uncertainty of control for a time, but as light, soft singing was encouraged, this uncertainty was never a source of annoyance or frustration.

We listened. We listened to recordings of singers, mostly male. Popular singers came first, then concert artists. "Notice the control of the crooner." "Listen to the resonance of this TV artist." "Hear the way this man approaches and sustains his higher tones." "Note how easy it is to understand this fellow's words." "Now boys, *you* try it— but in this key."

Or: "Here is a song you may be singing one day. This song is a favorite of baritones." "Here is a famous bass song that audiences always like." "This composition is just made for a good tenor voice." Always we sought to identify the boy with the singer or song.

We kept records and files. Each boy noted his own improvement from day to day. A periodic voice check, supplemented by a tape recording, verified his achievements. Physical data were recorded. By the end of the year each boy could note his progress and take pride in the changes that had occurred.

We read new music. These boys had read music in the elementary schools; the skills were there, ready to be transferred. An explanation of the bass clef, a look at the newness of the positions of flats and sharps, a song with simple rhythmic patterns and scale-wise progressions—and away they went! There were "mystery tunes" to be figured out silently. In the more mature groups we had a song or two with skips of fourths and fifths, and then the bass part of familiar songs, using the ubiquitous I-IV-V bass progressions, but transposing to the key the boys could negotiate. In the less mature group we used a tenor part in the typical

144

"sixth below the soprano," again transposed to fit the range of the class.
We did part-singing. Not right away, of course. Not until the classes
were "with us" and were able to sing unison songs with some degree of
musicality. A few rounds and canons first. (Did you ever hear "Row,
Row, Row Your Boat" sung in the deeper bass register? A most unusual
and intriguing sound!) Then the bass or tenor part to some familiar
Christmas carols, learned thoroughly until no pianist, playing the melody
loudly, could lose them. An invitation to the girls to come and sing the
soprano and alto parts resulted in a red mark on the calendar, for this
day we sang grown-up music for the first time. Of course we transposed
the carols to the proper key. Likewise, the introduction of the tenor part,
sung very softly since it lay in the "danger zone," was combined with a
similar invitation. There were some volunteers—and soon we had a
group singing all four parts very acceptably indeed.

* * * * *

TABLE I. NUMBER OF SEMITONES GAINED FROM SEPTEMBER TO MAY

No. of bass-clef semitones gained	57 boys 534 semitones average—9.4	30 boys 160 semitones average—5.3	23 more experimental boys gained average of 4.1 semitones more
No. of treble (falsetto) semitones gained	81 boys 250 semitones average—3.0	75 boys 66 semitones average—0.9	6 more experimental boys gained average of 2.1 semitones more
No. of over-lapping tones gained*	25 boys 144 semitones average—5.7	17 boys 74 semitones average—4.4	8 more experimental boys gained average of 1.3 semitones
No. of "lost tones" regained	24 boys 122 semitones average—5.0	7 boys 30 semitones av. loss—4.3	17 more experimental boys regained average of 9.3 semitones

*Overlapping tones are tones that can be sung both in the full, changed
voice and in the lighter falsetto or head-voice.

* * * * *

An invitation to put on a demonstration downtown gave the incentive for a combined chorus. Again, some manufactured arrangements:

melody in the bass, tenors on a light descant, parts worked out separately (because of divided classes). Then came a combined volunteer rehearsal at 7:30 one cold winter evening. Of our 84 boys over half were there— and on time! Over fifty appeared for the second meeting, and we began to "sound." The demonstration went well; the audience was impressed; morale went higher.

Then came a three-part song: melody in baritone (those boys who could now handle a high B-flat); deeper basses on a tonic *sol-fa*; "tenors" in typical "third above" harmony. By May we had at least two four-part barbershop quartets that sang acceptably, rehearsing on their own time and with a minimum of teacher help. "Let the visitors come. We'll show them we can sing."

Were we successful in our teaching? Enthusiasm and intense interest can tend to bias judgments, so we worked out the most objective measurements possible.

First of all, remembering our original problem, we watched registration for elective music in the ninth grade. Forty-four of our eighty-four boys signed up. That was over half—more than double the number in any of the five years previous. The most capable went into a mixed choir; twenty-four more went into an all-boy class to continue the work begun in the eighth grade.

Another measure we applied was to compare vocal development. Across town there was another junior high school where classes had proceeded as in previous years on a mixed and heterogeneous basis. We checked voices in the fall and in the spring. Then we counted the tones that each boy could sing easily. Table I shows what we found.

You will note that in every one of the four areas where we could increase the control of the voice, more boys in the experimental class gained, and they gained more tones, on the average, than did the boys in the control school who sang in mixed classes.

More vocal skill was not enough, valuable though that may be. So we measured the boys' attitude toward music. Under the guidance of the able and experienced test constructor Julian Stanley of the University of Wisconsin an attitude scale was constructed and checked for validity and reliability. Answered anonymously (to reduce bias) by all eighth-graders, one test in the fall and another in the spring, these instruments enabled us to compare the scores of various groups. Table II gives the results.

146

TABLE II. COMPARISONS OF MEAN SCORES ON THE ATTITUDE SCALE OF VARIOUS GROUPS BETWEEN SEPTEMBER AND MAY

Group	Mean Scores Fall	Spring	Mean Gain	Critical Ratio
Boys in experimental school	88.1	93.7	5.6	2.4
Boys in control school	86.7	85.0	—1.7	3.4
Girls in experimental school	98.5	98.6	.1	.4
Girls in control school	106.0	109.4	3.4	2.3

* * * * *

Apparently some changes in the attitude towards music of our experimental boys took place between September and May, while the boys in the control school, if anything, regressed. It also appears that the boys in the experimental groups had pulled up closer to their girl classmates, while the difference between girls and boys in the control school increased.

We had not emphasized the acquisition of knowledge very greatly in the experimental classes. We felt that our first emphasis was to be on the problem of the changing voice and that any increase in knowledge of musical notation, sight-reading, information, or criticism would be incidental. Nevertheless we measured the knowledge outcome too, giving an objective test in September and again in May. The results are tabulated here.

* * * * *

TABLE III. COMPARISON OF MEAN SCORES ON THE KNOWLEDGE TEST OF VARIOUS GROUPS BETWEEN SEPTEMBER AND MAY

Group	Mean Score Fall	Spring	Mean Gain	Critical Ratio
Boys in experimental groups	25.33	31.41	5.88	10.8
Boys in control school	26.67	27.52	.85	1.6
Girls in both schools	33.4	33.2	—.2	.3

* * * * *

It appears that the experimental boys started out slightly below the control boys and decidedly below the girls in the fall. By spring these boys in the experimental school had surpassed the boys in the control

147

school, and were only a small amount below the girls. In fact, the experimental boys were the only group who seem to have acquired any additional knowledge during this special year.

We feel that the results of our experiment are encouraging and that our hypotheses are defensible. More boys wanting to continue in music, more skill in handling the singing voices, a better attitude toward music in general and more knowledge acquired—all these make us think that we are on the right track.

Can any teacher use this approach to teaching boys music in the junior high school? With other boys of this age?

The answers to both are "Of course." If a teacher feels that it is *important* to have basses and tenors as well as sopranos and altos; if a teacher realizes that the adolescent male is just as responsive to music as anybody else, and that underneath an air of bravado or assumed indifference he is just as eager to perform well, achieve results, and participate in a successful group as are his schoolmates; if a teacher has some little knowledge of singing techniques and understands matters of range, breath-control, and register; if a teacher is willing to look around for suitable songs, recordings, and maybe even make up a few; most of all, if a teacher is willing to try something new, approach a situation with an open mind, not insist that a given class *must* sing a certain song in a certain key on a certain day because that is what the course of study says must happen.

The rewards can be stupendous. Musically it may go slowly; after all, tone-matching on the first-grade level means music of a pretty elementary sort—although there may evolve a great pleasure in the fragile out-of-this-world tone-quality possible in these immature deepening voices. But emotionally there is a satisfaction to be derived from a roomful of young boys—eager, loyal, responsive to discipline, and channeling their high spirits into a team project. Psychologically there is a satisfaction in piercing through the false outer shell of these young adolescents and in discovering that they are really uncertain, awkward, somewhat scared boys who would like to be young men but don't quite know how and would like somebody to help them—if it can be done without loss of face.

What a wonderful resource for school public-relations when forty or fifty young "colts" standing at attention, with faces scrubbed, hair slicked back, and fresh white shirt and tie instead of sloppy jeans and T-shirt, produce the deep bass tones or floating tenor notes that announce their crossing over into young manhood. What parent or teacher will not feel a tug of emotion?

148

Note 1. The Davenport Scale presents the course of sexual development in six stages. The first is pre-pubescence; stages two through five represent different degrees of development in the pubescent period; stage six is post-pubescence. See Frank K. Shuttleworth, *The Adolescent Period: A Pictorial Atlas.* (Monographs of the Society for Research in Child Development, Volume XIV, No. 2, Serial No. 50, Evanston, Ill., 1951).

Note 2. The grouping was done with the use of the photographs found in Shuttleworth, op. cit., pp. 31-33.

Note 3. For a description of this technique and the theory behind it, see Duncan McKenzie, *Training the Boys' Changing Voice*, p. 39. (New Brunswick, New Jersey: Rutgers University Press, 1956).

FREDERICK J. SWANSON
John Deere Junior High School
Moline, Illinois

OF SPECIAL INTEREST TO BOYS IN CHOIR

The Hebrews considered music as a means to an end—a means to establish communion between man and God. Women were not allowed to participate in the Temple service, where singing was done in octaves by men and boys. Biblical music was in antiphonal form, accompanied by musical instruments in octave unison, and possibly from time to time also by arpeggios on the harps. At given moments the singing ceased, and the orchestra played an interlude. Music was used on all great occasions: heroes returning in triumph (1 Samuel 18: 6; Judges 11: 34); music for a good friend setting out on a journey (Genesis 31: 27); leading a religious procession (2 Samuel 6: 5; 1 Chronicles 13: 8). The Talmud describes the role of these singing boys.

A useful source of information on this and other Jewish musical practices is *Of Jewish Music: Ancient and Modern* by Israel Rabinovitch (published by The Book Center, Montreal, Canada).

SPURS IN CATHEDRALS

An amusing old English custom was recently enforced on Prince Philip by a group of choir boys.

In many English cathedrals it is the custom for the choristers to claim a fine from persons who enter wearing spurs. This custom is a very ancient one, royalty not even being exempt, for one of the items in the Privy Purse Expenses of Henry VII is the following:

"In 1495, October 1—To the children, for the King's spoures, 4 shillings."

A similar entry occurs three times in the reign of Henry VIII, in the year 1550. The person caught has one chance of escape, for he can demand that the youngest chorister be brought before him, and should the boy not know his catechism well, the fine is not paid. In this way, the Duke of Wellington evaded the payment of a fine at St. George's Chapel.

In recent years one person complained to the magistrates at Hereford because the choristers had decamped with his hat when he refused to pay the customary fine. The magistrate decided in favor of the choir boys!

NANCY POORE TUFTS

The Youth Choir

JOE ADOLESCENT AND SALLY TEEN-AGER

1. Communication

Adolescence is not really a "disease," but a valley through which all must pass. Everyone must make the same journey during this period of growth and change. It is essential that adults working with adolescent groups help them toward understanding the seeming contradictions in their personalities and development; to adjust to other personalities; to realize the importance of love and the need for the approval of others (not just outsiders, but also of the family circle); to accept gracefully and with real knowledge their changing (maturing) voices; to weigh the proper relationship between work and play; and to plan for the future as to profession, courtship and marriage. These are some of the same problems that we adults have to face, but Joe and Sally do not have our years of experience, education, maturity, and self-control.

A successful Youth Choir director learns to communicate *with* them and not *to* them. Regardless of the extent of our knowledge of church music, unless we can get through to young people our efforts are wasted. Therefore we may need to spend some time in getting acquainted with Joe and Sally. What do they read? What are their likes and dislikes? What are the fatal attractions to jazz, rock 'n roll? Do we show interest in or attend their school games and musical productions? Youngsters of this age cannot be forced to participate in church activities; they have to be persuaded and interested by the enthusiasm of those whom they respect and like. An experienced choir director with an attractive and persuasive personality, who has learned to communi-

151

cate with and to admire Joe and Sally for their many fine qualities, will draw and hold a vital, enthusiastic and faithful group of singers.

Teachers! "Stop sounding off; listen! Look into their eyes and smile. And try to love and understand each one a little more." (The Rev. Victor Hoag, D.D., in *The Living Church*)

2. Preparation

Prepare thyself: No group is more enthusiastic and idealistic than teen-agers. Their enthusiasm and idealism need firm and effective guidance and leadership. Youth Choir directors must be especially well-prepared as to materials, music and teaching techniques, and well-braced for the unexpected. They must muster or develop a brand of resilient and infectious good humor. Webster's various definitions of "prepare" usually include the word "beforehand." Efficient teaching can only result from thorough advance preparation. Teen-agers are sharp, and the only way to stay ahead of them is to be sharper!

Enthusiasm: The leader's enthusiasm is another key to success in dealing with choirs of young people. "Enthusiasm" is derived from two Greek words meaning "God within you." What could be a more appropriate reminder to those whose responsibility it is to inspire choristers to praise God through music? Joe and Sally respond readily to a leader who has vision and high ideals, and is courteous, encouraging and enthusiastic.

1. Enthusiasm is infectious.
2. If you don't have it, act it until it becomes so.
3. Enthusiasm is the dominant personality characteristic of every really successful person in any field.
4. "As a man thinketh in his heart, so is he."
   "Positive thinking produces positive works;
   Negative thinking produces positively nothing that works."
5. Real enthusiasm is derived from inner spiritual sources.
6. "Believe that you possess significant reserves of health, energy and endurance, and your belief will help create the fact."
   (William James, psychologist)

Prepare thy choristers: A Fall Retreat for teen-agers affords an excellent opportunity to prepare them for the season's responsibilities as leaders in worship. A Retreat program might include: the relationship of the chorister to the choir; discussions of the plans for the year; the meaning of worship; a study of the hymnal; the duties and responsibilities of being a good choir member. The minister of the church should be enlisted to share leadership in this kind of Retreat.

3. Discipline

D ecide what *you* expect from teen-agers. What shall be the relationship between them and the choir director? The familiarity which results when an adult tries to be an adolescent can become a discipline problem. Cultivate their love and respect, but don't try to be one of the "gang"!

I nterest them in an orderly rehearsal, an orderly rehearsal room, and in a challenging leadership program. Here is the time and place to work; later, at social or recreation hour, is the time to play. Interest is maintained by a fast-paced rehearsal.

S elf-discipline, says Margaret Kendrick, is the only discipline worth having! Teach teen-agers to be proud of their desire and willingness for self-control.

C ontrol: Self-control begins with the director! How can we expect teen-age choristers to control themselves if we directors cannot control our own emotions and actions? The quickest way to lose control of *them* is to lose *our* self-control.

I dleness by an individual or section in rehearsal is potential trouble. Keep the minds and voices busy every moment.

P lan for twice as much material to be learned as you think really possible. The choristers will sense the urgency to make every minute count in the rehearsal.

L oud talking and shouting on your part only breed louder and more unruly behavior by the teen-agers themselves.

I nvest private time in two things: (1) Invest time in any chorister who seems to have problems, for it will pay tremendous dividends of increased group attention and interest. (2) Invest money and time in studying recommended books on teen-age psychology.

N ever expect anything of a teen-ager—either his time, his loyalty, his attention, or his love—that *you*, yourself, are not willing to give to him. Respect him as an individual, and he will do the same for you.

E xpectation is a wonderful part of living! Most people receive about what they expect. Expect the *best* of Joe and Sally and very rarely will you receive anything else.

153

4. The Changing Voice

The unchanging characteristic of Joe and Sally is that their voices do change! The problem is not so much working with the adolescent voice itself; rather it is how to help the adolescent understand and live with this natural phenomenon, the change in the speaking and singing voice.

Neither Joe nor Sally will fit into a pattern that says their voices will change at this particular month and year, and neither can it be said that this will happen when they are in a certain grade in school. I have known high-school juniors whose voices had not changed, yet on the other hand I have known 6th-grade boys whose voices had changed.

I feel it is right and our responsibility to keep teen-agers singing during the changing period. Church programs across the country, including my own, have really avoided the issue by having related musical projects or interest groups to supplant their singing participation. Two such projects, both excellent in themselves, are (1) the Choric Speech Choir (or Speaking Choir), which is undoubtedly an aid in learning good diction and other attributes of good singing; (2) the Handbell Choir, which furthers team work and musicianship. Worthy as are these activities, I still think it advisable for teen-agers to continue singing during the changing period.

Where shall we put Joe and Sally in the School of Choirs? It is perfectly possible to have a fine Girls Choir composed of 7th, 8th, and 9th-graders. As the girl's changed voice is more subtle, the mixing of the changed and the unchanged at this particular level can work extremely well.

Now where shall we put Joe? Boys must be treated individually, for a solo group of the comparative grades mentioned may be far from satisfactory. If the voice is unchanged, vocally he belongs with the Juniors, where he must have some added title or rank of leadership since he is older in years (something we must never forget). If Joe's voice has changed or is in the changing state, he will work out best in a high-school group.

What are we going to call Joe's voice during the changing years? Dr. Irving Cooper suggests calling him "cambiata," while Duncan McKenzie prefers "alto-tenor." I have found that it boosts the teen-age ego and helps him live in a community of adultism to call him "tenor." However, both the singer and the director must be aware of the ability and limitations of the voice at this phase.

What can I expect from this changing voice? While in the 9th grade I was a "triple-threat" man myself! At the same time I sang first tenor in

154

the High School Choir under Lara Hoggard, I sang second soprano in the Junior High Chorus, and baritone in the Junior Mixed Chorus! Fortunately both teachers knew how to handle the voice, so choral singing has long been remembered as one of the joys of my adolescent years. I have found that most of us do not expect enough of adolescent voices. They can carry the load in either a mixed choir or in separate groups.

This year I have the pleasure of working with 42 teen-age boys in Pembroke Country Day School, Kansas City, and am grateful for four changing voices in the first tenor section. I have not discovered many real tenors in early adolescents, so the changing voice is a wonderful asset to a choir as first tenor in the boys' group, or tenor in a four-part mixed group. The great danger lies in allowing boys to force the expansion of range or the volume prematurely.

WILLIAM W. LEMONDS, MUS.D.

TALK ABOUT TEEN-AGERS

Today's teen-agers are the focal point of much discussion: magazine writers forever quizzing parents on the handling of their offspring; PTA groups analyzing the teen-ager; the church struggling to challenge him. In short, everyone becomes an amateur psychologist probing into the mind and soul of this 20th-century phenomenon. Indeed, our teen-agers do face an unprecedented assortment of temptations, problems, and decisions, perhaps aggravated by this very attention. With the blossoming of scientific interest in our country, little boys have forsaken their traditional idols—the policeman or the fireman—and dream of becoming nuclear physicists! By their teens some of these boys are well on their way to this goal. Likewise, girls are no longer content to embroider samplers or turn out a perfect pie-crust. Our youngsters' interests are varied and sophisticated.

If the church believes in the development of the whole person, with emphasis on his spiritual nature, what then is the responsibility of the church musician to today's teen-ager? Is it enough for a youngster to proceed through the prescribed Sunday School classes and Sunday evening youth groups, with a few hayrides and summer camps thrown in?

Most churches confess to a sizable loss of young people during their college years. I do not believe this is because they are being taught that Christianity is outdated; I believe it is because the church fails to grow with them. Many 17-year-olds' concept of worship consists of someone struggling through a hastily selected prelude on a battered piano fished from someone's basement; a prayer; a few stanzas of some sentimental song selected because it "has a good beat"; a lesson read from the current literature; another song picked at random; and a benediction. Little wonder that they are ill-equipped to carry their religious faith through the critical college years.

It is on this basis that I believe that the church musician has an obligation to the teen-agers of his congregation beyond the teaching of music; rather it is to implant the principles of Christian faith through the avenue of music. It is commendable for your youngsters to master the mechanics of good choral singing, but it is more important that they appreciate our musical heritage, that they learn to evaluate a hymn, that they discover the joy of singing with understanding the great historic hymns of our faith. We dare not overlook the hymn as a powerful instrument for instilling the gospel (or questionable concepts as well!) into the youth of our congregations. Because our hymns combine doctrine and music, they are doubly effective in formulating our ideas about God, Jesus, and the church, and in creating Christian attitudes. This is true because hymns have the added emotional appeal of music, because they are sung repeatedly through the year (and often memorized), and because we are frequently unmindful of the concepts embodied in the hymns we sing.

Our young people are so receptive; they are accustomed to being taught. Let us take care to acquaint them with hymns which convey a worthy concept of God through dignified and reverent music. This is not to say that we must dissect every hymn in the hymnal in search of hidden heresies, but rather that we need to approach every hymn with intelligent appraisal.

High School Choir rehearsals and Sunday evening fellowship groups are natural opportunities for hymn-study sessions. Youngsters love to try new things and (unlike their parents) even new hymns! Children's and Youth Choirs should be instructed in the hymnal each year, and other youth groups could profit by an annual series of programs on this subject. Otherwise the result will be a generation of church leaders who are ignorant of the hymnal and indifferent to the beliefs they sing.

Far better, is it not, that we capture the imagination, the intellect, and the faith of our young people that they may earnestly sing, as did Charles Wesley:

156

"O for a thousand tongues to sing
My dear Redeemer's praise,
The glories of my God and King,
The triumphs of his grace!"

Shirley W. McRae
First Methodist Church
Collierville, Tennessee

A PROGRAM FOR A JUNIOR HIGH CHOIR

Our Junior High Choir, an enthusiastic group of 12, 13 and 14-year-olds, meets on Wednesday afternoons at 3:30 right after school. We have a recreation program for them first: ping-pong, shuffleboard, folk games, square dancing, charades, and other games. Rehearsal is held at 4:00 P.M. in the sanctuary. Rehearsal procedure outline is as follows:

1. Breathing exercises while standing with good posture.
2. Vocal exercises.
3. Learn hymns for the following Sunday service.
4. Practice anthems, working out the parts. This group is capable of singing in three and four parts.
5. Practice processing, sometimes with books on heads for good posture.
6. Practice with handbells.

At 5:00 o'clock the choir goes downstairs, where they first set up tables and chairs for supper, then hold a Youth Meeting with two graduate students as advisors.

At 5:40 they have supper, each paying 35c. Six menus have been worked out from a list the youngsters made of their favorite foods. One parent prepares the meal each week; this is usually done in the morning at home and brought to the church in mid-afternoon. I do the finishing touches. The young people do all the rest of the work, and three are assigned each week to clean up. After the supper we sing fun songs at the table, then wind up with a friendship circle and sing "Blest be the tie that binds" after the minister's closing prayer.

This program is very successful and well-attended. The young people are ready to go home by 6:40 P.M. The minister enjoys the contact with the youngsters at supper each week.

The Junior High Choir sings with the Senior High Choir at the early service every Sunday. Each group sings an anthem and the prayer responses alone twice a month, and both lead the hymn-singing. There are a few extra services and programs at Christmas and Easter.

157

In May the Junior High Choir visits a county church and presents a concert of sacred music, the best of all the anthems done during the year. The young people conduct the service, and give a talk on camping. The offering is used by the county church to send their own young people to camp. The choir looks forward to this annual event, when they can make a worthwhile contribution outside of their own church.

MRS. EARL F. SPENCER
University Baptist Church
State College, Pennsylvania

* * * * *

The First Methodist Church of Peoria, Illinois, has a similar program for the High School Choir. The Director, Mrs. George Becker, writes:

"The Wesley Singers (High School) sing at the 8:30 service on the first and fourth Sundays of the month. Their rehearsal is on Thursday, in conjunction with supper and a psychology study group. Most of them come directly from school, a habit established over the years in the younger choirs. The library and various rooms are available for homework, while others may attend study groups, or play. We have facilities for shuffleboard and ping-pong. The rehearsal is early (6:30 to 7:30), so that they can attend High School activities the same evening. We have students from five high schools. We receive a combined schedule of the high school games and activities at the beginning of the school year and plan around them."

YOUTH CHOIR REHEARSAL TECHNIQUES

The Senior High Choir is perhaps the most challenging group in the choir system. No group reacts so spontaneously to the music, is so quick to turn its attention from last night's date to the intricacies of a Bach chorus, or is so hard to "stir up" if the team lost last night's game! But when an anthem is reverently performed, no group is more conscious of its part in the service of worship.

At Westmont the Senior High Choir rehearses for one hour on Sunday evening preceding the Youth Fellowship meeting. Because of seating space in the chancel the choir is limited to 40 members. We have a system of training alternates who rehearse with the choir and sing when a regular member is unable to be present. This choir sings at the second service every third Sunday, at other special services during the

158

choir year, at church functions such as Family Night, and during Christmas on radio and TV.

When the call goes out in September, the first 40 to sign up and to be accepted comprise the choir. We strive for the best possible balance, but there is usually a shortage of boys. Anyone making later application is given the choice of serving as an alternate or of being placed on a waiting list. Luckily our rehearsal room is large enough to accommodate those who wish to be alternates.

A typical rehearsal is as follows:

1. Sing through the hymns for Sunday in unison.
   (This takes the place of any planned vocalization.)
2. Put finishing touches on the anthem for Sunday.
   "The Lord Is a Mighty God," Mendelssohn (Kjos #9)
   "Create in Me a Clean Heart," Mueller (G. Schirmer 8682)
3. Review responses to be used (Introits, Amens).
4. Anthems studied for future use (work out parts).
   "What Shall I Render to My God," Lovelace (Canyon)
   "God Be in My Head," Grant-Schaefer (Flammer 88508)
   "Lead Me, O Lord," Peery (H.W. Gray 1047)
   "Worship," Shaw (Novello MT967) (Sing through once).
5. Rehearse anthems and responses in the sanctuary for Sunday.
6. Close rehearsal with prayer.

We feel that there is no need for as many social events with this choir as with the younger groups. Christmas caroling and a Festival of Sacred Music in the spring comprise their extra activities. Refreshments are served occasionally following rehearsal.

The following must be taken into consideration when selecting anthems:

(1) Is the text suitable for your church, for young people? (2) Is the range of the voice parts within the capability of your singers? (3) Is it the type of anthem that will draw "That's the most" comments or unfavorable or neutral responses? In your search for suitable music, don't forget the unison and two-part anthems; sometimes these are even more effective than many written for three and four parts. Always be seeking for anthems that are "the most." The realization of a spiritual experience in singing or hearing a truly fine anthem is well worth the hours of going through stacks and stacks of music.

ANDREW FLANAGAN
Westmont Presbyterian Church
Johnstown, Pennsylvania

159

YOUTH CHOIR COVENANT: STANDARDS AND PROCEDURES
Bellaire Methodist Church, Bellaire, Texas
EARLE LOWDER, *Director*

WELCOME, NEW STEWARDS OF YOUTH CHOIR:

To be a Steward of Youth Choir, you should know about the procedures and organization. The Youth Choir is responsible for the 9:30 worship service each Sunday morning. Besides an anthem, each Sunday we sing the responses and hymns. Every two months we sing the full Communion ritual. Special programs and out-of-town projects are a regular part of our yearly schedule.

We have our full ensemble rehearsal on Sunday afternoon from 4:30 to 5:30. Sectional clinic sessions, to solve personal vocal problems and gain added knowledge of musical literature, are held weekly:

Soprano ....Monday ....5:00-6:00 P.M.
Alto ....Monday ....6:30-7:30 P.M.
Tenor ....Tuesday ....5:00-6:00 P.M.
Bass ....Tuesday ....6:30-7:30 P.M.

PURPOSE

The purpose of the Youth Choir of Bellaire Methodist Church is to supply worshipful music for the services of our church, and to find for the individual choir members spiritual enrichment through great sacred music. To do this we, Choir Stewards of the Youth Choir, do

COVENANT

1. To attend all rehearsals and services unless ill or otherwise unable to attend;
2. To notify our Section Head or call the Minister of Music at the church when unable to attend rehearsals or services.

Soprano Section Head	Name	Telephone
"A" Unit		
"B" Unit		
Alto Section Head		
Tenor Section Head		
Bass Section Head		
Minister of Music	(Earl Lowder)	

160

3. To conduct ourselves in services and rehearsals in such manner that our presence will contribute to the growth and effectiveness of the Youth Choir and to ourselves as Christian individuals.

NEW CHOIR STEWARDS

1. Must accept probationary status for one month before becoming active Choir Stewards.
2. Must attend at least three full ensemble rehearsals before singing in service.

NEWLY APPROVED STANDARDS

1. All active Choir Stewards must maintain an average of 70% attendance at rehearsals and services.
2. Members who do not come up to these standards will not sing in the first service of the following month; if the two rehearsals in that first week are not attended, then the member will not sing in the second service of the month, and so on through the month. After three successive months of sub-stewardship attendance, said Choir Member will be considered probationer and will be required to re-serve the beginner probationary period.
3. There will be no exception without the majority approval of the Executive Committee.

   The Executive Committee will meet each month on the Saturday preceding the first Sunday of the month to weigh each case of drop in stewardship level and to consider general Youth Choir plans, needs, and welfare.

   NOTE: These standards and amendments were approved by the Youth Choir on (dates); revised and approved (dates).

OTHER CONSIDERATIONS:

After you become an active Choir Steward (in accordance with the Choir Covenant) you will be eligible to sing in the Sunday services.

We begin warming up and robing at 9:00 on Sunday mornings. *It is important that you be on time.* Robes will be issued to all new members as they come from probationary status.

What to wear: There are no set rules for dress, propriety being left to the good taste of each Choir Steward. It is suggested, however, that boys wear white shirts and maroon bow ties to merge harmonically with our maroon choir robes; girls are requested to refrain from wearing earrings or elaborate hair ornaments, and to keep in mind the appropriateness of general dress in relation to the chancel setting and robe coloring.

EXECUTIVE COMMITTEE SALUTATION:

Your Executive Committee and Ministers of Music hope you find the joy in Christian service through great music that awaits all sincerely religious persons. Let us know when we can be of help to you; let us grow together in grace, knowledge, and usefulness.

/Signed/ YOUR EXECUTIVE COMMITTEE
and
MINISTERS OF MUSIC

N.B. A footnote from Norma Lowder: "These standards were written by the Youth themselves, and believe me, they are carried out. The Executive Committee wields a heavy blow!" (The fact that the Choir has 107 regular members is an indication that the Covenant is taken seriously. R.K.J.)

CHOIR MEMBER'S CREED AND RESOLUTION

I believe it my duty to my Church Choir to love it, to support its regulations, to accept its responsibilities, to respect its members, and to defend it against all criticism.

I will use the talent which God has given me to sing his praises during the year 196__, and will make every effort to attend all rehearsals and services as scheduled, God helping me.

/Signed/...............................
Choir Member

N.B. Try using this or a similar creed when organizing a High School Choir, or at the beginning of a season. This was quoted in *Let's Go,* the choir paper of St. Mark's Lutheran Church, Jacksonville, Florida. Hugh Alderman is the Director of Music.

YOUTH CHOIR FELLOWSHIP SUGGESTIONS

Several High School Choirs in Oklahoma City and Tulsa come together annually for a Choir Festival which is held alternately in the two cities. This is a splendid opportunity for a number of young people to establish friendships with other young people who have similar interests and whom they might otherwise never have met.

(R.K.J.)

In Cedar Rapids, Iowa, there is a city-wide Christian Vocation Conference for High School Fellowship members of all Protestant denominations. The conference includes a banquet, a service of worship, and an outstanding guest speaker. If this can be done for Youth Fellowships, why could it not be equally valuable for Protestant Youth Choirs, with the choirs prepared in advance to sing the service?

No activity is more conducive to concentrated rehearsal than an exchange of churches between two choirs. Singing in some church other than our own seems so much more important!

Certainly regular responsibility for one of their own church services is essential to a healthy High School Choir.

(R.K.J.)

* * *

The Choristers' Guild Chapter of Lynchburg, Virginia, sponsored the 11th Annual Youth Choir Festival, the Gymanfu Ganu, on December 2, 1962. It was "A Christmas Carol Sing" and is becoming a real community celebration. The Gymanfu Ganu started because the young people desired and earnestly requested a festival of their own after they outgrew the Junior Choir Festival in which they had participated as youngsters.

(R.K.J.)

CHRISTIAN SYMBOLISM STUDY FOR YOUTH CHOIRS

Resources:

1. *Christian Symbolism in Evangelical Churches,* Stafford, Abingdon Press.
2. *An Outline of Christian Symbolism,* Wilson, Morehouse-Gorham.
3. *Symbols of the Church* (filmstrip), Cathedral Films (series of six).
4. *The Church Year in Symbols* (color posters), Sacred Design Associates.

Purpose:

To introduce some of the historic symbols of the Christian faith in order to bring about deeper spiritual experiences in worship.

I. *The Cross*

Emphasize that this is the chief symbol of the church because it is a reminder of Christ's sacrifice for us. It should be noted that there

163

are more than 400 forms of the cross. Simple posters may be made to illustrate some of the commonest forms of the cross and can supplement the explanations, or a filmstrip may be shown.

Suggestions:

A. Latin cross
B. Graded, or Calvary cross
C. St. Andrew's cross
D. Greek cross

E. Celtic, or Ionic cross
F. Maltese cross
G. Papal cross
H. Russian cross

II. *Symbols of Doctrine*
This session may include any symbols not specifically dealt with in other sessions. Emphasize that a symbol is not a picture but a suggestion of a person, an event, or an idea. Explain how symbols, through the years, helped to proclaim our faith and communicate Christian truths. Here again, it is helpful to illustrate with colorful drawings or have the young people draw their own.

Suggested symbols for study:

A. Circle
B. Rose
C. Anchor
D. Pointed Arch
E. Pomegranate

F. Wheat
G. Grapes
H. Butterfly
I. Lamp
J. Crown and Cross

III. *Symbols of the Apostles*
Explain that most of the traditional symbols of the apostles indicate the manner in which they died. Since these symbols are frequently used in church decoration, it would be most helpful for the group to visit a church in which these are used. If no one is available to serve as a guide, be sure to explain these symbols thoroughly in advance. A filmstrip is practical here.

IV. *Colors and the Christian Year*
Explain that the Christian Year serves to remind us of the main events in the life of Christ and of his teachings. The color of the cloths on the altar, the pulpit, and lectern is a visible sign of these events or aspects of the Christian life. Information on these is found in the resources listed above.

Note: A fitting conclusion to this series would be a tour of local churches to see examples of the symbols studied.

164

THE TWENTY COMMANDMENTS OF RUSSIAN SCHOOLS

1 — To acquire knowledge persistently; to become an educated and cultured citizen and be of the greatest possible service to one's country.

2 — To study diligently and be punctual in attendance.

3 — To obey the instructions of the school director and teachers without question.

4 — To arrive at school with all necessary textbooks and writing materials, and be prepared for lessons before the teacher arrives.

5 — To come to school clean, well-groomed, and neatly dressed.

6 — To keep his place in the classroom clean and tidy.

7 — To enter the classroom and take his place immediately after the bell rings; to enter and leave the classroom only with the teacher's permission.

8 — To sit upright during the lesson, not leaning on his elbows or slouching; to listen attentively to the teacher's explanations and the other pupil's answers, and not to talk or let his attention stray.

9 — To rise when the teacher or the director enters or leaves the room.

10 — To stand at attention when answering the teacher; to sit down only with the teacher's permission; to raise his hand if he wishes to ask or answer a question.

11 — To take accurate notes in his assignment book of homework scheduled for the next lesson, and to show these notes to his parents; to do all homework unaided.

12 — To be respectful to the teachers and director; to greet them with a polite bow.

13 — To be polite to elders; to behave modestly and respectfully in school, on the street, and in public places.

14 — To avoid coarse expressions, smoking or gambling. (Coarse includes profanity, clichés, and slang expressions such as "wow," "real gone," and "yeah.")

15 — To protect school property; to be careful of his personal things and the belongings of his comrades.

16 — To be attentive and considerate of old people, smaller children, the weak and the sick; to give them a seat on streetcars, buses, trains, or make way for them on the street, being helpful in every way.

17 — To obey parents; to help in the care of small brothers and sisters.

18 — To maintain cleanliness and order in rooms; to keep clothes, shoes, and beds neat.

19 — To carry student record book with him always; to guard it carefully, never handing it to anyone; to present it upon request to the director or teacher.

20 — To cherish the honor of his school and class, and defend it as his own.

*   *   *   *   *

When Hugh Ansley, a young teacher at Glenridge Junior High School, Winter Park, Florida, read these Commandments to his class, and told the class that students in Russia must memorize them and are expelled if they do not observe them, there was at first a stunned silence. Then one of the students said, "Mr. Ansley, why couldn't we try that Russian plan in our class?" The class seconded the suggestion, and finally the teacher agreed that they would try it for the next seven weeks, the remainder of the semester.

The results were electrifying. The 285-page civics textbook assigned for the whole year's work was completed in the seven weeks. Grades went up 25%, and parents could hardly believe their offspring's changed behavior and study habits.

At the end of the seven weeks the class was so exhilarated by their first voluntary efforts at concentration and self-control that they asked, "Is there any reason why we can't have classes on Saturday?" The principal was willing, and Mr. Ansley offered to teach without extra pay. Students not in the civics class begged to be included, so with the permission of their parents, any student whose grades were "C" or above could enroll, and the Saturday classes would be in subjects not otherwise available to 9th-graders. A three-hour morning class in Logic was attended by 17 students, and a three-hour afternoon class in History of Philosophy was attended by 26. The course ran for 15 weeks, and the conversation and discussion of the children were proof that the subjects were not above their heads. The Twenty Commandments were the rule of the Saturday School.

After the first seven-weeks experiment, the 8th-graders came to Mr. Ansley and said that they would like to "pick up where the 9th-graders leave off," and would like to start this year!

When I read Stanley Roberts' report of this experiment in the *Family Weekly* of Feb. 1, 1959, I was acutely conscious of the small challenge we give our children in school, and particularly in choir. I wondered what would happen if our Junior and Senior High School Choirs were inspired to adapt these Commandments to their choir membership.

166

The greatest lack in most of our choir programs is the lack of challenge. We attempt to keep them interested and regular in attendance, but to what purpose? The strength of any choir is in the effort that each member brings to the common task. And unless we train our children to recognize their responsibility to the group, we will never have a strong choir, nor be meeting our own obligation to their development.

During the summer many students paid a $20 fee and gave up swimming and other vacation activities to continue classes in psychology, American heritage, geography, biology or art—all without academic credit!

The Children's Choir movement is growing rapidly, but it is growing on such thin soil that the first hot sun is likely to dry it out. We need to concern ourselves with the development of strong roots rather than priding ourselves on the large number of struggling, undernourished branches. There are those who recognize this same need throughout the whole church, and some few are beginning to cultivate the roots.

THE REV. ALBERT FAY HILL, pastor of the 295-year-old First Presbyterian Church of Elizabeth, New Jersey, makes the following requirements for membership in his church: Prospective members must attend at least ten instruction sessions and pledge themselves to a lifelong study of the Bible. They are asked to contribute time and talent as well as money. They are expected to pray daily for "the whole church of Christ," and to behave morally and ethically, and to "love and respect all of their brethren regardless of race, social status or past life." And each new member is urged to tithe. As the Rev. Mr. Hill says: "People have got to the point where they need know little, believe little, and do little to join the church."

Try rewriting these Twenty Commandments for your choir and for yourself.

RUTH KREHBIEL JACOBS

The Handbell Choir

GENERAL INFORMATION ABOUT HANDBELLS

WHAT IS A HANDBELL?

Any bell with a handle or handgrip that is light enough to be picked up and rung.

WHAT IS AN ENGLISH HANDBELL?

The musical or tuned handbell cast of bell metal, an alloy of copper and tin, with its clapper rigidly mounted and hinged so that striking is possible in only two directions, and with a retaining device which prevents the clapper from lying against the bell when held with the lip up, is English in origin. This type of handbell is known as an "English handbell" regardless of the manner in which it is played or the country in which it is manufactured.

WHERE CAN THEY BE PURCHASED?

Bells of David, David Workman, 7037 Indiana Ave., Kansas City 30, Missouri.

Petit & Fritsen Bell Founders, c/o G. Fritsen, 80 Larkdale Road, Deerfield, Illinois.

Schulmerich Carillons, Inc., Sellersville, Pennsylvania.

Trusonic Bells, Benard Mason, P.O. Box 31-111, Los Angeles 31, California.

Whitechapel Bell Foundry (Mears & Stainbank), 32 Whitechapel Road, London E- I, England.

WHAT COMPRISES A SET?

There is no rule. You may order one bell or sixty-one (five chromatic octaves, the total number manufactured). Ringers can normally handle at least three bells apiece.

However, the number of bells used by various groups tends to fall into about five categories or "sets": (1) The smallest practical set is 14 or 15 bells. (The melody alone of the "Star-Spangled Banner" requires 13 bells.) Simple harmonizations are possible. This set should range from middle C to G above the treble staff, plus F-sharp, B-flat, etc. (2) Two chromatic octaves (25 bells) from F or G below middle C and up two octaves. (3) Three chromatic octaves (37 bells) from C below middle C and up three octaves. (4) Four chromatic octaves (49 bells) from F or G an octave and a half below middle C and up four octaves; or the lowest four octaves from C to C. (5) Five chromatic octaves (61 bells) from C two octaves below middle C and up five octaves.

Warning: It is important to remember in ordering handbells that handbells are a transposing instrument, sounding an octave higher than the music written for them. Unless you are ordering all five octaves, build your order around the middle C used for writing purposes (523 vps, 4½″ in diameter), not the founder's middle C, or you will receive the low, heavy, more expensive bells. Check your order with an experienced handbell ringer.

WHAT DO ENGLISH HANDBELLS COST?

Approximate costs are listed below according to the tentative sets mentioned above. Write the founders for the latest detailed price lists. In the case of English-made bells the list-price is lower; however, the U.S. Customs duty must be considered in the total cost.

15 Handbells	$ 300.00
25 Handbells (2 octaves)	550.00
37 Handbells (3 octaves)	800.00
49 Handbells (4 octaves)	1200.00 and up
61 Handbells (5 octaves)	1500.00 and up

WHO RINGS HANDBELLS AND WHO CAN DIRECT HANDBELL GROUPS?

Although handbell ringing is popular and appropriate for groups of all ages, probably the largest number of ringers in America today are young people from 12-18.

Any patient individual with some musical and conducting training can become an effective leader of a bell group.

170

IS THERE A NATIONAL ORGANIZATION OF HANDBELL RINGERS?

Yes. The American Guild of English Handbell Ringers, organized in 1954, is the only such society in the world, listing members in nearly every State in the Union and in several foreign countries.

HOW CAN I JOIN THE AGEHR?

Anyone interested in handbell ringing may join this Guild by filling out an application form and by paying dues of $5.00 a year. Individual membership is $5.00 a year; group membership is also $5.00. (Directors must hold an individual membership.) Write the Editor: Nancy Poore Tufts, 9051 River View Rd., Washington, D.C. 20022

WHAT ARE THE PREREQUISITES OF MEMBERSHIP?

Those holding individual memberships receive a subscription to *Overtones,* the official magazine of the Guild; receive copies of other official publications; have the privilege of purchasing Guild insignia; are entitled to vote and to hold office. Group membership entitles the group to receive five subscriptions to *Overtones;* the privilege of wearing Guild insignia and of attending Guild meetings and festivals as planned by their directors.

WHERE CAN MUSIC BE PURCHASED?

Handbell collections, individual selections, duos with organ, and choral and organ numbers with handbell parts may be ordered through local music stores or directly from music publishing houses: Carl Fischer; J. Fischer; H. Flammer; Galaxy; Lorenz; H. W. Gray; G. Schirmer; or through Cokesbury, or Whittemore Associates of Boston. Mimeographed sheets of simple arrangements for handbells and more advanced music for the carillon (some of which can be arranged for handbells) are available through *Societas Campanoriorum,* Office of the Carillonneur, The Riverside Church, New York 27, N.Y.

HAVE ANY BOOKS BEEN PUBLISHED ON THE SUBJECT?

Yes. (See MATERIALS)

ARE RECORDINGS AVAILABLE OF HANDBELL RINGING?

Yes. (See MATERIALS)

NANCY POORE TUFTS

171

SERVICES OF DEDICATION FOR A SET OF HANDBELLS
No. 1

PRELUDE   "Bell Symphony"   Purcell
(Organ and Handbells)

PROCESSIONAL HYMN (with bells ad lib)

INVOCATION (Minister)

Dearly Beloved: We learn from the Holy Scriptures that devout men set apart temples for the worship of God and used musical instruments therein for his praise and adoration. We therefore assemble here for the purpose of dedicating these handbells for service in the worship of almighty God.

THE CALL TO WORSHIP

MINISTER: Surely the Lord is in this place.

CONGREGATION: There is none other than the house of the Lord: this is the gate of heaven.

MINISTER: Enter into his gates with thanksgiving and into his courts with praise.

CONGREGATION: O magnify the Lord with me; let me exalt his Name together.

GLORIA PATRI (said or sung)

PRAYER (Minister)

DEDICATION

(The bells may then be presented for dedication by the chairman of the Music Committee, the Choir Director, or someone designated for that purpose, in some such words as):

We present these handbells for dedication (if a gift or memorial so stating), the gift of _____, for the glory of God and in loving memory of _____.

Then shall the Minister say these or similar words of dedication, all the people standing and uniting in the responses:

MINISTER: In the Name of the Father, and of the Son, and of the Holy Spirit, we dedicate these handbells to the praise of almighty God.

CONGREGATION: Praise God in his sanctuary: praise him in the firmament of his power. Praise him with the sound of the trumpet: praise him with the psaltery and harp.

MINISTER: We dedicate these handbells for worship in this holy temple of the Lord.

CONGREGATION: Praise him with stringed instruments and organs. Let everything that hath breath praise the Lord. Praise ye the Lord.

172

MINISTER: We dedicate these handbells as instruments of praise, that joy and gladness may be found therein, harmony, and the voice of melody.

CONGREGATION: O sing unto the Lord a new song: sing unto the Lord all the earth, in psalms and hymns and spiritual songs, singing and making melody in your heart unto the Lord.

MINISTER: We dedicate these handbells to thanksgiving on festal occasions, and to such inspiration in the service of song that all people may praise the Lord.

CONGREGATION: It is a good thing to give thanks unto Jehovah, and to sing praises unto thy Name, O most High.

MINISTER: We dedicate these handbells to the healing of life's discords, and to the lifting of heart and soul to abiding beauty and joy by the glory of God's infinite love and good will.

CONGREGATION: That at the Name of Jesus every knee should bow, that every tongue should confess that Jesus Christ is Lord, to the glory of God the Father.

PRAYER (Minister)

O God, who of old didst appoint silver trumpets to sound in the temple: Bless now, we beseech thee, these handbells, that their music may come as a blessed benediction upon all who worship here; through Jesus Christ our Lord. Amen.

HYMN (with handbell descant)

ADDRESS

OFFERTORY ANTHEM: "The Old 100th Psalm Tune" arr. R. Vaughan Williams (Adult and Children's Choirs, trumpet or handbells ad lib)

RECESSIONAL HYMN

BENEDICTION

BELL AMEN (preferably from rear of sanctuary)

* * * * *

No. 2

The following Bell Dedication information appeared in the Church Bulletin of the Village Lutheran Church, Bronxville, N.Y. DORIS VOESTER is Director of Music.

This Service of Dedication comes from medieval times and consists of three steps:

1. THE WASHING OF THE BELL. This is to indicate that the bells are to be clean instruments of a pure and holy religion, and are thus cleansed before they are permitted to send forth a sound in the service of God.

2. THE ANOINTING OF THE BELL. The sign of the Cross is made with oil on the four opposing sides of the bell. The four-fold function denotes that the sound of the bell is to go forth to the four points of the compass to the praise and glory of God.
3. THE CENSING OF THE BELL. Prayer, in the language of Scripture, is likened to the smoke of incense rising to heaven and calling to God.

In ancient times this entire ceremony was performed on each bell. In our usage we use one handbell as a symbol of them all.

* * * * *

No. 3

An effective and appropriate Service of Dedication was held at the Indianola Presbyterian Church, Columbus, Ohio; ELDO NEUFELD, Director of Music. The sponsoring bell choir was the Pilgrim Bell Choir, First Congregational Church, also of Columbus; EDWARD JOHE, Choir Director. The service was a combined Epiphany Service, a Dedication of Handbells, and Recognition of Sponsorship of and by a sister Bell Choir. Here is a portion of the Service:

CEREMONY OF DEDICATION

SENTENCES

GLORIA PATRI

APOSTLES' CREED AND CHORAL RESPONSE

PRAYERS AND THE LORD'S PRAYER

THE QUESTIONS AND THE RESPONSES

MINISTER: These bells, as they find their place in the life of this church, could be symbolic of many things in the Christian faith:
. . . their clean, simple lines remind us of the simple virtues of faith, hope, and love.
. . . their clear, bright, ringing sound is characteristic of the pure sound of praise.
. . . and their requirement of being used in cooperation with others symbolizes the corporate nature of the worship of almighty God. (*Signaling everybody at the table to stand*): Mr. Pollock, you were inspired by the ringing of the Pilgrim Bell Choir in January 1958, and you then determined to provide such a set of bells for Indianola as a memorial to Mrs. Pollock. Do you now bequeath these bells to this church, with the hope that they may serve to give youth an added opportunity to serve God and his Church, and to inspire us to an appreciation of beauty in the worship of God?

174

MR. POLLOCK: I was so inspired, and I now bequeath these bells to this church.

MINISTER: Mr. Ervin, as chairman of the Music Committee of this church, do you accept this gift in the name of the church from Mr. Pollock, and do you promise to encourage the formation of a Bell Choir and to instigate such projects and ideas as may be necessary for its most successful functioning?

MR. ERVIN: I do accept this gift most gratefully in the name of the church, and promise that we shall treasure it with reverence and gratitude, encouraging its highest and proper use at all times.

MINISTER: Do you, young people of our Chapel Choir, accept the responsibility of becoming the first Bell Choir of Indianola, and do you promise to provide from time to time such inspiring and entertaining music as you shall be capable of?

YOUNG PEOPLE: We do accept this responsibility and we do so promise.

MINISTER: Do you, Bell Ringers of First Congregational Church, welcome the formation of a sister Bell Choir in this church, and do you promise to encourage its efforts in the making of music, in that sense acting as its sponsors?

PILGRIM BELL CHOIR: We welcome this choir and we promise such encouragement.

MINISTER: Do you, Mr. Neufeld, as perhaps the most constant custodian of these bells, accept the responsibility of their care and use, for the formation and training of bell choirs, and for the overall character and quality of their contribution to our worship and other services?

MR. NEUFELD: I do accept this responsibility.

MINISTER: And now, do you, the members of this congregation and others gathered here with us, concur in the acceptance of this gift of bells and their dedication to the service of God and his Church? If so, will you answer, "We do."

CONGREGATION: We do.

MINISTER: Praise ye the Lord. Praise God in his sanctuary.

PEOPLE: (Read 150th Psalm)

MINISTER: To the glory of God, Author of all goodness and beauty, Giver of all skill of mind and hand:

PEOPLE: We dedicate these bells.

MINISTER: In faith in our Lord Jesus Christ, who has inspired men to offer in his praise their best in music and song:

PEOPLE: We dedicate these bells.

MINISTER: Moved by the Holy Spirit, our Guide in the worship of God and our Helper in the understanding of truth and beauty:

PEOPLE: We dedicate these bells.

MINISTER: To kindle the flame of devotion, that the people of God who here assemble may worship the Father in spirit and in truth:

PEOPLE: We dedicate these bells.

MINISTER: To bear up the melody of psalm and hymn and spiritual song in such wise that men may go forth from this house of God with high resolve to do his holy will:

PEOPLE: We dedicate these bells.

PRAYER OF DEDICATION AND CHORAL AMEN

HYMN: "Praise to the Lord, the Almighty" (Lobe den Herren)

* * * * *

TINTINNABULATIONS

By Nancy Poore Tufts

1. Bells at Christmastide

Let nothing you dismay! Long rehearsals, tired feet and sore hands are quickly forgotten as we approach this season. Surely Christmas was made for bell-ringing. Why, the beloved carols almost play themselves!

Do you have your new bell choirs ring frequently during their first Christmastide? Even simple carol melodies, unaccompanied, are beautiful when played slowly on handbells. You will notice a tremendous improvement in technique, general interest and attitude as a result of holiday ringing. Make definite if not detailed plans *now* for a late January or early February program or appearance. Immediately following New Year's, while the ringers are still aglow and keenly interested, is the perfect time to introduce more advanced material, new ideas and arrangements. Foil that post-holiday slump with fresh approaches! Build on that aroused enthusiasm!

Do you have a touch-me-not attitude with your handbells, or does one group in your church have a monopoly on bell-ringing? What a pity not to share the joy of ringing, even occasionally, with others. A lady confided in me that the Women's Association of her church had worked for two years earning the means to purchase handbells, but that only a band of little boys was allowed to use them, that the choir director refused to organize other groups, or to permit any one else to pick up and sound a bell!

176

May I suggest that you consider launching a choir "Open House," or a "Carol-Sing," to be held either in the Parish House or in your home during the Christmas season? Almost everyone truly enjoys singing familiar carols and hymns in an informal atmosphere, but there aren't many opportunities nowadays to do so. You and your children's and adult choirs could make this possible, and such an occasion might become a popular tradition in your community.

If a large group is expected, the time might be extended from 4:00 to 7:00 P.M. or 7:00 to 10:00 P.M. and so on. A number of pianists and perhaps other instrumentalists, who will agree to play in half-hour shifts, should be rounded up. Choristers should be assigned definite periods to serve as hosts and to lead or reinforce the singing. The choirs should decorate, also furnish, prepare, and serve light refreshments. An occasional solo, choral, or bell number would lend variety and encourage would-be stars to shine!

One should feature handbells in all their splendor. The bells might be attractively displayed in an adjoining room, in charge of several experienced ringers. Impromptu teams, of all ages, could be rapidly made up and each in turn encouraged to play carols from simple music scores or charts—perhaps melodies alone, with a harmonized cadence. Several signs such as "Handle Carefully," "Grasp Handles Firmly," "Do Not Touch Metal," plus an instructor or two should be sufficient safeguards. Let no one be disappointed! Quickly-numbered charts or sheets could be prepared for those who do not read music. This might take you 10 or 15 minutes. Assign each ringer one bell and a number. The delight and appreciation in the eyes of the inexperienced will repay you ten-fold.

"SILENT NIGHT" (any key)
10 bells—Try C

5, 6, 5, 3 – – , 5, 6, 5, 3 – – ,
9, –, 9, 7 – – , 8, – 8, 5 – – ,
6, 6, 8, 7, 6 – , 5, 6, 5, 3 – – ,
etc.

"JOY TO THE WORLD" (any key) 8 bells—Try C or D

8, 7, 6, 5, 4, 3, 2, 1,
5, 6, 6, 7, 7, 8 –,
8, 8, 7, 6, 5, 5, 4, 3,
etc.

Be generous with handbells at Christmastime. You pass this way only once; sprinkle joy and stardust!

2. Ring in the New Year

"Oh, the weather outside was frightful,
But the tea was so delightful."

Ring the doorbell and come right on in and make yourselves comfortable by the fire. I am just having tea, and I'll get out cups for you.

Let's finish up these chewy bell-shaped cookies someone sent in for Christmas.

Isn't it good to relax and purr a bit now that our holiday programs are a fait accompli? Another happy Christmastide to add to our treasure-store of memories! We are reluctant to let the season pass—with its glamor, charm, and blessedness. The children's expectant delight, gaiety and excitement has rubbed off on all of us. They sang carols and rang bells like starry-eyed angels. Would that we might hold on to that special shine throughout the year!

Now is the time to assess and evaluate as well as to clear away and make a fresh New Year beginning. Before holiday recollections fade why not list the material that was most effective, that the choirs especially enjoyed. List other music you heard in churches, schools, or over the air that you wanted to remember at the moment and order one copy for your files. Jot down ideas that occurred to you about improving your program planning and building: planning and rehearsing for Christmas earlier next fall to avoid fatigue; ideas for different seating and processional arrangements; decorations; new robes and accessories; the retirement or inactivating of certain music or dramas that have become stale or outgrown; the elimination of, changing, or adding choir holiday entertainment (reward or burden?).

Our forefathers customarily wrote two words, "Laus Deo," on the first clean page of the New Year's ledger. And so, praise be to God, we have completed another cycle. Now we must stir our bones to plan our Lenten and Easter music, our spring wind-up, and our summer vacations, camps, and workshops. We should take advantage of this foggy, chilly, or snow-bound season to order and arrange music, mimeograph material ahead, write letters, make lists, practice, plan and execute something special in the way of a trip, party, project, or program to keep up the choirs' enthusiasm during the "dull" months. Have you ever promoted a music-mending party? This can be made fun. Or a robe-mending bee? Or a choir-room cleaning or decorating "house-party"? Or a bell-polishing party?

A seed for a song: Last year my children rescued the choir-room Christmas tree from the Twelfth Night bonfire and stuck it in the snow near the choir-room window. They decorated it with strings of cranberries and popcorn, pieces of apple, bread, and suet, then sprinkled seed around the base. The Bell Choir tied on a string of tiny bells that tinkled merrily in January's blasts. Every week some of the children brought bread scraps and "bird-burgers". . . . Let's all feed our birds this winter. If a few pennies of seed or grain will mean that just one

178

songbird will live to sing again, won't it be worthwhile? Could there be a happier exchange than "a seed for a song"?

Next time we shall chat about spring music, bell festivals and dedications over the tintinnabulary teacups. Hurry back! "God bless thy year."

3. Bells of St. Patrick

On March 17th hundreds of thousands of persons of every conceivable background will pause to celebrate and whole communities will turn out to do honor to the patron saint of Ireland. For "Everybody's a little bit Irish on St. Patrick's Day"!

St. Patrick, like St. Francis of Assisi, is "everybody's saint." The same quality of joy, concern, and Christian winsomeness that drew people to them during their lifetime draws people to them today. It is not the grim-faced martyrs but the messengers of Christian joy that are universally popular and venerated. If, seemingly, it is a superficial reaction to parade to "The Wearing of the Green," to acquire garden statuary and bird-feeders, framed prayers and greeting cards, at least it is a Christian reaction and recognition.

In Ireland some of the most revered holy relics are the portable bells used by the early Celtic saints. These are small, four-sided handbells of iron or bronze. The most ancient is St. Patrick's bell in its reliquary (case), which may be seen along with about forty similar bells in the National Museum of Ireland in Dublin. The six-inch bell used by St. Patrick in the 5th century and found in his tomb is made of two plates of sheet-iron fastened together by iron rivets and bronzed. The case, dated A.D. 1005, is made of 31 bronze plates, richly decorated with intertwining figures of animals and studded with precious stones (red and crystal).

A report on St. Patrick's bell, or the Celtic ecclesiastical bells, which are the oldest known handbells still in existence today that have been used in Christian service, would be a worthwhile assignment for a Bell Choir next March or anytime. A poster picture or a facsimile of the reliquary would be interesting and attractive. The National Museum in Dublin has postal cards on sale with pictures of both St. Patrick's bell and the bell of Armagh.

Several years ago I chose that lengthy but lovely and mystical hymn "I bind myself today" (tune "St. Patrick") as the March "Hymn of the Month." The Junior Choir rehearsal nearest the Saint's Day was concluded with a brief feature and a "wee bit of the creature" (refreshments). The tallest boy represented St. Patrick and was dressed in a long green cape and a high cardboard "mitre." He carried an old bell and a "crozier" made from a broomstick topped with a cardboard emblem. As the choir sang the hymn he entered and sat with great dignity. Then he stood and said:

"Hear ye! I have come to this beautiful green country of mountains, valleys, and lakes to tell you about Jesus Christ, the Saviour of mankind. Put aside the worship of false gods, the worship of animals, trees, and stones, and learn of Jesus Christ, the Son of God, and your true Friend and Brother. Glory be to the Father, etc."

This melodious tune "St. Patrick" lends itself beautifully to hand-bell ringing as does the tune "Slane" ("Be thou my vision") and the tune "St. Columba." Charles Burke's arrangement of "St. Patrick's Prayer" (Stainer & Bell, #2389, SATB) is most effective, even dramatic, with children's voices in place of the soprano solo indicated and in the unison tutti.

AN IRISH BLESSING

May the Saints protect ye
An' sorrow neglect ye,
An' the top of the morning
To all that belong t'ye.
An' long life to yer honour—
That's the end of my song t'ye.

4. Bells of Easter

Greetings to you on the threshold of this spring-ringing month and a weary farewell to bullying March! April is sun-silvered, smiling, relaxed, and brings hope and happiness.

We too shall bring joy and beauty to the services and programs of this important season as we ring Lenten and Easter hymns, carols, and spirituals. Have you ever tried repeating (echoing) pianissimo the first two lines of Palestrina's "The strife is o'er," then ringing the final Alleluia super-forte? Or connecting three familiar Easter hymns with a key modulation, either on the bells or on the organ, to make a longer number? Or arranging a high shimmering descant for the end-line Alleluias of "Jesus Christ is ris'n today"? (This is a brilliant effect.) Or ringing on the outside steps of the church or even in the church yard on Easter Sunday morning as the people arrive, then joining the choir procession or ringing the opening hymn from the rear of the sanctuary?

Bell Polishing: Of course you will want your bells clean and shining for Eastertide. Eleanor Thompson recommends polishing cloths which

180

may be ordered @ $3 per dozen from CLEAN-E-ZE Mfg. Co., Philadelphia 23, Pa. The Fink family applies GLASS WAX after polishing. Lacquer thinner has been used successfully to remove sprays and shellacs. Saddle soap is good for stained leather handles. (Incidentally, the new Schulmerich bells have polypropylene handles; Whitechapel is experimenting with a similar substance for clapper strikers.)

Hymn for Bell Dedications or Festivals: From our English ringing friends comes this excellent hymn: "A Ringer's Hymn" by Percy Amos. The words are based on Psalm 48. Tune: "St. Thomas" ("I love thy kingdom, Lord").

Proclaim the Church of God,
  To men of every land;
The bells we ring, the Gospel bring,
  With melody and hand.

Ye sons of Sion arise,
  As the pilgrims did of old;
Up to Jerusalem they trod,
  With psalms their praise foretold.

Set on His holy hills,
  The towers thereof we tell;
Within their walls a message calls,
  From every hallowed bell.

Give ear, good Christian men,
  Low and high, both rich and poor;
God's presence and His very self
Convey from shore to shore.
Amen.

5. Let Freedom Ring!

Before you are let out to pasture for the summer, please make two firm resolutions: (1) That your change of pace and scene this summer will definitely include periods of relaxation and recreation. By June many of us are either drained of energy, exhausted and apathetic, or so jangled of ears and nerves that we are jumpy and irritable. We owe it to ourselves and to our choirs to regain our resiliency, to rekindle our warmth and enthusiasm, to re-create our spirits and inspiration. Chew your cud thoughtfully! (2) That your plans will include one workshop or festival offering a course in Handbell Ringing. There are many to choose from in various parts of the country: Chorister's Guild Seminar, Montreat, NAFOMM, Glorietta, Alfred, Ipswich, and Regional or National Festivals of the AGEHR.

Bell Memorials. I have heard from two persons who have given handbells as memorials this spring. What a beautiful gesture! Their mellow music will bring joy and comfort to many a heart. Memorial bells should be handled with especial care and respect. I would urge that memorial bells be engraved, that there be a suitable Dedication Ceremony, preferably in the presence of the congregation and choirs.

181

Let Freedom Ring! You have all read in *This Week* and the daily papers about the movement to ring all bells in the Nation at 2 P.M. (EST) on every July 4th. Do haul out your handbells and ring "America" on the church steps. Arrange to have the church bells rung too. This is a worthy project; let's cooperate with patriotic fervor. For information write "Let Freedom Ring," Box 4140, Grand Central Station, New York 17, N.Y.

Time brings down this season's curtain. Well rung, thou good and faithful servant!

6. Planning Ahead

Greetings! Here's an old bell inscription for you:
"Think no cost too much
That you bestow of all
To bring to pass so good a thing
That mellow bells together ring."

Here we are on the brink of a fresh and exciting new fall season. Were you able to gather useful material, new ideas, different approaches to old problems, plus a bit of re-creation and stimulation for yourself this summer? Of course you did!

Today is a composite of the past, the present, the future, and today is the time to plan your choir and handbell schedules to the end of the season: your rehearsals, services, and programs. Write down your goals, your plans, your dreams; keep them in your mind's eye, and forge ahead! Your singers and ringers will respond, like magic, to your dedication, your cheerful encouragement, your skillful leadership. You're off to a wonderful ringing season!

Directors who have been working for some time with various groups of ringers realize that the modern educational method of activity teaching—"do it yourself," "discover it for yourself"—is a remarkably successful one. It has been my observation that most choir directors talk too much. Students fidget and their minds wander unless information and instructions are given clearly and briefly. A teacher with a strong personality may hold youngsters' attention for five minutes—for ten minutes it would require a hypnotist!

Today the "telling" technique is recognized as a less effective tool. Activity is the password today. In handbell ringing we have one of the finest examples of activity teaching. The skilled teacher will hold "briefings" to a minimum, stimulate the "will to drill," and conduct brisk, well-paced rehearsals. His students will "learn by ringing," and love every minute of it.

182

Are you approaching this exciting new season with thoughtful, creative plans for your Bell Choirs?

Bell Trees: Several readers have sent in descriptions and pictures of "Bell Trees" at Christmas. Robert Legler of Wauwatosa, Wisconsin, decorated a 3½-foot stainless steel tree with dozens of small brass bells. A bell collector of Tucson, Arizona, had a blacksmith design a large iron tree for her holiday display. Ellen Jane Lorenz of Dayton, Ohio, with the help of her Bell Choir, has decorated a 13-foot tree with over 100 bells for the past four years. The bells are made of gilded paper drinking cups, with pipe-cleaner clappers. Another director cuts a Christmas tree shape from a peg-board, surrounds it with a garland and decorates with small bells. Another idea is the wicker tree of various sizes sold in Mexican shops. These may be used also on other occasions for parties, showers, displays, as a "cookie" tree, and for an Easter Egg Tree. But please do not risk tying *handbells* to a tree! (Yes, it *could* happen!)

> As once again in praise of Him
> The joyful bells of Christmas chime,
> May Christ the Lord look down on you
> And bless you at this holy time.

CLAPPER COMMENTS FROM HANDBELL DIRECTORS

From JOHN HALVORSEN, Epworth Methodist Church, Norfolk, Virginia:

"I have been greatly concerned with the intermediate boys in my church. Twelve to fourteen is that awkward age when voices crack and wobble uncontrollably. These boys don't like to sing with the girls and there aren't enough to form a group of their own. Handbells seemed the answer to keep these boys interested in the program of the church. One of the adult classes in the church generously ordered a set of 37 bells from the Whitechapel Foundry.

"But until they arrive—what to do with the boys? I hit upon the idea of using pipes instead of bells. The local organ-maintenance man gave me a rank of wood flute pipes. Each boy had at least two pipes and when his number came up on the blackboard, he blew! I must say we sounded like a broken-down circus calliope, but we had fun. We have performed for several church banquets and even the Norfolk Chapter of the A.G.O. Aesthetically and musically this little group leaves much to be desired, but it has served to fill a gap until we receive the exciting news that our handbells have arrived." (Editor's Note: Other "expectant" bell groups have practiced with sticks, tapping glasses filled with water, plastic bells, resonator bells, and so on. There are many devices that can aid in developing coordination and rhythm.)

Directors of successful Handbell Choirs must necessarily be firm disciplinarians. Bell ringing engenders a remarkable esprit de corps which frowns upon dawdling, buck-passing and absentee-ism and the Bell Choir is proving a splendid training-ground for Christian youth that surpasses mere music-making.

DAVID V. WILLIAMS wrote that he demands of his Bell Choirs in Tulsa "discipline and loyalty" plus the ability to read music.

DAVID YOLTON (formerly at First Methodist, Bryan, Texas; now at Abington Presbyterian, Abington, Pa.) required the study of a mimeographed booklet containing basic essentials of handbell ringing. "Things to Remember" included:

Never put your hands on the bells; use gloves to protect the bells and your hands.

Set a bell down carefully and quietly; beware of touching two bells together.

Polish bells before putting them away.

Let the Bellmaster know immediately if a bell's mechanism seems to function improperly.

Several "Information Sheets for New Ringers" sent in, including that of MILDRED GLEESON, Marvin Memorial Methodist Church, Silver Spring, Md., used similar examples to emphasize the importance of perfect attendance:

Q. What would happen if a member missed a rehearsal?

A. It would be nearly impossible for the group to play; i.e. if you played bells G and A and the Bell Choir was practicing the hymn "A Mighty Fortress is Our God," the result would be something like this (in the key of C):

A mighty - - tress is - - God,
A bul - - - failing:
Our helper he - - mid - flood
Of mor - - - vailing;
For still - ancient foe
Doth - - - us woe;
His craft and - - - ,
- - - - el hate,
On earth - - - equal.

Mrs. Gleeson also wrote: "It would, of course, be extremely difficult for the group to perform without all present. Remember tha

184

even though the bells you hold may ring only occasionally, you are 'in' every note. This is a group effort, and each must be alert to do his part toward making a perfect whole. Our high purpose is to offer the best possible bell-ringing to the glory of God."

* * * * *

AN OLD RHYME FOR BELL RINGERS
Ye ringers all, that do come here
Give head and hand and heart,
The head for will, the hand for skill,
The heart for worship's part.

HANDEL'S MUSIC FOR CLOCKS

George Frederick Handel's name is so identified with the pomp and majesty of his great oratorios that many musicians fail to recognize the delightful humor which occasionally peeps through his less lofty endeavors.

Like Mozart and Haydn he was not afraid to experiment with unusual musical effects and new musical inventions. These great men were not esoteric esthetes but practical, up-to-date, hard-working musicians, eager and willing to embrace innovations.

In 1735 Charles Clay, Royal Clockmaker for George I of England, perfected a remarkable musical clock with a mechanical chime attachment—a barrel playing on a row of bells. He commissioned his friend Handel to compose tunes for this clock. Handel wrote "Ten Tunes for Clay's Musical Clock," also a set of four tunes as a "Sonata for a Musical Clock," and five other pieces. These tunes used 13, 21, and 36 bells.

This marvelous clock was exhibited before His Majesty and became the sensation of London. The inventive clockmaker was inspired to experiment further, and later turned out clocks with bells, a small pipe organ, and a harpsichord, some of which played Handel's arias. These instruments "not only played together, but alternately."

Visitors to Kensington Palace today are shown a magnificent clock-case on a heavy pedestal which is about four times the size of the average grandfather's clock. Every inch is elaborately gilded, ornamented, painted, or carved. A sign reads "Clay's Musical Clock, 1735," but alas, the clock mechanism, the bells and other instruments have vanished. Perhaps it all wore out; perhaps no one could make repairs. No one seems to know.

But Handel's original MS for "Ten Tunes" is still in existence at the British Museum. Most of these are obtainable from three sources: "Sonata for a Musical Clock" (13 bells), edited by Percival Price, is published by Carl Fischer; "Ten Tunes" may be obtained from James Lawson, Carillonneur of The Riverside Church, N.Y. City (15-18 bells); and Richard Purvis has arranged six tunes as a novelty number for the organ "Suite for a Musical Clock" (Flammer).

Advanced handbell ringers have found these Handelian tunes a welcome addition to their repertoire. Ringers capable of ringing these tunes at a lively clip can tackle anything. Why not use one of the "Ten Tunes" as a warming-up exercise in place of scales and arpeggios?

NANCY POORE TUFTS

186

Projects and
Special Activities

AUDIO-VISUAL AIDS IN CHILDREN'S CHOIR REHEARSALS

An effective tool of learning available to us as directors and teachers is a comprehensive use of audio-visual aids. Nearly 400 new church-related audio-visuals are now produced annually, many of which can be bought as well as rented.

What kind of audio-visual library now exists in your church? It is recommended that each church compile its own A-V catalog for use of its church workers as your own A-V library grows.

Surely we would all agree that A-V aids should not be ends in themselves, but means or helps for carrying out the purposes or goals which we hope to accomplish in our teaching and singing, while we are working with children, young people, and adults.

To be able to see and hear songs, characters, seasons of the church year, hymns, and so on illustrated, can mean so much more to children in their learning processes, perception, understanding, appreciation, and accomplishment.

Sometimes we simply cannot find the kind of A-V aid that we need. In fact, this is still such a new area which opens doors for children that we should enthusiastically encourage our denominational bodies to process more teaching aids, particularly those which can be so helpful in the ministry of music. (Why doesn't the Choristers Guild pioneer in this field?)

187

Have you ever considered making your own aids? Pictures can be cut out and mounted on posters; an artist might draw or paint what you need; or perhaps you might use the magic of photography and make your own colored slides.

Choir rehearsals can be greatly enhanced, speeded up, and improved by the use of a tape recorder—a most desirable aid for every church music department. Here each chorister can listen to and criticize his own efforts. The immediate playback of a tape, after recording, provides an excellent teaching method as well as a permanent means of recording programs.

Many "live" experiences can be shared through A-V aids as a service to others beyond the local church group. For instance, a group of our 3rd grade boys and girls learned Grace Noll Crowell's poem, "Thank You, God, for Your Beautiful World," which had been set to music and printed in a church school periodical. The children loved it. In studying the text, someone mentioned that Mrs. Crowell lived here in Dallas and wished that she might hear the group sing the song. So it was recorded, and a few members of the group were selected to take it to Mrs. Crowell and play it for her. She had never heard this poem sung before and was delighted, not only with the recording but with the thoughtfulness of the children in doing this for her and coming to see her. The children, in turn, were thrilled to share in this experience with Mrs. Crowell. This is an example of using an audio-visual aid as a means to an end rather than as an end in itself. The children benefited in this experience of helping someone else by showing their love and interest in her.

Most denominations plan their courses of study in the church school by units, usually quarterly. For instance, the Methodist *Forecast* lists aids resource guides for using A-V by age groups as supplementary materials. *Be sure to preview in advance what you want to use.*

Listed below are a few films and records selected at random from the *1960-61 Audio-Visual Resource Guide* * which might be used as supplementary aids for different projects to be studied by children's choirs.

Let's Sing About Christmas
How We Got Our Christmas Carols
Born in a Manger
Legendary Story of the Animals at Nativity
Stories About Our Christmas Carols

188

Christmas Around the World
Christmas Customs
Christmas Rhapsody
The Christmas Story in Art

At Easter Time (for the very young)
Easter Around the World
The Easter Season
He Is Risen
The Meaning of Lent (Youth)

Christ and the Fine Arts
Religious Masterpieces
Church Symbolism
Christian Symbols
Christian Worship
How and Why We Worship (filmstrip)
One God (filmstrip)
The Reformation
Albert Schweitzer
John Wesley
Martin Luther

Sing Unto the Lord (filmstrip)
Home and Church Songs (record)
Gladly Sing
Let's Sing About Seasons
The Heart That Sings (filmstrip)
Enjoying a Song
Holidays (Kindergarten)

The Children's Bible Series
The Children's Church Series
The Life of Christ Series
The Story of Jesus Series
The Stories of the Prophets Series

The Lord's Prayer (Youth)
Let's Try Choral Reading (filmstrip)
Prayer for Children (slides)

* Audio-Visual Resource Guide (5th edition, edited by Donald J. Kliphardt); published by Department of Audio-Visual and Broadcast Education of the Division of Christian Education, The National Council of the Churches of Christ in the U. S. A., 475 Riverside Drive, New York, N. Y. 10027.

REV. ROBERT E. SCOGGIN, Minister of Music
University Park Methodist Church, Dallas, Texas

CHURCH-WIDE SUNDAY NIGHT FELLOWSHIP

By HARRY R. HOOK, Minister of Music
First Methodist Church, Albuquerque, New Mexico

This church had been accustomed to a Sunday evening preaching service since its organization. But the people were not supporting Sunday evening services, for the average attendance was only 60 youth and adults. It was imperative that a change be made. We chose mid-September as the starting date and set up the schedule outlined below.

Until last year we had held rehearsals for our children's choirs on Saturday mornings. In a city as spread out as this it meant another trip from home to church, which some of the parents who live a good distance away were reluctant to make. Also, there were conflicts with school activities, scouts, family picnics, and the like. By holding choir rehearsals on Sunday evenings it made Saturday more of a family day.

The success of this new program far exceeded our expectations. While the Cherub, Carol, and Junior Choirs rehearse, the parents are in a study session with the minister or some of our community leaders. At six o'clock all dismiss and go into our dining room for a light snack (10c for children; 25c for adults) followed by a Hymn Sing, and closing with a devotional by one of our ministers. The program concludes at seven o'clock, giving the family ample time to be home by 7:30, and the smaller children in bed by eight.

We are so enthusiastic about this type of program that we are making plans to expand it next fall by adding more choirs and by doing more along the line of extended study sessions with outside programs and speakers. This program has definitely been the "shot in the arm" our church needed. To have continued in the old way would have meant a very limited program, and possibly closing the church doors entirely on Sunday evening. I can safely say that in this case the choirs have revitalized the life of the church.

Time	Kinder-garten	Carol Choir	Junior Choir	Junior High	Senior High	College	Adults
5:00 5:30	Story Hour	Choir	Choir	Snack	Snack	Snack	Study
5:30 6:00	Choir	Choir	Choir	5:30 6:15 Study	5:30 6:15 Study	Study	Study
6:00 6:30	Snack Crafts	Snack Sing-Song	Snack Sing-Song	6:15 7:00 Choir	6:15 7:00 Choir	Study	Snack Sing-Song
6:30 7:00	Crafts	Family Devo-tions	Family Devo-tions			Recrea-tion	Family Devo-tions

N. B. The word "Study" in the schedule does not mean homework but a class in some phase of religious thought appropriate to the particular age group.

✕ PROPER VESTMENTS FOR CHILDREN'S CHOIRS

Most people like the Negro spiritual "All God's Chillun Got Robes" and join heartily in singing it. Perhaps it is true that all of God's choir children do have robes, but what do some of them look like? What peculiar garments we sometimes see under the title "robe"! How much careful consideration has been given to the selection of style and materials? After all, are robes—let's call them vestments—necessary for children or are they just unnecessary expense? If we do have them, what style and color should be chosen?

Before we can answer any of these questions we need to review the reasons for having vestments for choirs. First of all, vestments set choir members apart from the congregation and designate them as co-leaders with the minister in the service of worship. They are a badge of service loaned by the church in recognition of the choristers' contribution to its services. They create a uniformity that is pleasing to the eyes of the congregation and that indicates to the choir member the oneness of their organization. No uniformity is achieved if one single item of apparel proclaims the individual. A colored hair-ribbon or other ornament on one child causes her to stand out from the group. Colored socks attract the same attention as do bracelets and necklaces and neckties. Earrings, no matter how small, attract attention to themselves.

191

We feel that choir vestments are as necessary for children as for adults and that they must be given the same careful consideration. Some churches, in an effort to economize, provide only a cotta or cotta-like garb for their children but would not think of asking adults to appear in this outlandish half-vestment! A reasonably uniform dress is far better than this haphazard attempt at vesting. Uniformity cannot be achieved unless a child's dress or suit is completely invisible.

A vestment is a garment that says to the child: "My church is proud of me and expects me to give of my best"—and it should be worn with pride. To the congregation it says: "Here is a group that is giving time and energy to the service of the church. We must support them in every way."

One-piece garments for children seem to be the most satisfactory from the standpoint of initial cost, upkeep, and ease of wearing. They should be dignified in appearance, avoiding all unnecessary embellishments. Each child should be carefully fitted for his vestment at the beginning of the choir year and the selected garment should be his alone for the year. The length and the shoulder fit will be right for him and, unless he grows unusually fast, will remain satisfactory for that period of time. Directors should instill in the choristers respect for these garments and require that they be properly cared for both by the children and the adults who assist them.

The wearing qualities of the cloth are important, for vestments should not need frequent replacing. The weight of the cloth depends somewhat upon whether the choir wears them only for the winter season or for the entire year. In addition to fully made robes special kits of pre-cut material are now available from the Ecclesiastical Arts Department of the Lutheran Church Supply Stores, 2900 Queen Lane, Philadelphia, Pa. 19129.

Let us remember always that vestments are to help choristers and congregation alike to "worship the Lord in the beauty of holiness."

MADELINE INGRAM

THE CHRISTIAN CHURCH YEAR
Seasonal Planning of Musical Programs

The Christian church year seems difficult for some to understand, and indeed to some others, quite foolish—too formal and stilted. But an increasing number of ministers and churches are finding it helpful and useful.

The church year is the attempt to organize Christian practices and

192

thinking into an annually recurring pattern. Centuries of usage and tradition are behind it. All Christian churches observe Christmas and Easter; many in addition observe Advent and Lent. Thus in actual practice the church year is followed and proves particularly helpful to church musicians in advance planning.

The Christian church year gives the Children's Choir director opportunity to explain Bible events in an orderly fashion. Children will understand a parallel between a school day or semester with the definite order and happenings of the church year. In many non-liturgical churches which follow the church year pattern the Trinity season is called "Kingdomtide," a period for stressing the church at work in the world.

In order for us all to understand the church year a bit better, the following is taken from Lutheran liturgical sources:

The church year begins with Advent Sunday—the Sunday nearest the 30th day of November. Advent means "coming" and the Advent season (including four Sundays) looks forward to Christmas, the day of Christ's coming. From December 25 to January 6 is the Christmas season.

January 6 is Epiphany, the beginning of the season which stresses Christ's coming to all people. This season continues until the 10th Sunday before Easter. It may include from one to six Sundays.

The pre-Lenten season (including three Sundays) is followed by Ash Wednesday which is 46 days before Easter and the first day of Lent. There are 40 weekdays and six Sundays in Lent. Easter is the first Sunday after the full moon which happens upon or next after March 21st. The Easter season is 40 days in length.

The 40th day after Easter is Ascension Day. Pentecost, 50 days after Easter, is followed by Trinity Sunday which begins the Trinity season including from 22 to 27 Sundays.

Explaining Ash Wednesday and Lent

For those of you whose churches observe Ash Wednesday and Lent, a few words may be in order to assist you in your work with boys and girls. Children absorb quickly, readily, and easily. At the Junior age level (possibly not before) explanations are in order about what the adults around them are doing. They see and feel more than we even dream of. The observance of Ash Wednesday and Lent should become a part of their normal growing experience.

The term Lent derives from an old Anglo-Saxon word *lengten,* which originally had no religious significance whatever. It meant

193

simply "lengthen." Since at that time of year the daylight hours were gradually lengthening, it soon came to denote the spring season. Lent begins on Ash Wednesday, the 40th weekday before Easter. Lent actually continues for 46 days, but six of these days are Sundays and are not reckoned as fasting days. There is considerable disagreement about the symbolism of the 40 days. Four principle views are held: (1) the 40 days during which Jesus fasted in the wilderness; (2) the 40 days spent by Moses on Sinai; (3) the 40 hours of Christ's entombment; (4) the 40 days between the Resurrection and the Ascension.

Since the 4th century Lent has been devoted to Christian nurture through discipline and penitence. In his book *Worship Resources* Charles L. Wallis says: "Objections to what may become a mechanical or spiritually blind observance of certain physical discipline ought not to lessen the possibility of making this period one of genuine spiritual restoration, commitment, and recreation." For Protestants Lent should become a period of *soul* refreshment—the forgetting of self and the doing for others.

For centuries, in nearly all religions, penitence has been a basic part of religious observance. The Jews, particularly, practiced intense penitence by sitting in a heap of ashes, clothed only in sackcloth (probably like our gunny-sack), and strewed ashes over their heads as they bewailed their personal and public sins. About 600 A.D. Pope Gregory the Great introduced the custom of dusting ashes on the foreheads of the penitent at the beginning of Lent and thus established Ash Wednesday in Christian practice. Whether we observe Lent and Ash Wednesday or not, our youngsters should learn the religious practice of others.

I would urge you not to give your Juniors (or even your Junior High group) all this information at once, and not even merely as information. Intertwine it with their learning of an anthem or a hymn. Make it a part of their experiences, if at all possible. Ash Wednesday and Lent can be as real to boys and girls as to adults. Never undervalue your youngsters' abilities!

RUTH KREHBIEL JACOBS

TIMOTHY, THE CHURCH MOUSE

(An Original Story for Young Choristers)

By TISSA ROBERTS

Once upon a time, many years ago in a large church called a cathedral, there lived a very devout little mouse called Timothy. Tim-

194

othy was among the first of a very long line of church mice, and perhaps best remembered for his goodness. It must be Timothy that mother is speaking about when she says, "Be quiet as a mouse," because not once, no not ever, did Timothy make a sound in church . . . except on one very important day.

Now Timothy dressed like the holy men of that time in a brown robe that tied in the middle with a rope. The robe even had a hood that pulled up over his head when the weather was cold; and especially made for Timothy was a long piece of cloth that fitted his tail like a glove. He loved to climb up to the rafters high above the floor where the stained glass windows shed their many colors. And it was a very high place, because the church was very large, and it seemed almost a mile down to the shiny marble floor. There he could see all that happened. He could watch the priests perform their daily duties and the people come and go at the altar. He could see the candles burning and the beautiful pictures and drapes against the stone walls.

But most of all Timothy liked to listen to the music. He enjoyed listening to the Boys Choir so much that he would often sit dangerously near the edge of the rafter so that he could hear and see better. And that is where our story begins.

This was the day that a saint beloved by every man and by all nature was to visit the church. His name was Saint Francis of Assisi. He preached and sang to all people of the land and to the creatures of the forest. He spread joy wherever he went, and he was coming to the cathedral where Timothy lived.

Everyone was terribly excited, and Timothy most of all. He scampered up to the highest rafter and sat down to wait for Saint Francis. And he did not have to wait long, for he had barely made himself comfortable when the great doors of the cathedral opened and the Boys Choir began to walk down the aisle singing. And following right behind was Saint Francis. Timothy was so happy that he could hardly sit still. The choir was singing his favorite hymn and he leaned over to listen more closely.

> "All creatures of our God and King
> Lift up your voice and with us sing."

And he did! . . . Timothy did sing with them after that. He happily chimed in:

> "Alleluia! Alleluia!
> Thou burning sun with golden beam,
> Thou silver moon with softer gleam,
> O praise Him! Alleluia!"

The choir was passing right under Timothy now, and he leaned over just a little bit more so that he could see them, when he felt himself starting to slip. He tried his best to hold on, but it was no use. All of a sudden he was falling head over heels through space and headed right for the hard, shiny marble floor way down below.

Timothy closed his eyes and squealed as loudly as he could. Then he prayed with all his little heart. He prayed and he prayed, and he was still praying when he landed, ker-plunk, right in the hood of St. Francis' robe! Saint Francis said not a word, but reached into his hood and pulled Timothy out by the rope around his middle. He was surprised, but he smiled and winked at Timothy and slipped him back into the soft folds of the hood. There Timothy stayed until the service was over, and then Saint Francis again pulled him from his hood and held him in his hand while he talked to him, telling him about Jesus who loved everyone. Then he shook Timothy's tiny hand and told him goodbye.

Timothy climbed to his place on the rafters again and sat down to think. He decided that he would try to be as good and as kind as Saint Francis and tell others about Jesus. And I'm not so sure he was not successful, because if you listen closely, you might hear the mice speak of a Saint Timothy who lived in a large church called a cathedral many years ago.

(Written by Tissa Roberts while a student at Southwestern University. Tissa is now assistant to Bob Scoggin at University Park Methodist Church, Dallas, Texas.)

TIMOTHY, THE CHURCH MOUSE, MEETS THE PIPE ORGAN
(An Original Story for Young Choristers)
By John Scholten, Choir Director
Camp Hill Presbyterian Church, Camp Hill, Pennsylvania

(Toll chimes slowly twelve times).

The chimes in the church tower were striking twelve and all was dark, when out from behind the pulpit peered Timothy, the church mouse. (Play some high notes on a 2' stop.) "Ho-hum," he yawned, "time for a midnight snack. I think I'll eat Hymn No. 365—that's one of my favorites." He spied an open Hymnal on the music rack of the organ and was about to take a big bite out of "Onward, Christian Sol-

196

diers" when a deep voice complained (play some low notes on a 16' stop): "What's the big idea? How am I supposed to lead the people in the hymn-singing on Sunday if you insist on nibbling at my music?"

"Who are you?" asked Timmy. "And what's the big idea scaring me like that?"

"I'm Reginald, the Organ," answered the deep voice. "And what's the big idea disturbing me?"

"Oho," said Timmy, "so you're the one who makes all that noise on Sunday mornings when I'm trying to sleep."

Reggie, the organ, was really mad now. "Noise! Well, I like that! Music is what I make—beautiful music!"

"I really like to listen to you; I was only teasing," said Timmy, "but I don't understand much about you. One day I peeked over the shoulder of Mr. Piper, the organist, when he was practicing, and I saw so many knobs, buttons, and other do-dads that I got dizzy."

"Well, I *am* a bit complicated," said Reggie proudly, "but if you're really interested, I believe I could explain it—even to a simple-minded mouse like you. First of all, the part of the organ on which Mr. Piper practices is the console. The rooms over there from which you can hear my voice speaking are the other part of the organ. They are called the organ chambers."

"How is it that you have so many voices?" asked Timmy. "Sometimes you have a loud voice, sometimes a soft one; sometimes you have a low voice, and sometimes a high."

"Just a minute—let me explain," interrupted Reggie. "In each chamber there are many different pipes. There are small pipes and big ones, fat ones and skinny ones—and all of them have different voices. Hey, Timmy, what are you doing?"

Timmy looked embarrassed. "I just pulled out this pipe to see how it works. It looks like a whistle." (Blow on a pipe you have removed from the organ.) "Toot-toot! Hey, it *is* a whistle! An organ is nothing more than a roomful of whistles."

Reggie sighed. "Won't you ever learn to call things by their proper names, Timothy? It is a *pipe*, not a whistle! It is something *like* a whistle, but think how many people you'd need to blow all the whistles—pipes, I mean; now you've got *me* doing it!—all the *pipes* in this chamber. But I can play many of them at once. My big motor works the bellows that blow the air through the pipes.

"The pipes have many different sounds. Listen! I can sound like a trumpet . . . clarinet . . . oboe . . . flute . . . violin. (Play some notes on each stop.) When I put all the pipes together, I can make a loud

197

sound—like this. (Play full organ.) Or I can make my voice very soft—like this," explained Reggie. (Play on softest stop.)

"How interesting!" said Timmy. "But how do you make the music sort of fade away until I can hardly hear it?"

"Well, one wall of the chambers has wooden shutters that look like venetian blinds. When I open the shutters, the music gets louder—like this. (Illustrate.) And when I close them slowly, the music gets softer—like this." (Illustrate.)

"But how do you open your shutters, Reggie? I don't see a cord to pull them up and down."

"We'll have to go back to the console to see how that works," replied Reggie.

"I've always wondered why an organ has so many keyboards," said Timmy. "Mr. Piper has only two hands. How can he play on three keyboards at once?"

"Unless it's a very tricky piece he doesn't have to," Reggie said. (Illustrate, if you feel up to it!) "But sometimes Mr. Piper wants to change the sound of the organ very quickly—like this. (Have manuals prepared with three different tone colors.) And sometimes he wants to make an echo effect—like this. (Great—forte; Swell—mezzo piano; Choir—pianissimo.) You'd be surprised how many times he needs all the keyboards, or manuals, as organists call them. The top manual is called the Swell, the middle one the Great, and the bottom one the Choir."

"Say, is that a keyboard 'way down there, Reggie? Don't tell me Mr. Piper plays music with his feet!"

"Of course he does. All organists do. Look at how much bigger the keys are down there. They make it easy to play the lowest part of the music with the feet. Sometimes Mr. Piper will even play a tune with his feet." (Play a tune the children have been practicing.)

"What are all those knobs with the funny names on them?"

"Some of the names may seem strange to a mouse—Quintadene, Nachthorn, Bourdon, Dulciana; but others should be familiar to you—Trumpet, Oboe, Clarinet, Flute. All of them are names of different pipes in the organ. Do you remember the sound of a trumpet? Well, this knob, or stop, as it is called, makes the organ sound like a trumpet. Each stop makes a different kind of pipe sound."

"What are those little round buttons?"

"They are *pistons,* my friend, *not* buttons! Oh, what am I going to do with this stupid mouse?" said Reggie under his breath. "The pistons help Mr. Piper change many stops quickly. Look how fast the

198

pistons can change them. (Illustrate.) If Mr. Piper had to do it all by himself he'd need more arms than an octopus!"

"I believe I know all there is to know about an organ now, Reggie—but wait! What are those three pedals down there near the keyboard for the feet? What do they do?"

"They work the shutters we talked about—remember? When you push down the pedals, the shutters open. When you draw them back, the shutters close. See?" (Illustrate.)

"The last pedal lights up that little green light, Reggie."

"Yes, it is the crescendo pedal which makes all the stops—from the softest to the loudest—join in, one at a time, till all of them are playing." (Illustrate.)

Timmy's whiskers were trembling. "My, that's loud," he said. "Do you think I could learn to play the organ? It looks like fun."

"It is fun, Timmy. But tell me, do you know how to play the piano very well?"

"Well, I take lessons, but sometimes I forget to practice. I'm kind of rusty now."

"Shame on you, Timmy. You'll never learn to play the organ until you're a good pianist. You march right downstairs and get to work. Maybe some day Mr. Piper will let you play the organ. And here, take 'Onward, Christian Soldiers' with you. No fair nibbling on it, though—not until you've learned to play it!"

EASTER EGG TREE

Why not an Easter Egg Tree? Will you join me in reviving, encouraging, and promulgating this charming and traditional Easter custom?

The ancient practice, going 'way back to pagan times, of decorating and coloring eggs as symbols of the blossoming season became for the early Christians a symbol of the Resurrection. Christians saw in the empty or apparently "dead" egg a happy symbolism of the empty tomb from which Christ had risen to new life in glory.

Little wonder then that it became a family tradition, especially in Western European countries, lavishly to decorate blown eggs as well as wooden and china eggs, which were carefully preserved and even venerated. Artists and craftsmen were inspired to design wondrous and fanciful egg-shaped objets d'art. Fabulous examples of this art are the Faberge Easter Eggs, created for the Russian Czar Alexander III, of which 53 are in the possession of Kremlin, Metropolitan and British Museums, and of private connoisseurs.

The Pennsylvania Dutch are keeping alive today the old-world custom of the Egg Tree. In many homes the eggs are kept from year to year and added to and improved each Easter season just as you and I might add to our Christmas tree ornament collection. The traditional German Egg Tree was also decked with wild-bird eggs as well as hen, goose, and turkey eggs—all carefully colored and decorated, and hung by ribbons or wires, or impaled on ends of twigs. Decorations might also include cooky figures (usually birds, rabbits, lambs) and tinsel. Under the tree is inevitably a magnificent Easter Nest presided over by a huge rabbit or lamb. Large trees, both family and community, are often outdoors. The Berks County Historical Society of Reading, Pennsylvania, has revived the custom of annually decorating a 10-foot Egg Tree with some 1400 eggs.

The Metropolitan Museum of New York City and department stores and libraries in New York and Washington displayed egg trees last season. In fact, the Metropolitan Museum now has a pamphlet on *Easter Eggs—25 Designs* available for 25c. Current magazines invariably carry attractive egg-decorating articles and pictures in the spring. But who needs to tell children how to decorate Easter eggs? Turn them loose with dye and glue, ribbons, pipe-cleaners, glitter, sequins, artificial flowers, and odds and ends of tulle, mesh, braid, rickrack from the sewing basket!

Last spring, "egged" on by my enthusiastic Junior choristers, I made my first Egg Tree. Although it would not have been difficult to have cut a good-sized bare tree or a large branch and brace it in a bucket of rocks or sand or a Christmas tree holder, I decided to start out with a table model. I found a big wicker florist's basket with handle (though a vase would do), filled it with rocks and stuck in several large bare branches having lots of twigs. I painted basket and branches a dreamy pink, tied huge pink bows around the basket and on the handle, and covered the rocks with green paper grass.

I had previously asked the choristers to save eggs for several weeks. A number of them did so, and regularly "blew out" breakfast eggs through pinholes, replacing the shells in egg boxes. The choir held several decorating sessions following rehearsals, and the results were "fabulific." We preferred hanging the eggs with narrow pastel ribbons of varying lengths. An attractive nest with huge paper folding-eggs was arranged around the base of the basket. Vases containing long branches of forsythia and flowering peach blossoms filled in the background.

The whole effect was exquisite; the children were enthralled. Many pictures were taken, and the Egg Tree was borrowed by other organizations in the church for meetings and parties. It was of course the center of attention at our annual Junior Choir Easter Egg Hunt and Mad Hatters Party. When the tree was dismantled, those wishing to save their eggs carried them home in egg-containers. (Eggs should have marks of identification.) Several families announced the intention of starting the custom of a family Egg Tree.

Although my initial effort was somewhat of a party decoration venture, there were no Disney-like or cheap effects, and we tried to keep it tastefully festive. (I have since decorated several larger trees, more formally, for church vestibules and for the Children's Museum.) The Egg Tree is a delightful part of the observance and celebration of Easter and deserves a place in our culture. Why not an Easter Egg Tree?

In *Russian National Songs* (1877) occurs this Easter song:

Easter eggs! Easter eggs! Give to him that begs!
FOR CHRIST THE LORD IS ARISEN.
To the poor, open door; something give from your store!
Those who hoard can't afford—moth and rust their reward!
Those who love freely give—long and well may they live!
Eastertide, like a bride, comes and won't be denied.

NANCY POORE TUFTS

A BEETHOVEN'S BIRTHDAY PARTY

SALLY LEASE, Boulder, Colorado, directs a Junior Choir that has a party every semester. The choice one fall was either a Halloween, a Christmas, or a Beethoven's Birthday party. The children unanimously selected the Beethoven party.

Anticipation piled high as the choir studied about Beethoven and his music, sang his "Ode to Joy," planned the supper menu, and decided to bring "birthday presents" for German refugee children. "The roof blew right off when I announced that Beethoven would be present in person," wrote Mrs. Lease, and she found it necessary to send the parents a note of clarification after several incredulous mothers called to make inquiries. One child drew a remarkable portrait which was posted under the sign telling how many more days until Beethoven's Birthday.

The party was held after the regular Tuesday rehearsal. First on the program was a game that divided the choir into small groups of five or six. Mrs. Lease called out a letter of Beethoven's name, and each group tried to be the first to form the letter. The second game was "Symphony

Upset," usually known as "Fruit Basket Upset." Instead of fruit names, each child was assigned a note name, staff part, or music symbol. The symphony "upset" when the leader called out "Beethoven."

Following the games, the children placed their chairs at the long U-shaped table and stood waiting for the Guest of Honor. Pretty spry for his 189 years, Herr Beethoven (recognized with some difficulty as our Minister of Music, Dr. Everett J. Hilty) was ushered to the head of the table amid cheering and lusty singing of "Happy Birthday, dear Ludvig." Dr. Hilty's costume consisted of a cane, a straw-cornucopia ear-trumpet, his son's tuxedo, his wife's lacy blouse, and a mop wig which he had starched, curled, and sewed to the top of a nylon stocking and stretched over his head.

The gifts were then presented and all sat down to supper, which cost about 35c a child. When Beethoven had blown out the candles on his birthday cake, each child received a piece with a candle and the number 189 on it.

The tables were covered with white paper tacked down at the edges. A staff of crepe-paper with clef signs and bar lines was stretched out the length of the tables. The notation of the table "symphony" was concocted from three pounds of that awful candy assortment found in dime stores before Christmas; colored toothpicks formed the stems and leger lines. After dessert the choir devoured the "symphony"!

Religious Drama and Choral Speaking

"THE GOOD NEIGHBOR"

The Parable of the Good Samaritan

A Playlet for Children's Choirs   Songs by James Stewart Boles

Cast:

NARRATOR	PRIEST	LEVITE	INNKEEPER
MAN	LAWYER	SAMARITAN	ROBBERS

GOD HAS TAUGHT US

Choir: 1. God has taught us how to love.
     Christ knew this all else above.
     Love for friends is not enough;
     Love your neighbor, though it's tough!

    2. "Thou shalt love thy God, the Lord."
     Jesus spoke to all this word.
     How he meant it let us see
     In the phrase "Be neighborly."

Narrator: One of the stories Jesus told was meant to show people how they should feel toward other people. He made it a very striking story because he chose a Samaritan to be the hero. The Samaritans were very much hated by the Jews. One day a lawyer had been asking questions he thought Jesus might not be able to answer. He wanted to know what he should do to be sure that he would have eternal life. Jesus asked him if he read the scriptures, and if he did, what he read in them.

Lawyer: You must love God with all your heart, and with all your soul, and with your whole strength, and with your whole mind; also, you must love your neighbor as yourself.

Narrator: Jesus told him that he had given the right answer to his question; if he lived up to it, he would really live. But the man was looking for a good excuse instead of an answer. He asked another question.

Lawyer: Who is my neighbor?

Narrator: Then Jesus gave us this story:

Choir: 3. Questions, questions, Christ was asked.
Giving answers is a task.
Jesus knew the man's intent.
Now let's see what Jesus meant.

Narrator: There was a certain man who was traveling from Jerusalem to Jericho. (*Man enters with baggage on his back. Robbers appear on other side.*)

Robber: Look, there is a lone traveler! We can take his things without much fuss. Come on, men! Let's get him! (*They attack, beat, and rob the man. Robbers take loot and head for the hills.*)

THOU SHALT NOT STEAL

Choir: "Thou shalt not steal," our God has said.
Yet some can't get this in their head.
Why must some people robbers be,
When God has taught us honesty?

(*Priest enters from Jerusalem direction.*)

Priest: Oh my, look what has happened here! I wonder if he is dead? Well, I better keep away from him. After all, if he's hurt he needs a doctor more than he needs what I can do for him. (*Passes by on the other side and leaves.*)

SONG OF THE PRIEST

Choir: I'm solemn, reverent, dignified;
By me these traits are glorified.
If people would be more like me,
Just think how fine God's world would be!

Man: Oh, who will help me in this time of need? I'm very badly hurt and in need of help. Surely someone will come along the road and give me aid.

204

Choir: A Levite strong and proud am I.
My fame is in my voice so high.
In holy worship I must lead!
When my voice sounds, all people heed.

Levite: (*Enters from Jerusalem direction.*) What has happened to that man? Is he a criminal? I wonder if he is one of my friends? (*Looks.*) Well, I don't know him from Adam. Someone else will come along and take good care of him. I had better hurry and get to the Temple so I can pray for opportunities to do good deeds. (*Leaves.*)

Man: Help me, someone please help me! O Father in heaven, please look upon this thy servant. Send aid to give me the chance to live. (*Enter the Samaritan and goes to wounded man.*)

SONG OF THE CHORUS

Choir: Now this is truly strange to see;
This injured man's a Jew, you see.
Samaritans and Jews each hate
The other with a hate that's great.

Samaritan: (*calls out*) Innkeeper, come quickly! This man needs rest and care. Give us a room, and send things so that I may take care of his wounds. (*Enter innkeeper.*)

Innkeeper: Yes, sir, right way, sir! (*Aside to himself*) What is happening here? One of these men is a Samaritan. What on earth is he doing helping a Jew? This indeed is very strange. Ah well, the world is full of unusual happenings these days. Who knows what someone will come up with next? (*Innkeeper goes off, returns with bandages. The Samaritan bandages the wounded man and helps him off to the inn.*)

Narrator: All through the night the Samaritan cared for the wounded man. He bandaged his wounds and cared for him as best he could. The next morning, the Samaritan spoke to the innkeeper. (*Innkeeper and Samaritan enter.*)

Samaritan: I must go on with my trip today. Please take care of this man. See that he gets all the good care he needs, and don't spare anything that he should have. Here's money for his room, food, and other things. If it isn't enough to cover all the cost, let me know when I come back from my trip. (*Samaritan leaves.*)

Narrator: The lawyer had been listening to a very different answer from the one which he had thought he would get from Jesus. "Who is my neighbor?" Not just people he knew on his street, or in his town. His

205

neighbor was any man who needed his help. "Which one of these was neighbor to the man who fell among thieves?" Jesus had asked him another question. The lawyer had the answer to this question: "The one who took pity on him." Jesus answered and said: "Go and do likewise, yourself."

FROM TALES OF CHRIST

Choir: From simple tales of Christ like these
The family of Christ now sees
That we must love folks everywhere.
The love of God is meant to share.

"THE DRAMA OF MUSIC"

(A program designed and presented by ROBERT McGILL, Grace Methodist Church, and LORRAINE DUGGINS, University Church, both of St. Louis, Missouri.)

Music is many things to many people. *Drama* in its most literal sense derives from a Greek word meaning "to do." To do music is our purpose this evening; to present music in the various forms in which it can be most effective in creating an atmosphere of worship for youth. It is our intention to utilize the fundamental elements of music such as rhythm, harmony, tone-color, and pattern, and to present them in several different forms. Thus we find unison singing, three and four-part harmony, the speaking voice in choral reading, the Rhythm Choir, and the rich coloring added by the instrumental voices of oboe, trumpet, and organ.

Because all religious art and drama come through man's seeking to reveal his awareness of God, we respect its revelations through sacred music, painting, sculpture, poetry, drama, and symbolic movement. In our program we have included two of the oldest and most neglected of the arts of the church, both of which are capable of revealing spiritual truths to us and of deepening our emotional living. These are the arts of the Speaking Choir and of the Rhythm Choir.

The art of the Rhythm Choir, which uses symbolic movements, knows no barriers of creed or dogma, but humbly and joyously offers itself as a way to worship and glorify God. Although it has deep and valuable spiritual meaning for adults, it is with youth that it can most easily and naturally achieve esthetic and psychological effects. It is a very real experience of consecrated participation at a period when young people want to give themselves fully—body, mind and soul—to a cause.

206

In the early days when chanting of psalms became a part of worship in the Temple, there were speaking choirs to help carry on the ritual of worship. One responded antiphonally to the other. We have included an antiphonal arrangement of singing and speaking voices, and a reading in unison.

It has been said: "Everything points to God." It is with this thought in mind that we present this offering of music.

THE DRAMA OF MUSIC

Title	Source	Composer or Author
O GOD OF YOUTH—(Church Music Review)		Glenn Darst
LIKE AS A FATHER—The Choirs (SAB, Belwin)		Cherubini

LET US PRAISE GOD—The Singing Choir and the Speaking
Choir (Schmitt, Hall & McCreary) _____Olds
BE THOU MY VISION—The Choirs—(Kjos) _____arr. Young
PRAISE TO THE LORD—(Concordia) _____Rohlig
     Choral Concertato with Choirs, Trumpet, Organ and Oboe
A WORD OF GREETING _____Host Minister
NOBODY KNOWS THE TROUBLE I SEE _____Negro Spiritual
THE READING OF THE LORD'S PRAYER
LONESOME VALLEY _____White Spiritual
     The Rhythm Choir, The Speaking Choir, and Solo Voice
A WORD ABOUT YOUTH CHOIRS _____Dr. Duggins
NEGRO SPIRITUALS:—Speaking and Singing Choirs
     Poor Man Lazrus—(Bourne) _____arr. Hariston
     Climbin' Up the Mountain—(Kjos) _____arr. Smith
     Swing Low, Sweet Chariot—(Music Press, Tuskegee) arr. Dawson
     The Battle of Jericho—(G. Schirmer) _____arr. Bartholomew
     The Old 100th Psalm Tune—(Oxford-Gray) _____arr. Williams
          Choirs, Congregation, Organ, Trumpet

CHANCEL DRAMA CYCLE

The Chancel Drama Cycle, sponsored by several of the Episcopal churches of Washington, D.C., and now in its sixth year of a ten-year experiment, has proved a remarkably successful means of Lenten education.

Last year there were 76 requests by churches of various denominations for a scheduled cycle of plays during Lent. There were only eight plays available, which meant that each cast was committed to about ten performances. Six plays came from Episcopal churches, one each from a Lutheran and a Presbyterian church. The plays ranged from a medieval mystery play to Ionesco's *The Bald Soprano*. Two plays were original; an aim of the Cycle is to encourage the writing of Religious Drama or plays with true meaning.

The churches receiving the Dramas incorporated them in a Lenten program on every Wednesday or every Sunday evening. Each Drama is preceded by a brief service in which the players participate, sitting in the choir. The Order of Service is: "Processional Hymn, Opening Sentences, Introduction or Explanation, Dedication, The Play, Offering, Benediction, Recessional Hymn."

Following the service (and this is a most important part) is a Coffee Hour and Discussion Period in the Church Hall. The cast also participates in the discussion, but does not dominate. Chairs and tables are arranged "in the round," and a clergyman (preferably) is the moderator. The meanings and motives of the play are discussed rather than the merits of the production or the acting. Invariably questions and opinions fly thick and fast; the young people and the timid are encouraged to speak up. The moderator should guide and tie-in the discussion, and call time. Most of the discussions I have attended have been so enthusiastically received that the same people are drawn to return each week and attendance grows. The casts usually deport themselves with dignity and dedication. It is a splendid and rewarding experience for older teen-agers as well as for adults on all levels of life.

These chancel dramas are a means of Lenten education: a deeper dimension of reality than a sermon can reveal is brought before the altar as an offering of the people. (Advent is also an appropriate season of penitence and self-examination in which to offer chancel dramas.) The plays are short and are often "of the people" in language and content. Actors and congregation have here the opportunity to see the true state of our lives and ourselves in truth—our motivations as we strive to find our way to the light or to turn from the light. Here we may express and recognize our highest hopes, our gravest problems, and know God's grace at work in the hearts of men.

In many churches the music department is consulted about or participates actively in dramatic productions, especially at Christmas, in Lent, or at Easter. Even straight dramas often require musical backgrounds or special effects. If you are helping with or directing plays, I suggest you think seriously of interesting your minister and other churches of your area in promoting a Chancel Drama Cycle, a truly worthwhile project. And remind those who object to Drama in the sanctuary that the first drama in the Western World was presented in the church by the clergy! This is no innovation: it is a return to an ancient practice. Religious drama is as old as the Christian church.

NANCY POORE TUFTS

"NOYE'S FLUDDE"
A "Noah's Ark" Play

Noye's Fludde (Noah's Flood), the 14th-century Chester miracle play, set to music by Benjamin Britten in 1958 and published by Boosey & Hawkes, was given its premiere at the 1958 Aldeburgh Festival. Its first American performance took place at Union Theological Seminary, New York City, in March of 1959. This attractive musical play has since been presented in several cathedrals of England and in a number of churches and schools throughout this country.

Choir directors with imagination and originality (and dozens of young choristers) should consider this outstanding and worthwhile musical pageant. It is not only "an opera for children," but a wholly appropriate and deeply moving setting of the Biblical story. It is both entertaining and practical—even the audience joins in now and then!

This engaging work by Britten calls for a cast of about 150 player-singers, a unique orchestra of some 60 pieces, an Ark that can be assembled during the pageant, dancers (if desired), costumes for 46 different kinds of animals, costumes (or props) for waves, wind, lightning, sun, moon, and stars. There are only three adults in the dramatic cast: Noah, Mrs. Noah, and the Voice of God. Noah's three sons and their wives sing in unison and three-part harmony (SSA or SAT), the chorus in unison.

This musical play is a remarkable achievement. In an age when music seems to grow increasingly elaborate and complicated, Britten's ideas are so utterly naive that one wonders why no one has thought of them before. Britten equals Haydn in shaking from his sleeve ingenious and imaginative effects. The orchestration includes strings, trumpets, flutes, recorders, tympani, drums, organ, slung mugs, a whip, a gong, sandpaper, and handbells. Drums signify the wrath of God; recorders and tinkling triangles make magical sounds when the dove returns to the Ark; handbells and organ announce the rainbow's appearance. The musical treatment of the deluge is remarkably dramatic and awe-inspiring. At the climax, amazingly, Dyke's great hymn "Eternal Father, strong to save" comes sailing in with a marvelous sense of grandeur and rightness.

209

The refreshing sweetness of the play can best be summed up by the final words of the Voice of God to Noah: "And nowe fare-well, my darlinge deare."

* * *

Production Notes: This play could be done on a smaller scale, but must be done well, or not attempted. The orchestra is the greatest problem, but many churches, especially in cities, can set up a good amateur group. The costumes for the children were the simplest sacks, about knee-length, with cords at the waist. These had been dyed elementary crude colors. All wore those tights most kids have now. The children can make their own masks of cardboard to be worn like hats and pulled down over the face to represent different animals.

Noah and family have the same type of costumes of rough cloth, tied at the waist. Noah must be a fine singer, a baritone. School or choir voices are adequate for all the rest. Mrs. Noah should be a good actress.

Men of the church could make the panels of the Ark which is assembled before your eyes onstage. Use props of long pieces representing wind, waves, and lightning that can be moved or seesawed back and forth by stagehands in costume. Or let dancers (if permitted) with veils and special lighting effects represent these dramatic episodes. Either is "good theater."

The sun, moon, and stars can be brought in like huge signs or mobiles. For the stars, especially, a huge mobile of wires suspended from a tall stick with golden stars (maybe tin-can stars) floating on wires or strings can be stunning. The rainbow may be like a banner, with a pole at each end, and should rise spectacularly at the finale.

A "Noah's Ark" would make an interesting project for an entire year for a school, or religious education department, or choir. An Ark and the animal figures might be constructed or collected by the children, pictures and posters might be made, the scenery and costumes for the play might be made, and there might be a trip to the nearest zoo.

NANCY POORE TUFTS

"HEROD"
A Medieval Nativity Play

Herod, a 13th-century liturgical drama written for the Christmas season, has been transcribed, edited, and translated into English by W. L. Smoldon for unison voices, various solo voices, and optional instruments (organ, recorders, strings, trumpets). Published in 1961 by Stainer & Bell, Ltd. in octave booklet form, it is available through Galaxy, and is not expensive (75c). Performance time is one hour. Cuts are feasible.

Actually *Herod* is a Nativity opera, since it is sung throughout. Music directors interested in undertaking an authentic and worthwhile production, with no insurmountable problems, could make of this drama a wholly satisfying work of art in performance. Although the contrasting colors of mature voices are more desirable, this play could perfectly well be presented with young people. Even older children could sing the male solos an octave higher.

Herod appears in a very scholarly edition of two of the delightful 13th-century music dramas contained in the "Fleury Play-Book" from an Orleans MS. Dr. Smoldon, who is a leading authority on liturgical drama (see his article in New Oxford History of Music, Vol. II), has arranged a practical version in English of the two plays dealing with the Shepherds and the Wise Men ("Magi" versions), with excellent suggestions on production, costumes, accompaniment, etc. Incidentally, the usual day for a "Magi" performance was Epiphany, January 6.

The scene of the first performances was the monastic church of Fleury. And it is the medieval "station" technique—five distinct sites for dramatic action, well-separated from each other—that will intrigue and challenge the imaginative director. The true setting, therefore, is within church walls, although it could be adapted to a spacious church hall—if not "in the round" perhaps "in the star"!

Of course it must be remembered that the medieval church made no concessions to such human weakness as chair-seating, and the audience was free to follow the players from site to site. A characteristic medieval feature was the actors' call upon the onlookers to approach, to behold, to worship. However, a modern production of the separate scenes would not be difficult. The ancient story follows the familiar outline with some charming and even amusing innovations such as the action at Herod's Court and the progress of the Star.

The modern producer must brace himself to provide a smooth and dignified mobile star. The "Magi" playwrights insisted on a mobile unit, suspended and following (tracking) each scene. A Rouen text describes it as a "star-shaped cluster of lights," evidently a candelabrum drawn by cords. Another challenge: to match the inventiveness and daring of the medieval producers!

The music of the original MS consists of a single melodic line on a four-line stave in Gregorian neums. The text is in Latin, interspersed with occasional stage directions. Two melodies are borrowed from the

211

liturgy, and several of the texts from the Gospels of St. Matthew and of St. Luke. Choristers unfamiliar with plain-chant can be taught to sing clearly and expressively by rehearsing their lines in normal speech-patterns before attempting the musical setting. Five selections written in rhythmic verse are reminiscent of the troubadour songs of the period, and harmonized accompaniments are provided here. Pitches may easily be transposed to suit available voices, or to divide sentences among Shepherds or Magi—a useful dramatic device.

The Fleury MS makes no reference to the use of instruments. Since other dramas of the period mention drums, harps, pipes, and strings, Dr. Smoldon has added slight accompaniments here and there: shepherd's tunes, interludes on the recorder, snatches of flourishes for the Court of Herod, cymbals for Herod's "raging." He suggests "discreet instrumental prompting" and even doubling a vocal part on an instrument, such as a recorder. An occasional "drone" or pedal-point might be employed. Instruments may be played backstage or by extra actors.

The work concludes with a moving climax, the singing of the Te Deum. There are plainsong versions in several Protestant hymnals. An ancient familiar hymn (seasonal) to be sung by players and audience could be substituted. The players should assemble in a central group to lead the final number, or sing antiphonally. At one point the players should depart and the music fade into the distance. A little judicious organ support would be helpful here. Dr. Smoldon writes that the 10th-century *Regularis Concordia* mentions the use of bells at such performances.

Herod is recommended to experienced and discriminating music directors.

NANCY POORE TUFTS

212

Hymns and Hymn Study

THE HYMNAL AS RESOURCE

One of the requests we hear most frequently is for materials. I know of no better source of material than the denominational hymnal. Next to the Bible itself the hymnal will most adequately express your Christian beliefs.

When our children are promoted from Primary Choir to Junior Choir, they are presented with a copy of *The Methodist Hymnal*. This hymnal, along with the Bible which they receive at the same time as a part of church school promotion, becomes one of their most prized possessions, used at every rehearsal and service thereafter.

In our hymnal, as no doubt in yours, there are hymns of many types and of varying caliber. One of our jobs as choir directors is to be selective. What are the qualities of a good hymn? Dr. Austin C. Lovelace lists the following:

1. It has simplicity of thought, text, and language.
2. It contains a balance of feeling and thought.
3. Ideas are drawn from the familiar.
4. The hymn is capable of being sung sincerely.
5. It is reverent.
6. It is dignified.
7. There is beauty of thought and truth.
8. There is a unity of thought, yet variety in its presentation.
9. The approach is positive.
10. It is the best possible expression of a given truth.
11. The melodic line must have quality and character.
12. Rhythm must undergird and carry forward the text.

213

13. Harmony must move so that all parts have interest.
14. Text and tune are equally important.

Recently I had occasion to discuss at some length the field of church music with a retired minister in Houston. Especially important in his evaluation of hymn singing was the suitability of text. Vivid in his memory was a revival held in another state during which two ten-year-olds sang: "I was sinking deep in sin, far from the peaceful shore." "What," said the minister, "could these children possibly know about sinking deep in sin? Oh yes, granted they were singing a catchy tune! But what about the text?"

He further urged that we examine the hymns we sing to be certain that we can sing them with sincerity. " 'Are ye able,' said the Master, 'to be crucified with Me?' No, I don't really think I am; yet I sing 'Yes, I am able.' Surely I don't mean it."

Yes, in the selection of hymn tunes, we who dare to teach must never cease to learn. In our church we select hymns to be sung as hymn-anthems (the second anthem on every other Sunday). Included in this year's list were:

Sing praise to God who reigns above

Immortal, invisible, God only wise

Praise my Maker while I've breath

All creatures of our God and King

Come, ye faithful, raise the strain

The God of Abraham praise

For all the saints who from their labors rest

Once to every man and nation

O my soul, bless God the Father

Now thank we all our God

These hymns, along with ten others, were studied by members of every choir from Junior age up, and used in other phases of the church and church school as well. During the summer months we are repeating many of them as hymn-anthems. While this is not a "Hymn-of-the-Month" plan as carried on successfully in many churches, it serves approximately the same purpose.

We should remember that the hymn learned today is the tradition of tomorrow. The little child has no tradition except what we pass on to him. He has no basis at first for judging values; leaders are responsible for that. He takes what we give him. It is up to us to choose that which is a sincere, true, and reverent expression of the faith that is ours.

NORMA LOWDER

214

TEACHING JUNIOR CHORISTERS HOW TO USE THE HYMNAL

It is important that children become familiar with the "feel" of using the hymnal; that they know the various indices, and that they are at home in the mechanical as well as the spiritual use of the book. This can best be taught in the Junior Choir. In fact, I am reasonably sure that I spend from one-half to one-third of my Junior rehearsal time with *The Methodist Hymnal*.

After periods of study we devise questions and reviews in the form of games. These may be used during the rehearsal, preceding it for those who are early, or at one of our occasional parties. As an example, here are a few that we used last May:

FROM WHAT HYMN DOES THIS PHRASE COME?
1. Come and reign over us. (*Come, thou almighty King*)
2. His kingdom is glorious and rules over all. (*Ye servants of God*)
3. On earth is not his equal. (*A mighty fortress is our God*)
4. Awake, my soul, and sing of him who died for thee. (*Crown him with many crowns*)
5. Well supply thy sons and daughters, and all fear of want remove. (*Glorious things of thee are spoken*)
6. All ye who hear, now to his temple draw near. (*Praise to the Lord*)
7. Give to us peace in our time, O Lord. (*God, the Omnipotent*)
8. Sons of men and angels say, Alleluia. (*Christ, the Lord, is risen today*)
9. Yet in thy dark streets shineth the everlasting light. (*O little town of Bethlehem*)
10. God in three Persons, blessed Trinity. (*Holy, holy, holy*)

IDENTIFY THIS HYMN UPON HEARING THE RHYTHM CLAPPED:
1. For the beauty of the earth
2. Fairest Lord Jesus
3. Prayer of thanksgiving
4. Silent Night
5. All creatures of our God and King
6. Joy to the world
7. Come, ye thankful people, come
8. Rejoice, ye pure in heart
9. Soldiers of Christ, arise
10. This is my Father's world

IDENTIFY THE HYMN UPON HEARING ANY ONE PHRASE PLAYED:
1. Joyful, joyful, we adore thee
2. Praise the Lord, ye heavens adore him
3. Now the day is over
4. Immortal, invisible, God only wise

215

5. Now thank we all our God
6. Hark, the herald angels sing
7. Faith of our fathers
8. All glory, laud and honor

9. In Christ there is no east or west
10. For all the saints who from their labors rest

During the year our Juniors chose as their favorite hymns: (1) A mighty fortress is our God; and (2) Praise to the Lord. Yes, the only limitations of our children are those we put upon them. The depth of their appreciation is impossible to measure.

NORMA LOWDER

PLAN FOR HYMN-LEARNING

Last season MARVIN E. PETERSON, Minister of Music, First Methodist Church, Marysville, Ohio, devised a simple plan for learning hymns. In late May each Junior Choir and Junior High Choir boy and girl who completed the plan received *The Methodist Hymnal* with his name stamped in gold letters. While the plan uses denominational hymnals, most hymns are included in the *Choristers Little Hymnal*.

Early in May Mr. Peterson wrote: "To date, 726 hymns have been checked off by the 16 Junior Highers and 35 Juniors. If all of these come through, there will be a total of 1530 hymns. Five Junior Highers and three Juniors have checked off all their thirty, each. Another 15 or 20 are near enough to completion that I expect they will carry through.

"Although I have encouraged the Choir members to get hymns checked off during the course of the year, many are leaving it to the last minute. (Usual, isn't it?) Last Saturday two different youngsters sang 24 hymns each, and another sang 23. That was really a marathon day, with six hours devoted to this program. Eleven persons sang a total of 136 hymns. The previous Saturday I listened to 60 hymns. I can only imagine what the next three Saturdays will be like."

Many of the hymns in our Methodist hymnal are suitable not only for adults but also for children to use. The list entitled "The Basic Thirty" contains 30 of the great hymns of the church which use language simple enough for children to understand, yet are used continually by young people and adults in the regular services of worship. All of these hymns are simple enough for a Primary child to learn, but they are meaningful for adults as well. A number of the great hymns of the church do not appear in the list because they contain words and ideas too difficult for Primaries and Juniors to understand.

216

Following the name of the hymn in "The Basic Thirty" list is its number in *The Methodist Hymnal* and the name of the tune associated with the hymn in that volume. There is also a line for your choir director to sign when you have learned the hymn and sung it for him.

Since we are Methodists "The Basic Thirty" hymns were all selected from *The Methodist Hymnal*. In some cases other hymnbooks used by our choirs have different tunes for some of the hymns, and sometimes the words are different from those in our hymnal. In all such cases the words and music of *The Methodist Hymnal* have been chosen.

The plan this year is to learn the *tune* and *first stanza* of as many of "The Basic Thirty" as possible. A notebook sheet for each of these hymns will be prepared. Each sheet will have on it the melody and first stanza of the hymn. There will also be interesting information about the hymn and a few blanks to fill in. If there is room, other stanzas of the hymn will be included also.

Whenever you have learned a particular hymn and can sing it without any help from the piano, check with your choir director. He will listen to you and then check off the column marked "Learned" in your notebook. He will also record your achievement on a chart of his own. At the end of the choir season, an award will be presented to all those learning "The Basic Thirty."

Your notebooks may be taken home to study the hymns in them if you wish. However, if you do take your notebook home, be sure to bring it to choir with you. *You will always need your notebook at the regular afternoon choir rehearsal.* If you can't remember to bring it each time, better leave it at the church.

"The Basic Thirty" will be used this year not only in our choirs but also in the Sunday morning services of worship. If other members of your family don't know all 30 of these hymns, help them to learn the ones they don't know. You can help us have a "singing church."

THE BASIC THIRTY

Hymn	Tune	Learned
1. All creatures of our God and King	Lasst uns erfreuen	....
2. All glory, laud, and honor	St. Theodulph	....
3. All people that on earth do dwell	Old 100th	....
4. All praise to thee, my God, this night	Tallis' Canon	....
5. Away in a manger	Mueller	....
6. Christ, the Lord, is risen today	Easter Hymn	....
7. Come, ye thankful people, come	St. George's, Windsor	....
8. Fairest Lord Jesus	Crusader's Hymn	....

9. Faith of our fathers	St. Catherine	....
10. For the beauty of the earth	Dix	....
11. Hark, the herald angels sing	Mendelssohn	....
12. Holy, holy, holy	Nicaea	....
13. How firm a foundation	Foundation	....
14. I love thy kingdom, Lord	St. Thomas	....
15. In Christ there is no east or west	St. Peter	....
16. Joyful, joyful we adore thee	Hymn to Joy	....
17. Now thank we all our God	Nun danket	....
18. O come, all ye faithful	Adeste, fideles	....
19. O for a thousand tongues to sing	Azmon	....
20. O God, our help in ages past	St. Anne	....
21. O little town of Bethlehem	St. Louis	....
22. O worship the King	Lyons	....
23. Praise to the Lord, the Almighty	Lobe den Herren	....
24. Rejoice, ye pure in heart	Marion	....
25. Silent night, holy night	Stille Nacht	....
26. The God of Abraham praise	Leoni	....
27. The Lord's my Shepherd	Martyrdom	....
28. This is my Father's world	Terra beata	....
29. We gather together	Kremser	....
30. When morning gilds the skies	Laudes domini	....

THREE HYMN STUDIES FOR YOUNG CHORISTERS
By CHRISTINE KALLSTROM

1. "Holy, holy, holy, Lord God Almighty"

Words by
Reginald Heber (1783-1826)

Tune: NICAEA by
John Dykes (1823-1876)

DEAR BOYS AND GIRLS:

Surprise! My name is Charley the Choirboy, and I'm in a choir just like you.

How would you like it if we learned to sing some of the same hymns? O.K.? Then let's get started right now!

The very first hymn I ever learned is . . . but wait! Your choir teacher will hum it and see if you can guess what it is.

Did you know "Holy, holy, holy"? I bet you didn't notice that two lines of the tune are just exactly alike! It is the first line and what other line?

218

My real reason for liking "Holy, holy, holy" so much is that it shows how I feel when I wake up extra early some mornings as the earth is beginning to turn toward the light of the sun. Perhaps this was how Isaiah felt when he wrote Isaiah 6:3. Why don't you stop and read his words right now?

The last line, "God in three Persons, blessed Trinity," really stumped me at first—but now I know that this means:

GOD THE FATHER—who created the earth with the intention that some day the whole universe should be united in love.

GOD THE SON —who came to earth to teach us about God's plan of love.

GOD THE SPIRIT —who lives within each of us and makes us able to teach others about God's love by the way we live.

What other hymns do you know that name the Trinity?

One day in choir, my teacher sang the words while we showed the meaning of the words with movement. Could you show the meaning of the first stanza?

In these cold winter days, as you see the glistening snow and the shimmering icicles and the many other wonders of God, why not sing along with me this wonderful, warm hymn:

"Holy, holy, holy, Lord God Almighty!
All thy works shall praise thy Name,
in earth and sky and sea;
Holy, holy, holy, merciful and mighty,
God in three Persons, blessed Trinity!"

Your new friend,
CHARLEY THE CHOIRBOY

2. "If thou but suffer God to guide thee"

Words by
Georg Neumark (1621-1681)
Tr. Catherine Winkworth (1829-1878)

Tune: NEUMARK by
Georg Neumark (1621-1681)

DEAR BOYS AND GIRLS:

School is out where I live! Mother's first summertime job for me was to clean out the closet.

I threw away an old Davy Crockett coonskin hat and a big red hula

219

hoop that I no longer play with because the "fad" is over. A "fad" is something that is very popular for a short while—and then it goes out of style.

One reason I love learning the great hymns of the church is that—unlike fads and popular songs—good hymns last forever. Look through your hymnbook to see how many hymns were written in the 1800's or the 1700's or even longer ago than that!

Just imagine! Over 300 years ago, when your great-great-great-great-great grandfather was about your age, he was singing the same hymn that you and I are learning together this month: "If thou but suffer God to guide thee."

This hymn teaches us something we will always want to remember: that if we let God be our guide in the choices we make as we grow up, then he will give us the strength to bear us through any troubles or evils that we might meet throughout our lifetime.

This promise must have worked for our grandfathers because, since they were little boys, our world has been through at least a dozen wars, many earthquakes and floods and tornados, and many different sicknesses—and yet, you and I have a more wonderful place to live than grandfather ever dreamed could be possible.

Isn't it good to sing the second and third stanzas and know that we have been chosen by God for his very own, and that God needs us to sing, pray, and live so as to teach others about his ways?

It might be fun for you and your choir friends to discover in what countries your own great-g-g-g-g-grandfathers lived. What language would he have spoken? Can you find his country on the map? Is it a free country today, or do we need to pray to God to help the people there to re-discover the meaning and the opportunity for freedom?

Why not make a list this summer of all the hymns you know and try to discover in what country they were first written? When I grow up, I'd like to travel around the world singing hymns so that Christians in every country would recognize the tunes and sing along with me . . . in their own language, of course! Have a happy singing summer!

Your friend,
CHARLEY THE CHOIRBOY

3. "Our church proclaims God's love and care"

Words by
Mabel Neidermeyer

Tune: TRURO L.M.
Psalmodia Evangelica

HI, BOYS AND GIRLS:

Whew! we barely made it back to America in the 1960's before running out of fuel on our long rocket journey back into time.

It's good to be home—and yet I see happening around me right now the same things I saw in every century we visited: People building things! People making music! People worshiping God!

One important difference is that *now* churches are working together to proclaim God's love and care to children of every land: "Her hands reach out in service through kind, helpful deeds that Christians do to show God's children of every land the world of love that he has planned."

Churches are working together not only in missions but in writing vacation church school books—and some in making better children's choirs around the world. Did you know that your own director is one of nearly 2,000 members in the Chorister's Guild—an undenominational organization of children's choir leaders around the world? Ask her to tell you more about it!

Let's pretend that all the children of all the directors are singing right now the hymns we've studied together. I'll be the announcer and you be the choirs. O.K.?

Announcer: All through the centuries Christians have sung praises to God, as in this hymn written in Greece in A.D. 220.

Choirs (sing): "Shepherd of tender youth"

Announcer: The monasteries helped keep Christianity alive during the dark ages. Here is the Lord's Prayer, sung as a chant.

Choirs (sing): "Our Father who art in heaven"

Announcer: The Middle Ages was a time of castles and knights and spirited folk-tune hymns like "In Dulci Jubilo."

Choirs (sing): "Good Christian men, rejoice"

Announcer: There were hard times during the Reformation, but the hymns of Christians showed us that their faith was strong.

Choirs (sing): "Now thank we all our God"

Announcer: When the English spread throughout the world, they took the teachings of Christianity with them.

Choirs (sing): "Jesus shall reign where'er the sun"

Announcer: Ancient Ireland gave us this beautiful tune.

Choirs (sing): "Be thou my vision"

Announcer: Inventions and factories changed the world, but not the
   Christian faith.
Choirs (sing): "Life is good, for God contrives it"
Announcer: Camp meeting songs were full of rhythm and fun to sing.
Choirs (sing): "Wonderful words of life"
Announcer: This hymn of consecration was written at the turn of the
   century.
Choirs (sing): "Just as I am without one plea"
Announcer: Let us all join hands with the prayer that we may truly
   proclaim God's love throughout the world.
Choirs (sing): "Our church proclaims God's love and care"

   I wish my pretending *could* come true and I could hear each of you
sing these hymns together! It's been a wonderful journey!

Your friend,
CHARLEY THE CHOIRBOY

PROGRAM FOR DEVELOPMENT OF A SINGING CHURCH

Why a Singing Church?

1. It is an opportunity for active participation.
2. It opens resources of helpful, comforting, strengthening thoughts.
3. It requires active participation which is physically vitalizing.
4. Hymns emphasize the essence of basic religious truth and experience. Hair-splitting theological niceties do not make good music.
   The whole Christian world meets on the foundation of fine hymns.
5. It unifies. Why do service organizations have song leaders? Why
   do colleges have school songs?

What conditions encourage a Singing Church?

1. Acoustics. Do I feel surrounded by tone, or as if I were singing
   a solo?
2. The prevailing atmosphere. Are others around me singing with
   enthusiasm? Is the choir singing with me, or at me?
3. Organ. Does it lead the congregation, or drag it along? Does it
   reflect the text, or play all the stanzas like a steam calliope? Does
   it over-dramatize the hymn? Is the Amen a summation of the
   thought and mood, or a dismal appendage?
4. Familiarity and personal association. We can't blame people for
   preferring hymns associated with their childhood and early religious
   experiences. Our job is to replace rather than discard.

222

What can you do to encourage a Singing Church?
1. Have the vision, patience and persistence to educate the congregation.
2. Plan a Hymn Study Program for a whole year for the whole church. Plan with the minister.
   Set the Music Committee to the task of a survey. Find out:
   a) Hymns used during past years; how often used?
   b) Favorite hymns of the congregation.
   c) Hymns used in church school; any progressive plan?
   Get together a representative committee to select the hymns to be used.
3. Process of selection:
   Present a larger list from which the committee is to select.
   Have a selected group of singers present them effectively.
   Give them information about the hymn.
   a) In which denominational hymnals is it used?
   b) Any special association with our denomination?
   c) How is it particularly suitable for our church program?
   Give each member of the committee a hymnal and a scoring sheet.
4. Character of hymns to select:
   a) Variety—prayer, praise, seasonal, etc.
   b) Something suitable for each age.
   c) No involved symbolism.
   d) Text and musical phrase well mated.

Promoting the Hymn Study Program
1. Mimeograph a booklet with the hymns and pertinent information.
2. Distribute it through the whole church.
3. Hold a training session for hymn leaders.
4. Get several books on hymns for the church Library.
5. Ask each organization to report on its use of the hymns.
6. Hold Hymn Sings at informal church functions.
7. Use the Church Bulletin to keep interest alive.
8. Use the hymns in the services whenever suitable.
9. Use anthem arrangements of the hymns.
10. Make use of posters. Have a poster contest.
11. Climax the year with a Hymn Festival.
12. *Don't* use the morning service of worship to teach the beginners.

The Children's Choir and the Hymn Study Program
1. See that every child has a *Chorister's Little Hymnal.*
2. Give a certificate to those learning all the hymns selected for the year.

3. Use "Hymn Study" pages in their notebooks.
4. Encourage them to learn to play the hymns.
5. Find anthem settings of the hymns and use them in the service.

The Festival of the Singing Church

1. Family Night—an informal gathering of hymn enjoyment.
    a) A display of hymnals.
    b) Hymn-tunes on the paper table-cloths.
    c) Hymn Singing relay: Table 1 sings first phrase, Table 2 the second, etc.
    d) Guessing game: Play 2nd or 3rd phrase of hymn; guess name of hymn. Clap rhythm; give name of hymn.
    e) Prize to family giving most interesting rendition of hymn.
    f) Presentation of prizes to those learning all the hymns.
    g) Introduce hymns for next year's study.

2. Hymn Festival in Sanctuary
    a) Prelude, Offertory, Postlude, based on selected hymns.
    b) Use all the choirs.
    c) Have choirs sing from memory.
    d) Include congregation liberally.
    f) Make use of instruments on climaxes.
    g) Keep it uplifting and dignified.

RUTH KREHBIEL JACOBS

WAYS TO USE HYMNS AS ANTHEMS

1. Sing it as written.
2. Melody in unison.
3. Men sing melody alone.
4. Women sing melody alone.
5. Solo voice or section on melody; other parts as background.
6. Alto, tenor, and bass on melody; soprano on descant.
7. Soprano and alto, or soprano and tenor as duet.
8. Tenor and bass on melody; alto on alto and soprano on tenor 8va.
9. Duet, trio or quartet of solo voices as contrast.
10. Antiphonal treatment.
11. Round or canon.
12. Organ or instrumental descant.
13. Free accompaniment. (*Free Accompaniment to Hymns*, 1st Book, Bairstow; 2nd Book, Thiman; Oxford University Press)
14. Fauxbourdon (melody in tenor)

224

15. Organ prelude arrangement; choir sings melody against it.
16. Use hymn as choric speech.
17. Use as antiphon: minister—speech; choir—sing.
18. Have congregation sing on last stanza.
19. Change key from stanza to stanza.
20. Use interludes between stanzas.
21. Use women's chorus (SSA).
22. Use men's chorus:

	or
1st tenor on alto	1st tenor on tenor
(where written)	2nd tenor on melody
2nd tenor on tenor	baritone on alto
baritone on melody	(octave lower)
bass on bass	bass on bass

23. Use a combination of these methods within the stanza.

AUSTIN C. LOVELACE

CHILDREN'S CHOIRS AS HYMN LEADERS IN THE ROMAN CATHOLIC SERVICE

From "Cantate Domino" by ELEANOR DuBUISSON FOSSICK

"It is Lent!" How often preceding the glorious Day of Resurrection is the Catholic child reminded that he should forego this or that pleasure or delicacy to discipline himself by small sacrifice in honor of Him whose death we will commemorate on Good Friday.

Children show quite as much fortitude as adults in following the liturgy during the Lenten season. Their young minds, unclouded by doubt, unwarped by ambition, find delight in making an extra effort to "be good" for forty days. For those who make it to the end of Lent, with no broken resolutions, the struggle will be easier afterward. Once the liturgy is understood and loved, it permeates our worship and carries over into daily living. When we have attained the true spirit of the liturgy, we no longer experience rebellion over the so-called "new rules" as promulgated in the September 1958 Decree on Participation in the Mass.

In truth the liturgical movement is not new at all, but a restoration of public worship as it was when the church was young. Superficial, half-hearted assistance at Mass must give way to an active and reverent participation with the celebrant. Priest and congregation, praying together, have been called an "antidote against Communism," and it is also a weapon against Catholic egoism.

In the case of the restored Easter Vigil the idea of lay participation is as old as the church itself. The new decree simply states that the people are to have restored to them that which is rightfully theirs, but the people—being what they are—will put up resistance to an order that requires them to bestir themselves from their lethargy and give voice to their worship. They will blame the pastor for interfering with their comfort. They will castigate the choirmaster for his "new-fangled" ideas; and it is for him quietly, but firmly, to pursue his course and assume the monumental task of educating the congregation to pray and sing. This will mean hard work, discouragement, imperviousness to criticism, and a feeling of hopelessness and helplessness. However, if the long-suffering director will persevere, his reward will come when at long last he finds himself a member of a praying, singing congregation.

But where shall he begin? With the children, of course! By teaching the children the Dialogue Mass with appropriate hymns, as well as the Proper and Ordinary of the Missa Cantata, the choir director is preparing the future congregation in the way it should go, while the youngsters are subtly leading their elders on Sunday morning. Small groups of children, placed at strategic points throughout the nave and assigned the task of distributing Mass cards and hymn-books, constitute the first step. For the first few Sundays the children and their director will be singing alone in a hostile environment. Then, here and there, a hardy individual will decide to join them; eventually more and more members enter the participation, and lo! the director will know the happiness of hearing a glorious surge of voices rise to heaven as one. This I have known, together with the months of heartbreak that went before.

Do not underestimate the ability of children's choirs. They are capable of singing the best hymns and any of the Chant Masses that you may select, particularly the easy Mass XVI, with Gloria XV and Credo I or III. This is the selection made by the 1958 Decree Commission to be learned by Catholics throughout the world so that they might participate in singing the Mass in any country.

Teach the choirs the Holy Week Chants. If you need simplified arrangements, the cards for Palm Sunday through the Easter Vigil (published by the Gregorian Institute, Toledo, Ohio) are Nos. HW-1, 3, 4 and 5, priced from about 25c to 50c each. Teach them "Parce Domine." They love this plaintive chant; have them sing it before and after Vs. 1, Ps. 50 (Miserere) instead of "Laudate Dominum" after Benediction during Lent. Another Lenten jewel is "Attende Domine," a lovely, meaningful chant that fills many places: as an Offertory supplement, a

226

Processional or Recessional hymn, etc. Both of these chants may be found in *Pius X Hymnal* (McLaughlin) and in the *Parish Hymn Book* (World Library of Sacred Music). A beautiful and appealing English Lenten hymn is a 17th-century Hungarian melody, with text by Shane Leslie, in *Pius X Hymnal*, No. 209. I have seen the eyes of choir boys glisten with unshed tears as they sang the last two lines: "Jesus of Galilee, stricken and torn, give us a share in thy crown of thorn."

HYMN-PLAYING AT THE ORGAN

By A. Eugene Ellsworth, Minister of Music

East Dallas (Texas) Christian Church

There is probably no situation in which one person has more power of sound at his disposal than that of the church organist at his console. At his finger tips are literally thousands of tone-producing pipes capable of sounds from a whisper to an ear-splitting roar. He can create and maintain a worshipful atmosphere, allude to the theatrical, or sink to meaningless dawdle. He can enhance or he can mar worship. No person, not even the minister, wields more control over the service, once it has begun, than does the organist. Pace and continuity are his responsibility and privilege, but this carries with it the necessity for judgment, technical proficiency, and good taste.

Probably the most vital requirement of the church organist is a mastery of the art of playing hymns. It is common knowledge that the capacity to play an excellent organ recital does not guarantee the performer to be a good service organist. (But it is not a bad qualification!) A recital glorifies the organist and the composer. A service glorifies God.

In the proper playing of a hymn the organist becomes at once not only the accompanist but the leader of the congregation in the singing of that hymn. He must announce the hymn with an introduction, set the pace, and hold a steady rhythm. He must allow opportunities for the singers to breathe (especially between stanzas) and give adequate tonal support to the congregation—but without drowning their voices in a torrent of sound. How then does an organist play aggressively enough, with neither too much nor too little tone? How does he keep the congregation moving at a reasonable pace without dragging? How does he help express the meaning of the hymn and how does he inspire the layman to sing enthusiastically?

First of all, the organist must become an integral part of the

227

congregation. Carl Halter, in *The Practice of Sacred Music* (pub. Concordia), says: "The organist must strive to play *with* rather than *for* the congregation." Ideally, the sound of the organ and the singing of the congregation are welded into one unit, but the organist is the conductor of the singing.

To accomplish this ideal there are a number of factors that play important roles, all of which become second nature to the experienced organist. These include choice of key, the hymn introduction, registration, such technical considerations as tempo, touch and accuracy, phrasing and the ways of achieving variety.

CHOICE OF KEY

To many this may seem an irrelevant point. After all, hymnals have been prepared and edited by committees of musicians and clergy with hymn settings appropriate for congregational singing. But the simple fact is that many of our hymns are published in keys *too high* for unison singing by average voices. Evidence of this is seen in a number of recently published hymnals in which many well-known hymns are transposed to lower keys than are found in earlier editions. (Note especially the new Baptist hymnal).

The musician may argue that a higher key sounds brighter and more jubilant, but if our congregations will sing when the keys are lower and remain silent when they must strain to sing the high notes, what then?

It should be a basic part of every organist's training and acquired technique to be able to transpose a hymn at least a step down or up. If he feels uncomfortable or insecure in transposing from the printed page he may write out the transposition in the desired key. A safe top note for congregations is a fourth line D or fourth space E-flat. With this as a maximum high note, it is not likely that a hymn melody would ever go too low. Few hymns ever need more than the transposition of a major second or, rarely, a third.

Whatever the means of getting the music in the right key, this must be a first decision on the part of the organist. Once the key is set, the organist moves into the actual playing of the hymn.

HYMN INTRODUCTION

It is generally agreed that the best introduction to any hymn is to play it once through in its entirety at the tempo in which it is to be sung and in a manner to suggest the spirit of the text. However, in many services the element of time dictates a shorter introduction; in this

228

event whatever introduction is played should end with an appropriate cadence, not an abrupt or misplaced dominant to tonic (V to I).

A short introduction may include only a phrase or two, but it should state the opening melodic line unless the hymn is especially well known, in which case the last phrase may be adequate. Frequently an introduction may be formulated by playing the opening phrase followed immediately by the final phrase, which ends with a cadence that naturally leads the congregation to the first notes of the hymn.

The organist should avoid an introduction that ends with a cadence on the dominant of the key, because this leaves the singer uncertain as to whether he should begin singing or wait for the organist to play further. The organist should avoid the trap of finding himself in dominant tonality and trying to "ad-lib" chords to reestablish the original key. The wise organist not only will have practiced the hymns before the service, but will have decided on the exact introductions he intends to use.

REGISTRATION

Carl Halter, in *The Practice of Sacred Music,* defines registration as "an art analogous to the choice and use of color by a painter." The term "registration" is the organist's word for "instrumentation" as used by the orchestral arranger. To lead a congregation effectively the organist must choose stops that will give support and will lead and inspire. A clearly defined registration of sufficient body and texture can usually be found on most organs that will support the singer, yet allow him to hear his own voice without causing him to feel he is singing a solo.

Because no two organs are exactly alike in specifications, voicing, and acoustical environment, the organist must prepare hymn combinations appropriate to the particular instrument and sanctuary in order to provide adequate volume needed for the size of the congregation and the type of hymn to be sung. He should choose the clearest-toned stops available. On most organs this requirement is met by the Diapason chorus: Diapason (or Principal) 8', Octave 4', 12th, 15th, and possibly the Mixture. A variation in the basic 8' tone may be the Gedeckt in place of the Diapason, but the 4' tone should be of Diapason quality because the Flute 4' is swallowed up in the overtones of the Diapason. Each manual may be set up with one clear-sounding stop on each pitch desired (8', 4', 2', etc. to Mixture) and coupled to the Great as desired. Four-foot couplers may be used on smaller organs or when there is a scarcity of voices above 4' (sometimes above 8'). Reed stops (especially Trumpets) and Mixtures may be added for brilliance and sonority.

Heavy, overpowering registration tends to overwhelm the singer and drown him out, making him feel it is useless to try to sing against it. Avoid using multiple 8' stops, or multiple stops at any pitch, because this tends to make the ensemble muddy without adding effectively either volume or ensemble. In addition *avoid* the following: use of 16' stops on the manuals (except possibly an occasional light 16' Quintaton), Celeste stops, including Unda Maris, and tremolos. Carl Halter, in *The Practice of Sacred Music* adds: "Complete instructions for the use of the tremolo in hymn-playing: *Don't!*"

The pedal should balance whatever is played on the manuals, including 16' stops and 8' couplers to the manual sounding. On electronic organs it is usually better to omit Flute stops in hymn combinations because they frequently muddy the ensemble.

It is suggested that the organist consider the opinion of one or two musically informed members of the congregation regarding the amount of tone used on hymns. Such persons might listen to and criticize various combinations, or one person might be asked to play a hymn on prepared combinations so that the organist can listen from different locations in the sanctuary. The organist should find the clearest ensemble available on his instrument by whatever means necessary.

TEMPO

How does the organist arrive at the correct tempo of a hymn? It must be vigorous, steady, and sharply rhythmical. The organ must lead, not follow, the congregation at a tempo neither too fast nor too slow— neither as a race horse nor as a dray horse. (Sometimes he may feel more like a plow horse!)

Some hymnals, such as the *English Hymnal* and the *Christian Science Hymnal,* give metronomic markings. James R. Sydnor in *The Hymn and Congregational Singing* gives markings for a number of representative hymns as he would play them. However, the markings vary considerably, as shown by one example: "Ein' Feste Burg," which is indicated 40 beats to the minute in the *English Hymnal,* 69-76 in the *Christian Science Hymnal,* and 80-86 by Sydnor.

The following may help determine the correct tempo for a particular hymn:

1. Avoid prejudice toward any tempo which may be either too fast, too slow, or even medium speed.
2. Note any particular tempo indications on the music: "Majestically," "in flowing style," "with joy," "with quiet dignity," "reverently," "in moderate time," etc.

230

3. Identify the mood of the text and tune. Read aloud the text. Sing a few bars of the hymn to yourself before beginning the introduction.

4. Try to find the "natural" tempo, the tempo that "feels right" for the particular hymn-tune. Obviously there may be considerable variation of opinion, but a right tempo usually develops for each tune for every congregation.

5. Study the harmonic structure of the tune. Tunes that change harmony on almost every beat, with many chords in fundamental position, are usually played in a broad and dignified manner. Such hymn tunes include: "St. Anne" (O God, our help in ages past), "Lobe den Herren" (Praise to the Lord), "Old Hundredth" (The Doxology), and "Leoni" (Praise to the living God). Hymns with repeated chords or less frequent harmonic changes tend to move a little faster. Examples include: "Hymn to Joy" (Joyful, joyful we adore thee), and "Sabaoth" (Holy, holy, holy).

6. Respect the conditions or situations which may influence the tempo of hymns. The size of the congregation: a large congregation may require a slightly relaxed pace. The age of singers: children often sing at a faster tempo than adults. The acoustics of the sanctuary: a long reverberation time may require a slower tempo.

TOUCH

The usual rule for touch is that each voice part should be played legato; all repeated notes should be tied except those in the melody, which should be played disjoined at approximately half their given time-value or by cutting off the last half of the unit of count, whichever gives the shorter break in time. For example:

MERRIAL

However, this rule does not fit every situation. Certain types of tunes tend to lose motion when following the rule strictly, and every hymn requires phrasing (which is later discussed). The following are exceptions to the legato rule stated above:

1. When two or more notes of a chord are repeated in the following chord (in the same voice parts) it may be desirable to separate them.

LOBE DEN HERREN

2. When the same bass note is sounded on two or more successive beats of a measure it should be struck on alternate counts or on the first and last beats of the measure.

3. When chords are repeated with the same voicing, the upper three voices may be disjoined. (See "Coronation" as illustrated previously.) If the first of the two chords is an up-beat the whole chord should be separated.

232

4. When it is necessary to reinforce the rhythm or to establish and maintain the tempo (particularly when the congregation tends to drag), the organist may detach all voices other than the melody line, which should be played according to the legato rule.

ACCURACY

The organist should be meticulous in the correct playing of both notes and rhythm. The former is purely a matter of technique and the latter of keen sensitivity and musicianship. Both may be developed and improved with reasonable practice. Today's man-in-the-pew is accustomed to hearing accurate performance of music. Radio, television, school music, and community concerts have exposed enough people to well-performed music that the church musician must be thoroughly prepared if he is to command respect.

The usual manner of playing hymns is to do the soprano, alto, and tenor parts on a manual and the bass on the pedals. The bass part should be played as written. Avoid the practice of the "left-foot" organist who continually adapts the bass line to allow one foot to play in only the lower octave of the pedal board. Correct pedaling requires the use of both feet as necessary to secure a legato statement of the bass line. The left hand need not duplicate the bass part when it is played on the pedals.

The main problem in rhythm accuracy is that of the unsteady beat. The use of a metronome and persistent attention to the regular pulse can correct such irregularity.

Other errors in time heard frequently in hymn-playing include:

1. Improper dotted-note rhythm. Often the dotted eighth and sixteenth notes are rounded off as triplets, perhaps in an attempt to give the hymn more dignity. Whether or not this is justified is a matter of opinion and probably depends upon the hymn-tune in question. Usually the dotted note and the accompanying short note should be played in exact time. Such rhythms in hymns like "Neander" (Open now thy gates of beauty), "Antioch" (Joy to the world), and "Lobe den Herren" (Praise to the Lord) should certainly be done with correct time-values.

2. Improper sustaining of long notes. This problem occurs in hymn phrases ending on a long note of three or four beats. (The long note at the end of a *final* phrase offers no difficulty.) Examples include: "Italian Hymn" (Come, thou almighty King), "Arnesberg" (God himself is with us), "Leoni" (Praise to the

233

living God), "Belmont" (The Lord be with us as each day), "Finlandia" (We would be building), and "Forest Green" (All beautiful the march of days). (Notice the up-beat on the last phrase of this hymn, which is a half note instead of the usual quarter.) The long notes in all of these hymns should be given full count.

3. Errors in observing the time-value of rests. Rests in hymns usually occur at the end of a phrase following a long note, whereby the singer has time for a breath. Give both the note and the rest their full time-value. Examples include: "National Hymn" (God of our fathers), "Ar Hyd Y Nos" (God that madest earth and heaven), and "Rathbun" (In the Cross of Christ I glory). Other hymns with rests occurring *during* the course of the phrase include: "Sine Nomine" (For all the saints), the "Gloria Patri" (especially the tune by Meinecke), and "Poland" (The Lord is my Shepherd).

PHRASING

In hymn-playing phrasing may be considered the art of making the organ "breathe" along with the singers. The writer recalls hearing a certain organist play the hymns of a service with no break in strict legato from beginning to end. The effect was a feeling of breathlessness or of gasping for a breath during most of the hymn.

The organist should sing (mentally, at least) the words of the hymn along with the congregation and release the keys for a fraction of a second of silence at each point in the text where the congregation should logically take a breath. This not only suggests the acceptable places for the congregation to breathe but helps to maintain the tempo and to keep the singing spirited and energetic. Phrasings are usually done at punctuation marks (but not necessarily at *every* one) and must be done without breaking the rhythm. Simply "steal" a bit of time from the note preceding the break. Occasionally a phrase-ending should be executed where there is no punctuation mark: this occurs when the musical phrase obviously requires it or when the phrase of the text is too long for the congregation to sing it in one breath.

There is considerable misunderstanding regarding the fermata (⌢). Originally placed in hymns to mark the end of a musical phrase, it was not intended as a "hold" or interruption in the rhythm. This usage was a characteristic of the early chorales of the Protestant churches. Today's singers and musicians have tended to interpret the fermata as a hold, and the result is that the final note of a phrase is often held unduly long.

234

The *Episcopal Hymnal* of 1940 has eliminated the fermata but gives the fermata note an extra beat by actually changing the printed value of the note. Many organists and choir directors follow this practice in performance.

It is necessary for the organist to allow a reasonable break in rhythm between stanzas of a hymn. This need not necessarily mean the addition of any definite number of beats (as the counting off of an extra measure of time), but it should be sufficient to allow the singers time for a breath and to shift their eyes to the beginning of the next stanza. There should be no ritard at the end of a stanza.

The "Amen" should be sung without dragging the rhythm but also without rushing. Generally speaking, it should be sung in rhythm as indicated by the time-values of the printed notes.

Ways of Achieving Variety

To play a hymn of several stanzas with the same registration and in the same manner throughout can result in unnecessary monotony. There are a number of things the organist can do to offer variety, the most practical of which have to do with changes of registration. Occasionally unessential embellishment of the harmony may be desirable. The following are suggestions:

1. Change combinations (probably by piston) to provide change of color more than change of volume. A change of the basic 8′ stop (perhaps from Diapason to Gedeckt) or the addition of an 8′ reed (Trumpet) may give a desirable change. The addition of a 16′ reed in the pedals is another good change.

2. Play an occasional stanza on one manual only (such as the Swell) without pedals. Care should again be taken to avoid too great a contrast in volume level.

3. Play the melody as a solo on one manual using a strong combination or solo stop (Trumpet 8′, possibly with 4′ and/or 16′ couplers). The left hand plays the alto and tenor parts on a second manual, the pedals play the bass line.

TOULON

235

4. Double the melody line at the tenor octave in the left hand. This may be accomplished with both hands on one manual, or the left hand may play a contrasting combination or solo stop on a second manual. The right hand must fill in the essential harmony.

AUSTRIAN HYMN

5. Let the congregation sing a stanza without the organ, but be sure to advise both the congregation and the choir beforehand. The choir should sing out firmly and resolutely.

6. Alternate stanzas between the congregation and the choir, the former singing one stanza with the organ, then the choir singing another a cappella, perhaps in parts. The organist may also take a turn at playing a stanza alone. Again, the congregation and the choir must be prepared in advance.

7. Provide a descant (either on the organ or by the voices) to one stanza to heighten musical effectiveness.

8. Insert organ interludes between stanzas, sometimes with a modulation to a higher key (step or half-step) for a final stanza. Many people frown on this procedure which tends to call attention to the organist's ability to improvise a modulation and to transpose. It is acceptable, though, when done in a dignified manner and for such a purpose as "lifting" the mood of a congregation.

9. Prepare carefully any unessential embellishment of the harmony used for variety. Sometimes the addition of passing tones is possible and desirable. (Avoid excessive use of this device, which may make the harmonization sound trite.)

10. Provide a free organ accompaniment to one of the stanzas (probably the last one). The choir and congregation should sing this stanza in unison. A number of excellent published arrangements are available, such as the two volumes by T. Tertius Noble. Some organists improvise their own free harmonizations, but these must be carefully prepared in advance or the results

could suddenly become tragic (and embarrassing)! The congregation should again be advised when free accompaniments are used. Not more than one stanza to a hymn should be so treated.

A final word on playing hymns: Be consistent! Keep a uniform tempo throughout the hymn and avoid ritards. Make the pauses between stanzas of uniform length. Seek variety in registration and playing, but avoid sudden changes that may disrupt the congregation and stop their singing altogether. It is a great privilege to be a church organist, but also a great responsibility. The organist who truly leads his congregation in the spirited singing of hymns is making one of the greatest possible contributions to the service of worship.

Special Services
and Festivals

ORGANIZING A CHILDREN'S CHOIR FESTIVAL

A Children's Choir Festival, to be successful, needs the "look-ahead." Probably the largest number of requests for help and information coming to the Guild office pertain to Children's Choir festivals, particularly those involving community participation. "How do I start?" "Who selects the program?" "How do I follow up?" These and other related questions are answered in the following articles or at least guidance is given, for each situation offers varying problems. A successful Children's Choir Festival does not just happen. It is first a dream, then a plan, and then organization, all welded together by hard work. In no area of Children's Choir work does the axiom apply more aptly: "Plan your work, and work your plan."

The following two articles bring you the help of two people: one an "old pro" in organizing a community-wide festival, Louise B. Whitman; the other, an amateur (self-styled, however), Carla Bunting. The second plan outlined is very detailed; the first is more general. Both, however, possess one basic quality in common: careful planning and vigorous organization. Many more communities need the thrill and inspiration of a Children's Choir Festival. A spark-plug is generally all that is needed. Suppose *you* be that vital bit of mechanism!

(A.L.J.)

239

1. Problems of Planning and Performance

By CARLA BUNTING

(Written when Children's Choir Director of First Presbyterian Church, Amarillo, Texas.)

First, let me tell you that I am no authority on the techniques of holding a Junior Choir Festival! It was my first attempt at such a thing, but I was surprised that it was so easy—after careful planning and organizing, however.

A festival for Juniors is a glorious experience for those listening as well as for those singing. When I brought up the suggestion of a Spring Festival for our Juniors at the January meeting of the Choir Directors Guild of Amarillo, it fell, I thought, upon deaf ears, and no one shared my enthusiasm. "We haven't had time to relax since our Christmas programs," they said. "Easter is facing us and we'll have special programs then too." "We Baptists have Choral Contests to practice for." And on it went.

The next few days, however, revealed that there *was* enough enthusiasm to make further plans. I contacted all churches in the city that had Junior choirs, and ended up with nine choirs for the Festival. We nine directors had a luncheon meeting to make plans. In order to save time at the meeting I prepared an agenda for discussion: date, time, place, theme of festival, program outline, anthems, arrangements, hymns and responses to be used, guest ministers to serve, conductors to lead anthems, organist, publicity, programs, greeters and ushers for the Festival. As I knew our meeting time would be short, I prepared as much ahead as possible. For instance, I mimeographed a suggested Festival Program which I found in the CGL, made lists of possible hymns, anthems and responses, the names of ministers and organists who might be approached. The program was accepted unanimously! In the music chosen we included a number of anthems that were on the Baptist Contests lists; four of our anthem arrangements were hymn-tunes. Each of the areas of responsibility was assigned at this time, too.

Within a week after our meeting, I mailed to the nine directors minutes of the first meeting, a copy of our planned Festival Program, a list of all anthems to be used, including arrangers and publishers with publishers' numbers. In the case of hymns and responses I listed the arrangement or typed out the words, since often the text differs in hymnals of the various denominations.

A month before the Festival I called each director to check on the choir's progress. All reports were favorable. The overall cooperation was wonderful, and this is of the greatest importance to the success of a

240

festival. Our Festival went off with very few problems or mistakes because of this excellent cooperation.

One problem that I could foresee, with over 200 children involved, was how to handle the music quietly without distraction. The solution was to prepare for each child a sheet, folded like a book, with the Order of Service, the words of the hymns, anthems and responses. With this booklet program there was no music or hymnals for little hands to contend with. Of course the ideal is memorization, but our time was limited. This brings to mind another suggestion: don't wait until January to decide to have a festival in the spring! Plan it in September, work all year, and utilize festival anthems in individual church services.

A joint rehearsal was held one week before the Festival at the same time and in the same place as the actual Festival. Apparently directions for this rehearsal were not made clear, for 75 more choristers turned up at the Festival than at the rehearsal! This led to our only real difficulty, that of getting all those children in place to begin the service. The director in whose church the Festival was held did a fine job assigning each choir to a separate room for robing and lining up, but the children who were not at the rehearsal confused the processing.

The Festival Service itself went smoothly without further problems. The singing was glorious and showed the splendid cooperation and inspiration of the directors.

I feel that there is a real need for Junior Choir festivals in most communities, especially where smaller churches are involved. It makes a really worthwhile project for the children to anticipate and to work towards.

2. Details of Planning and Performance

By MRS. O. L. (LOUISE) WHITMAN, Director of Youth Choirs,

Glendale Presbyterian Church, Glendale, California

There are several kinds of Junior Choir festivals: those whose choirs combine to sing all the anthems; those that present each choir separately; and those in which each choir, or each director's several choirs, sing a number or two, with one or more numbers sung by the entire group of choirs. The Festival may be planned and carried out by a community group with committee chairmen and with all local churches invited to participate; or it may start with one church hosting the Festival, inviting others to take part, and handling all the mechanics through its director and Choir Guild.

We followed this latter plan in 1958 when the Choir Guild encouraged the director to issue invitations to a March Festival, the first in

Glendale in eight years. The burden of responsibility in establishing this annual Festival actually strengthened our already efficient Guild, and assured our choristers the experience of contributing something fine to the community life each season.

Like a wedding any festival must be set up months in advance and the details worked out in a logical sequence, so that those in charge may face the big day calmly. You may easily transpose this procedure to fit your dreamed-of Festival. It works! Try it!

PLANNING

March (1960) —Set date (Sunday, March 5, 1961 at 3:30-4:30 P.M.) Clear with Minister or Director of Christian Education and put on Church Activity Calendar, also Church Administrator's Book.

Clear with Session for use of facilities:
Sanctuary
Pipe Organ
Designate use of offering above Festival expenses.
Arrange for host church's organist to play.

Summer and early Fall (1960) —Select guest conductor (who may be a participating director) (If a Guild chapter or other community group puts on the Festival, the group chooses the conductor and consults with him on theme and repertory. If entire Festival consists of anthems sung by massed choirs, the choice of anthems should be announced by *early summer*.)

After consulting with you, the conductor will select:
1. Theme
2. Congregational hymn (our "Hymn of the Month" for March, if suitable; add interesting feature, such as descant by several choirs; Tallis' Canon, etc.)
3. Two anthems to be sung by combined choirs (theme).

September —Mail dittoed form *Letter #1* to directors of 15 Junior choirs (Grades 3 through 6, or to voice change) of churches in area inviting them to participate; each to sing one anthem separately; two numbers by combined choirs as listed (giving octavo numbers). Include copy of last year's Festival Program for directors who have not participated before. Include return postcard covering name of director and choir, and enrollment; name of anthem and composer.

242

September (1960)	—Announce Festival date to Choir Guild. Include in year's Choir Calendar and Choristers' Notebooks.
November (1960)	—Phone directors who have not yet replied. Then mail more invitations to other directors farther away, if necessary to be sure of 12 to 15 choirs. (Sanctuary seats 1300 plus 60 in choir loft.) Arrange for participating ministers.
December	—Drop Festival planning temporarily.
January Choir Guild Meeting (1961)	—Chairmen cover Festival responsibilities; group makes decisions. Recruit men from Guild and from Christian Education Committee of Session to assist processional marshal in patrolling line of travel, halls, patio.

Arrange for Church Nursery 3:15 to 4:45 P.M.

Assign hostesses: one for each church. Escort guest choirs at weekday rehearsal from sanctuary to line-up room via assigned route. Stay with them during Sunday massed rehearsal, recessional, robing, line-up and processional. (Watch for chewing-gum just before Festival!)

Arrange for Guild photographer to take pictures: color slides for Choir Families Dinner; one candid shot of two or three choristers about Festival for newspapers afterwards.

Guild chaplain offers prayer with our own group 15 minutes before Festival.

Processional marshal and *one* narthex assistant (*only*) wear black robes. Other processional assistants, general chairman and hostesses wear Choir Guild badges (made of paper by Guild crafts chairman to be used each season; distributed that P.M. by chairman; returned afterwards to Youth Choirs office).

Arrange for Junior High Girls Choir to usher. Their Choir Guild chairman and church head usher to rehearse them in narthex before Festival at 2:45 P.M.

Plan making of posters; hall signs to direct guests to line-up rooms and rest rooms; large card signs to label pew sections for choir seating (use each season). Line-up room directory (blackboard chart) for entry hall.

| Late January or Early February (1961) | —Mail each participating director dittoed form *Letter #2*. Include a reminder to advertise Festival to congregation: nursery open; parking for cars adjacent; location of rest rooms. Instructions for weekday rehearsal in sanctuary with date (to confirm earlier telephone arrangement with |

243

director). Sunday massed rehearsal instructions: assigned robing and line-up room. Performance instructions: seating in sanctuary; processional and recessional rules. Letter #2 enclosure: dittoed chart of sanctuary with exact block of pews labeled for choirs of director receiving letter. Letter #2 enclosure (optional): Return postcard requesting information regarding director's background and choirs (for newspaper publicity).

Schedule all weekday rehearsals in sanctuary on Church Calendar for custodians (include our choirs and guest choirs). Mail Festival organist *written* schedule. Get titles of organists' Prelude, Offertory, Postlude, with names of composers. Keep guest director informed of enrollment in Festival. Request glossy prints of guest director for newspapers.

WORKING OUT DETAILS

Early
February

—*Mail-outs*: Simple 8½ x 11 colored mimeo sheet, including: illustration, Festival name, place, date, list of churches and choirs participating, guest conductor. Deliver or mail several to each church for posting on their bulletin boards; mail to each chorister of your church *two weeks before* Festival; also place in church school teachers' boxes; mail to interested musical friends, etc., about *10 days before Festival.* Send to newly organized Junior Choirs inviting them to attend Festival and consider participating next season. (This is better than inviting them uninitiated to participate.) A Guild chapter or other organization might distribute quantities to participating directors for Choristers' Notebooks.

Mid
February

—*Program*: Arrange complete order of Prelude, Anthems and Offertory, with choirs seated on left and right side of center aisle *alternating* in performance (Offertory two-thirds of way through program ideally). Schedule Prelude, Invocation, Anthems, Offertory, Congregational Hymn, Benediction, Postlude and Recessional to fill about one hour. Alternate the boy and girl choirs, the lively and quiet anthems. Consult with another church musician if things get involved.

Give printer double-spaced copy at least 10 days before Festival. Proof-read. Order 1000, purple ink for Lent

244

(1959 cost was $16.64). If printing is done earlier, you may include one copy with each packet of mimeo mail-outs to choir directors, etc. (Smaller festivals may choose to mimeograph programs).

Mid
February
—*Publicity*: Write (always type double-spaced!) one comprehensive story about Festival, covering in first paragraph who, what, where, when, why. Name every choir, church, director, organist, host minister, other ministers, guest conductor; history of Festival; Choir Guild chairman, hostesses, processional marshal and assistants; any pertinent facts about conductors and choirs.

Rewrite this story with community emphasis for local newspapers; rewrite a streamlined version for church paper.

Have mat made from glossy print for church paper; then send glossy print to local newspaper for issue within week of Festival, with story and suggested heading. (Newspapers do their own engraving.)

Last
Two
Weeks
—*Host Church Paper*: Announce Festival date *early in February*. In last issue before Festival, run full Festival story with picture of conductor (guest or local) *first page*. Headline the Festival with a banner across top or at bottom of first page.

Note: If no combined anthems are to be sung or no "headliner" director, then pose three (only) choristers from three choirs in a *candid* shot (no vestments) and submit to newspapers.

Church Bulletins: Adult church and church school departments type copy announcing bare facts of Festival (what, when, where, and nursery when open) for Sunday morning of Festival and the preceding Sunday.

Bulletin Board Notices: Post mail-outs, etc., in Choir Room (for Adult Choirs), Christian Education office, other bulletin boards about church.

Posters: At least one poster carefully planned, to be used from year to year, with date on separate card attached at bottom.

LAST MINUTE DETAILS

Last
Two
Weeks
—Give head custodian list of days and hours when *risers and platform extensions* are needed in sanctuary on weekdays and Festival Sunday.

245

Ten Days Ahead	—Mail dittoed "Festival Instruction for Choir Guild" to about 20 hostesses, processional marshal and assistants.
	Arrange line-up rooms for guest choirs' *weekday rehearsal,* same number rows of chairs as pews reserved in sanctuary (but *no* center aisles).
	During week before Festival hold meeting of directors, guild chairman, processional marshal and assistants.
	Rehearse own church's Junior Choirs in sanctuary with organ at regular rehearsal hour within two weeks of Festival, after schedule accommodates guest choirs.
Sunday Before Festival	—*Church Technician:* Typed request: Remove earphones from pews before massed rehearsal, replace after Festival; place "mike" for massed rehearsal and Festival for use *only* of guest director, ministers, violins, and other obligato instruments; record entire Festival on tape from mike or recorder in balcony.
Last Week:	—Mail postal reminder of Festival schedule to our own Junior Choirs; also to Junior High Choir ushers.
Monday	—Give Choir Guild men typed instructions and chart for setting up chairs in line-up rooms, plus our choirs' seating chart and *chair labels*; hall labels, pew labels; masking tape. (3 men)
	—*Custodian:* Written request to lock business office (central storage spot for guest choristers' valuables, coats, etc.)

THE BIG DAY

11 A.M.	—Attach signs with masking-tape to doorways and along halls to line-up rooms and rest rooms; each church's name on door of its room. Place master directory of all churches' room numbers in entry hall. Place several Festival programs *for adults* on music stand or lectern in line-up rooms. (Sunday church school has entirely vacated rooms by this time.) During second service of worship arrange chairs in line-up rooms according to charts; no center aisles; same number of rows as pews assigned in sanctuary; pianos angled correctly; lectern or music stands in position.
	Attach name-cards to our choirs' chairs, referring to special seating chart.
	After church is dismissed: strap post-type labels to pew, identifying block section reserved for each church. Place

246

music stand center aisle, first pew; another at balcony rail at side, for directing combined anthems; package of programs to narthex table.

In letter a week earlier director is to give written information on guest director (3 x 5 card) to minister who will introduce him at time of Offering.

2:00 P.M. (not vested) or 2:15 P.M. in Vestments — *Massed Rehearsal*: Director welcomes guest director; introduces him to combined choirs; introduces organist, marshal.

Choristers come directly to sanctuary (no vestments if 2 P.M. rehearsal; or to line-up rooms, put on vestments, and to sanctuary at 2:15). Sit according to church; precise seat not necessary now. Rehearse with director *and* organist. (If massed rehearsal is at 2:15, one choir from a distance may rehearse separately, vested, from 2 to 2:15 while choristers assemble; 45-minute rehearsal for two anthems and the hymns.)

2:45 P.M. not vested (or 3:00 P.M. in Vestments) — Leave Sanctuary in orderly recessional, center aisle, marshal in charge; hostesses lead each church group to line-up and robing room where each choir has run-through of its separate anthem. If there is spare time, choirs may relax with fun songs; most choristers go to rest rooms. (Refreshments unnecessary and a liability under this schedule.)

—*Processional*: Marshal starts first choir into hall route at 3:20; hostess first, director and perhaps accompanist follow; then the choir, *all single file*, to entrance to narthex; wait. Marshal goes to next room and next, starts them. Half of choirs follow one route, other half another, for traffic control. When all are in halls, marshal goes to narthex, and with man assistant (both black-robed) starts the long unbroken queue down *center aisle* of sanctuary, spacing them. Order: Ministers, guest director, director of first choir, her choristers; next director and choristers, etc. Continue single file into pews at right, 1, 2, 3, etc.; then left side, per seating chart.

Processional assistants have definite posts in halls and patio. Choristers are never out of sight of them.

Labeled assigned seating for choirs, ministers, choir guilds.

—*Festival*: No choristers hold programs unless director assumes responsibility; she may get them in narthex

247

ahead of time and pass them to choristers *after* they have sung their separate anthem.

Choirs sing combined numbers standing at pews facing director in balcony at rear.

Each choir singing separately goes to platform (front) via outer aisle; sings; returns same route while choir from other side of center aisle goes up via its outer aisle, etc. Choir in loft will sing from that spot.

—*Recessional*: As rehearsed following massed rehearsal.

FOLLOW-UP

Late Sunday P.M.	—Choir Guild men remove all posters, bulletin board notices, hall and room signs, pew labels; store in Youth Choirs office.
Monday or Tuesday	— (Optional) Glossy print (or press-type camera's undeveloped film in film-holder) to newspaper with caption only; group of two or three choristers about Festival area; no news story. (State facts only.)
Within a Week or two after Festival	—Choir Guild chairman writes courtesy note to ushers and technician.
	Director sends dittoed *Letter #3* to directors thanking them and their choirs for participating; share anything noteworthy that has come to you pertaining to Festival's success; tell amount of offering, amount realized above expenses (nursery, custodial help, programs, guest conductor's honorarium, etc.).
	Mail check to designated organization.
	Director writes courtesy note to guest conductor, organist, ministers.

Keep a carbon copy of everything.

Check against this procedure book, month by month.

To determine number of choirs needed for a satisfactory Festival:

Glendale Presbyterian Church seats 1360 including choir loft.

Choristers are seated in loft and entire main floor except under balcony.

Fifteen singing choirs, one Handbell Choir: total enrollment—550 (from nine churches of Pasadena, Eagle Rock and Glendale; 10 directors).

Choristers actually attending—460.

Estimated attendance, choristers and congregation—1330 (in 1960).

248

1959 Theme—Bicentennial of Death of Handel (observed in combined
anthems and hymns)
1960 Theme—Reformation Hymns (congregational hymns)
1961 Theme—The Life of Jesus Christ (theme observed by individual
and massed choirs and in hymns)
Scritpure Reading before each category (Praise, Advent, Christmas, His
Life and Ministry, Lent, Palm Sunday, etc.) by ministers from participating churches. Two choirs under same director sing together to conserve time.)
Repertory: More easily chosen if there is a theme.

(Sample Correspondence)   FORM LETTER #1
          Glendale Presbyterian Church (Host Church)
              219 E. Harvard St., Glendale 5, California
                              September 28, 1960
Dear ....:
    The fourth annual JUNIOR CHOIR FESTIVAL will be held on
Sunday, March 5, 1961, at 3:30 P.M. in the Glendale Presbyterian Church.
We would like you to bring two of your Junior Choirs to sing (grades
3 to 6, or to voice change).
    Muriel Alford will be guest conductor. She needs no introduction to
those directors who have attended our Festivals, but for you new
people: Muriel is Director of Children's Work, including five choirs, at
the First Methodist Church of Glendale. A graduate of Westminster
Choir School, she writes the "Music for Juniors" in the Methodist *Music
Ministry,* and also directs the choir of the "Faith of Our Children" TV
program. Her boy and girl choirs and Wesley Bell Ringers have made a
real contribution to our past Festivals.
    The Theme of this year's Festival is "The Life of Christ." Mrs.
Alford will lead the massed choirs in singing two numbers:
INTROIT: "Vesper Hymn," Bortniansky-Stevenson, p. 26, *Book of
    Handbell Music, Set 1,* Watson, with handbell and pipe organ
    accompaniment (H. W. Gray). We will use words on enclosed
    sheet. Tune: Vesper Hymn (sing unison) found in *The Methodist
    Hymnal,* No. 45; Presbyterian, *The Hymnbook,* No. 67; *Rejoice and
    Sing* songbook, No. 6; *The Chorister's Hymnal,* No. 62 (Chorister's
    Guild). Tempo: slowly and smoothly.
CONCLUDING ANTHEM: "Let All the World in Every Corner Sing"
    by Claude Means, p. 7 in *Anthems for the Junior Choir, Book 4*
    (Westminster Press.) (Omit voice II which will be sung by the
    choirs in the choir loft.)

                                                    249

The Festival will be a Service of Worship complete with Scripture read by ministers from participating churches; congregation and choirs singing the *Doxology* (tune: Old 100th, original rhythm).

Each director will present his choirs, singing one anthem. To conserve time it is advisable that two choirs under the same director sing as a combined group. Arrangements should be made with me to rehearse your church's choirs with the Festival organist, Dr. R. Donald Curry, on a weekday afternoon. Rehearsal of massed choirs will be held at 2:00 P.M. the afternoon of the Festival.

The offering, above expenses, will go to the Choristers Guild.

Mimeographed instructions complete with sketches will be mailed in February.

Please return enclosed card promptly; don't let choice of anthem hold it up, but let us know as soon as possible, because we want to cover the theme, which of course parallels the Christian Year.

Telephone Numbers:	Sincerely,
Residence................	/s/ LOUISE B. WHITMAN
Church................	*Director of Youth Choirs*

FORM LETTER #2
(Mailed early in February)

JUNIOR CHOIR FESTIVAL—Sunday, March 5, 1961—3:30 to 4:30 P.M.

GLENDALE PRESBYTERIAN CHURCH, 219 E. Harvard St., Glendale 5, California

Fourteen singing choirs; one Handbell Choir; MURIEL ALFORD, *Guest Conductor*

Church Nursery will be open.

Please invite your church families to attend, through your Church Bulletin.

WEEKDAY REHEARSAL IN SANCTUARY:

Your Choirs: ..................P.M. sharp, to ..................P.M.
Dr. Donald Curry, Organist. Enter sanctuary; be seated as directed by Choir Guild hostess. After rehearsal on risers or platform, choirs will be guided to robing room assigned your church for Sunday.

SUNDAY, March 5th:

MASSED REHEARSAL: At 2:00 P.M. *all choirs* assemble (not vested) in labeled pews. Choristers sing combined numbers standing at the pews with conductor in rear balcony. At 2:45 P.M. dismissal to rest rooms and robing rooms. Your choirs go to room #.............. on ....floor.

PERFORMANCE:

PROCESSIONAL: Starts at 3:20 P.M. Marshal leads director and choir *single file* into hall, through narthex and sanctuary aisle to assigned pews; remain standing until seated by the conductor.
Your choirs will sit in _____ section to the _____ of aisle as you enter.

SINGING: *Individual choirs* and directors. A choir seated in RIGHT section will go to front via RIGHT aisle; stand on platform and/or risers; sing; return same route to same pews. *While they are returning,* a choir seated in LEFT section will go to front via LEFT aisle, wait for minister to read Scripture; sing; return same LEFT aisle, while another choir at RIGHT goes front, etc. *Massed Choirs:* Choristers stand at pews and face director in balcony.

RECESSIONAL: As directed by marshal moving several choirs at once through all exits from sanctuary.

PARKING: City parking lot on Harvard Street, west of church.

REST ROOMS: Follow the signs, or ask any Choir Guild member wearing green badges.

REFRESHMENTS: Please do not serve after combined rehearsal. Reason: Time.

PROGRAMS: For *adults only* during *performance.* Available in narthex *after* Festival for choristers.

REMINDER: These are to be memorized by each choir:
Introit: "Vesper Hymn," Bortniansky-Stevenson (word-sheet available).
Congregational Offertory Hymn: The Doxology, (Old 100th, original rhythm).
Concluding Anthem: "Let All the World in Every Corner Sing," Means, in *Anthems for the Junior Choir, Book 4* (Westminster Press), p. 7, Voice I only; Pasadena Presbyterian choirs in loft sing Voice II.

Sincerely,
/s/ Louise B. Whitman,
Director of Youth Choirs

Telephone Nos. _____

PLAN ON A FESTIVAL THEME

Many communities contemplating a Children's Choir Festival for the first time are faced with the problem of finding music that will not tax the inexperienced choir, but create a coordinated service built on a theme meaningful to both congregation and choirs. The following may be of value as a possible pattern for such a Festival Service. (R.K.J.)

A Choral Meditation on the Life of Christ

Organ Prelude
Processional Music (organ only, no singing)
Call to Worship
Hymn: Fairest Lord Jesus (choirs and congregation)

PROPHECY

Minister: O thou that tellest good tidings to Zion, get thee up into the high mountains; O thou that tellest good tidings to Jerusalem, lift up thy voice with strength, lift it up, be not afraid. Say unto the cities of Judah, Behold your God. For unto us a child is born, unto us a son is given, and the government shall be upon his shoulders, and his name shall be called Wonderful, Counsellor, the Mighty God, the Everlasting Father, the Prince of Peace.

Choirs: O come, O come, Emmanuel; *or*: Come thou long expected Jesus (Tune: Hyfrydol)

NATIVITY

Minister: Luke 2: 8-11, 13-14.
Choirs: What child is this (hymn)
The snow lay on the ground—Sowerby (Gray, 2238)
A Carroll—Jacobson (Birchard, 965—omit SSA section)
As with gladness men of old (choirs and congregation)

MINISTRY

Minister: Matthew 4: 23-24; Luke 18: 15-16; John 21: 25.
Choirs: O Master of the loving heart (No. 83, *Hymns for Junior Worship,* Westminster Press)

Minister: And it came to pass that as He was praying in a certain place, when he ceased, one of the disciples said unto him, Lord teach us to pray, as John also taught his disciples . . . And as He taught his disciples, let him teach our hearts to pray with humility and sincerity:
Our Father, who art in heaven (all)

252

Minister: Mark 11:1-10.
Choirs: Hosanna, Gregor-Bitgood, *Anthems for Junior Choir, Book 1*
(Westminster) All glory, laud, and honor (choirs and congregation)

EASTER
Minister: Luke 16:1-6.
Choirs: Christ the Lord is risen today, Davis (Remick, 10-G 185) and/or
Spring Prayer, Caldwell (Birchard, 2113)
Minister: O Lord and Master of us all, whate'er our name or sign, we
own thy sway, we hear thy call, we test our lives by thine.
Choirs: Prayer of St. Richard of Chichester, White (Oxford Press, E 43)
Hymn: All hail the power of Jesus' Name (Tune: Coronation); descant
and trumpet fanfare in *Youth Hymnary*, p. 42 (Faith & Life Press,
Newton, Kansas)
Benediction

CHOIR FESTIVAL LITANY

The 17th Annual Choir Festival of the First Presbyterian Church
of Hollywood, California, was remarkably coordinated. I was impressed
and inspired. Under the direction of Dr. Charles Hurt and his wife
Lucy the 391 members of the seven choirs were maneuvered from
balcony to choir loft for their individual numbers, and back again without the slightest confusion. The movement of choirs was so orderly and
quiet that one's attention was never distracted from the service. The
choir loft is large enough for one choir, even though only one choir
has less than 50 members. Half the large gallery that runs around the
church on three sides was used to accommodate the choirs. With
scarcely a sound or any wasted time each choir sang its individual
number from the choir loft and returned to its balcony seats for the
massed numbers.

A fitting ceremony, just before the closing hymn, was the dedication
of the new officers of the choirs.

The service opened with this *Call to Worship*:
Minister: I was glad when they said unto me,
"Let us go into the house of the Lord."
People: Enter into his gates with thanksgiving,
And into his courts with praise.

This was followed by the *Doxology*, the *Creed*, a *Prayer Anthem* by
the Carol Choir (grades 3-5), an *Anthem* by the combined choirs,
Scripture Reading, and this special *Litany*.

253

Litany for the End of the Church Year

Minister: For all gifts from our heavenly Father who in diverse ways manifests his love and reveals new beauty unto us:

People: We give thee thanks, O God.

Minister: For the songs of the Church handed down through the centuries from parent to child, kindling anew the fires of devotion in the hearts of each generation:

People: We give thee thanks, O God.

Minister: For self-expression in music, for the quietness and poise which music gives us in a hurried, restless existence, for speech and song capable of expressing our innermost feelings:

People: We give thee thanks, O God.

Minister: For the finer searchings of the human spirit which lure us on to each new-found beauty, for assurance that as we stand quietly before God, he will reveal himself to us in new ways:

People: We give thee thanks, O God.

Minister: For the inspiration of lives consecrated to thee, for hours spent in achieving excellence of expression, for the great historical tradition of sacred music, for the love of God revealed in the beauty of song, for leaders consecrated to Christian tasks, for a Church which harbors and nurtures the upward searching of the spirit, for the simple directness and ineffable beauty of our Lord Jesus Christ: we give thee praise in the Master's Name. Amen.

* * *

Each of the 391 choir members was listed, with a star for the Honor Roll, an asterisk for perfect attendance, bold-face type for those graduating to another choir, and numerals for the years of service.

(R.K.J.)

A FESTIVAL SERVICE OF HYMNS

(All hymns as found in *The Chorister's Little Hymnal*)

ORGAN PARAPHRASE ON AN APPROPRIATE HYMN

PROCESSION OF CHOIRS

CHORAL INTROIT: "God himself is with us" (p. 56—preceded by chimes until church is completely quiet)

CALL TO WORSHIP: Minister

"O sing unto the Lord a new song," etc. (Psalm 96:1-9)

254

HYMN: "All things praise thee" (p. 38—Choirs)

HYMN: "Praise the Lord" (p. 10—Choirs, congregation, and trumpet)

CALL TO PRAYER: Minister

LORD'S PRAYER: (Hymn, p. 57—Choirs)

PASTORAL PRAYER: Minister

"O God, the giver of every good and perfect gift, we thank thee for the beautiful gift of music. The song of the birds, the murmuring brook, the deep cadences of the sea, the silence of the stars, the sighing of the gentle breezes, the roar of the storms, the cooing of the happy baby, the songs of rejoicing throughout thy world—all speak to us of thee. Through music may heavy hearts be comforted, burdens lightened, joys become greater, and ideals more noble. May all of life become richer through music. Help us to use this gift to sweeten the lives of others, and to bring the sunshine of thy love into every corner of our own lives. We ask it in the name of Him, whose life was a psalm of victory and of love. Amen.

—From *Youth Hymnal* (Hall-Mack Co.)

SPEECH CHOIR: "Come, thou long expected Jesus" (p. 24)

HYMN: "O come, O come Emmanuel" (p. 23—Choir)

ORGAN RESPONSE: "Silent Night"

SPEECH CHOIR: "And there came wise men from the East," etc.

HYMN: "As with gladness" (p. 25—Choir)

MINISTER: "Behold the Lamb of God . . . He was despised . . . Surely, . . . All we like sheep . . . Worthy is the Lamb . . . Blessing and honor . . . forever and ever. Amen."

ORGAN RESPONSE: Last adagio phrase of Chorus No. 26 from Handel's "Messiah"

HYMNS: "Fairest Lord Jesus" (p. 22—Choir)
"Hosanna, loud hosanna" (p. 28—Choir)
"O sacred Head" (p. 30—Choir)
"O sons and daughters" (p. 34—Choir)
(These four hymns all linked with short organ interludes)

HYMN: "All hail the power of Jesus' Name" (p. 33—Choir, congregation, and trumpet)

OFFERTORY ANNOUNCEMENT and PRAYER

SHORT ADDRESS

HYMN: "Praise to the Lord" (p. 2—Choir, congregation, and trumpet)

BENEDICTION

RECESSIONAL

(R.K.J.)

255

THE APOSTLES' CREED IN HYMNS

(All hymns as found in *The Choristers' Little Hymnal*)

MINISTER: I believe in God the Father Almighty:

Hymn 2—"Praise to the Lord"

MINISTER: I believe in God the Father Almighty, *Maker of heaven and earth*:

Hymn 15—"This is my Father's world"

(or) 38—"All things praise thee"

MINISTER: I believe in God the Father Almighty, *And in Jesus Christ, his only Son our Lord*:

Hymn 22—"Fairest Lord Jesus"

(or) 46—"Jesu, joy of man's desiring"

MINISTER: I believe in Jesus Christ our Lord, *Who was conceived by the Holy Spirit, Born of the Virgin Mary*:

Hymn—"Silent night" (played quietly on the organ)

(or)—"O little town of Bethlehem" (Organ)

MINISTER: *Suffered under Pontius Pilate*:

Hymn 30—"O sacred Head now wounded"

MINISTER: Suffered under Pontius Pilate, *Was crucified*:

Hymn 53—"Christ, we do all adore thee"

MINISTER: Suffered under Pontius Pilate, Was crucified, *dead, and buried*:

Hymn—"There is a green hill far away" (Organ)

MINISTER: *The third day, he rose again from the dead*:

Hymn 34—"O sons and daughters"

(or) 31—"Jesus Christ is risen today"

MINISTER: *He ascended into heaven, and sitteth on the right hand of God the Father Almighty*:

Hymn 32—"Jesus shall reign where'er the sun"

MINISTER: *From thence he shall come to judge the quick and the dead*:

Hymn 39—"Let all mortal flesh keep silence"

(or)—"Upon the Day of Judgment" (Organ)

MINISTER: *I believe in the Holy Spirit*:

Hymn—"Come Holy Ghost, our souls inspire" (Organ)

MINISTER: *I believe in the Holy catholic Church*:

Hymn 40—"The Church's one foundation"

MINISTER: *I believe in the Communion of Saints*:

Hymn 43—"For all the saints who from their labors rest"

MINISTER: *I believe in the Forgiveness of sins*:

Hymn 18—"Grant us true courage, Lord"

256

MINISTER: I believe in God the Father Almighty, etc. . . . *the Resurrection of the body and the Life everlasting. Amen.*
Hymn 33—"All Hail the power of Jesus' Name"

* * *

In The Apostles' Creed Service the minister should remain in the pulpit throughout and read with a clear, unhurried, convincing voice. Before the final hymn he will read the whole of the Apostles' Creed. It should be indicated in the program when the congregation is to stand or sit, so that no announcement or gesture need break the continuity of the service.

The effectiveness of this festival service depends much on good timing: the way in which the minister relates his readings to the service portions following them, the way in which the organist leads into the hymns, the alertness of the choir, the smoothness of their standing or sitting together. It is attention to details that makes a successful service.

(R.K.J.)

A CHILDREN'S SERVICE FOR GOOD FRIDAY

"Has the Children's Work Committee of the United Churches ever considered having services for children on Good Friday?" a friend asked me about eight years ago.

I replied that as far as I knew, the matter had never been considered, possibly because most of the experiences of Good Friday are beyond the understanding of young children.

"I realize that," she said, "but I am concerned about our Protestant children. The public schools are closed on Thursday and Friday before Easter as well as the following week. The Roman Catholic children, whether or not they understand what's going on, are in their churches. But for our boys and girls, this is just another holiday."

These remarks posed a challenge which we debated at the next meeting of the Children's Work Committee. The criticism certainly was true, but we wondered if we could do anything that would be meaningful for children. Confining our efforts to children between the ages of 8 and 12, we tried to think of Holy Week as they see it.

So starts an article "A Children's Service for Good Friday" by Helene M. Suiter, who is Associate Secretary and Director of Children's Work, United Churches of Lackawanna County, Scranton, Pennsylvania, in the January 1961 issue of the *International Journal of Religious*

Education. Get a copy and start something in your community which will have a long-range effect. A copy may be secured by writing the *Journal,* 475 Riverside Drive, New York 27, N.Y. Single copies @ 75c.

(R.K.J.)

WE WOULD SEE JESUS
An Easter Hymn Festival
(Presented by five choirs of Dallas, Texas, in 1958)

This is a service of hymns and readings from the Scriptures. It is a simple service, and may be a pattern for use by any church, small or large. Done with finish, style, and a sense of the dramatic, it would be most effective. Possibly a hymn or two by choirs and the congregation should be added. Explanatory notes on the program were taken from *Lyric Religion* by H. Augustine Smith (Fleming H. Revell Co.), from *Canyon Hymnal for Boys and Girls* (Canyon Press, Inc.) and from *Our Hymnody* by Robert G. McCutcheon (Abingdon Press). The Scripture passages and the poem were presented as choral speaking by various choirs, or by individuals. Different choirs or groups of choirs sang the various hymns. The service included an Organ Prelude, Invocation, Prayers, Offering, and Benediction. The processional hymn was "All Hail the Power" (Coronation). The program outline was suggested by the hymn "We Would See Jesus" (Cushman). Based on the life of Christ, each stanza tells of a different period: His Infancy, His Childhood, His Teaching Ministry, His Healing Ministry, His Resurrection and Presence in our lives.

HIS INFANCY
SCRIPTURE: Luke 2: 8-16.
HYMN: "There's a song in the air" _____Christmas Song
CHORALE: "Ah, Dearest Jesus, Holy Child" _____J. S. Bach

HIS CHILDHOOD
SCRIPTURE: Luke 2: 40-51 and Luke 2: 52.
HYMN: "O sing a song of Bethlehem" _____Kingsfold
HYMN: "O Master Workman of the race" _____Petersham

HIS TEACHING MINISTRY
SCRIPTURE: Matthew 5: 1-12.
HYMN: "Saviour, teach me day by day" _____Innocents
HYMN: "Fairest Lord Jesus" _____Crusader's Hymn

258

His Healing Ministry

SCRIPTURE: John 9:1-38.

HYMN: "Immortal love, forever full" _____Serenity

HYMN: "My Jesus, as thou wilt" _____Jewett

His Triumphant Entry

SCRIPTURE: Psalm 24:7-10.

HYMN: "All glory, laud and honor" _____St. Theodulph

His Crucifixion

SCRIPTURE: Matthew 27:32-54.

HYMN: "There is a green hill far away" _____Meditation

HYMN: "O sacred Head, now wounded" _____Passion Chorale

His Resurrection

SCRIPTURE: John 20:1-18.

POEM: "An Easter Reveille" _____Slater

HYMN: "Jesus Christ is risen today" _____Easter Hymn

RECESSIONAL HYMN: "Thine is the glory" _____Handel

THE BLESSING OF THE ANIMALS

A charming and ancient church custom, revived a few years ago at Holy Trinity Church, Hereford, England, has now been adopted as a traditional service by Salisbury Cathedral and by other churches in England and in this country. The Blessing of the Animals service commemorating the life and works of St. Francis of Assisi is usually held on the patronal day dedicated to St. Francis, October 4 (which is also World Day for Animals) or on the Sunday nearest this date. Such services are testaments to St. Francis' words that "whole aeons of love will be needed to compensate the animals for their services to us."

Parishioners, mostly children, bring in their cherished pets including horses, ponies, dogs, cats, rabbits, parakeets, hamsters, and even goldfish and turtles, for recognition and blessing. The service is usually held in the church yard or garden, although at Salisbury the service is now held within the cathedral, and all the animals (except horses) are invited in with their owners!

This can be made a beautiful and impressive service. The animals seem to understand the solemnity of the occasion and are invariably on their best behavior during the outdoor sermon. Perhaps some one has thoughtfully invited representatives of the local Society for the Prevention of Cruelty to Animals, the poundmaster, the veterinarian, and other friends of animals to attend. A brief service with children's

259

choirs, handbell ringers and other instrumentalists might be planned as follows:

PROCESSIONAL

INVOCATION

HYMN: All creatures of our God and King (St. Francis' Hymn)

SCRIPTURE

PRAYERS for Animal Welfare

HYMN: All things bright and beautiful (Royal Oak)

SERMON: "Blessed Are the Merciful"

THE BLESSING OF THE ANIMALS

HYMN: All things that live below the sky (see below)

BENEDICTION: "Bless, O God, we pray thee, our friends the animals, and help us to love them for the sake of him who was born in a stable, thy Son, Jesus Christ our Lord. Amen."

* The Society for United Prayer for the Prevention of Cruelty to Animals, of Great Britain, publishes *A Collection of Prayers for Animal Welfare* which includes a selection of hymns. The following hymn by Edward John Brailsford is sung to the tune "Rodmell" which is unfamiliar to most Americans. Any well-known Common Meter (8,6,8,6) tunes such as "St. Anne" or "St. Peter" could easily be used in its place. (N.P.T.)

1. All things that live below the
    sky,
    Or move within the sea,
    Are creatures of the Lord most
    High,
    And brothers unto me.

2. I love to hear the robin sing,
    Perched on the highest
    bough;
    To see the rook with purple
    wing
    Follow the shining plough.

3. Beneath His heaven there's
    room for all;
    He gives to all their meat;
    He sees the meanest sparrow
    fall
    Unnoticed in the street.

4. Almighty Father, King of kings,
    The Lover of the meek,
    Make me a friend of helpless
    things,
    Defender of the weak. Amen.

FESTIVAL OF THE MASKS

A number of churches have become more actively concerned about the celebration of Halloween.

In an Episcopal church where I served for four years Evensong was always held on All Hallow's Eve, followed by a gay costume party

260

in the Parish Hall. It was a family occasion. The children were encouraged to attend the service dressed in their costumes and masks. In fact, at one point in the service they processed, costumes and all, behind the crucifer and choir around the church. The Junior and Youth Choirs sang, and many a pajama, pantaloon, and boot peeped from under robes.

This was a service that seemed to speak to the children. They were impressed with the Rector's explanation (interpretation) of All Hallow's Eve, pleased with their part in the service, and of course delighted with the later secular festivities. Hymn-singing, led by the Children's Choirs, was particularly hearty. Such hymns as "I sing a song of the saints of God," "For all the saints who from their labors rest," "Ten thousand times ten thousand," "The Son of God goes forth to war," are especially meaningful at this time.

The Rev. William Baxter, Rector of St. Mark's Episcopal Church of Washington, D.C., has arranged a "Festival of the Masks" that has been used effectively at nearby St. Christopher's, Lanham, Maryland, for several seasons. I believe that a similar Service, planned with musical participation by the Children's Choirs, as above, might be even more effective.

At St. Christopher's the men, women, and children wearing homemade masks walked in a long line behind a crucifer up the main aisle to the altar rail where the masks were taken off and laid on the altar step. The processional hymn was "Christian, dost thou see them on the holy ground?" Each mask laid before the altar represented the besetting sin of the person wearing the mask. Following the Processional, the Rector read appropriate selections from the Litany and gave an address. He picked up each mask, identified the demon it represented and pointed out that "All of us have things in our lives which make us feel ugly, afraid, or driven. The saints themselves, whose day is to follow, also knew the meaning of fear, failure, and the assaults of demons. They brought their lives just as they were to the altar of God, offering themselves to him and finding strength and courage."

After this interpretation the congregation joined in the Collect for Purity: "Almighty God, unto whom all hearts are open," and the service closed with the singing of "I sing a song of the saints of God."

From a noisome and destructive Halloween GOOD LORD DELIVER US!

NANCY POORE TUFTS

261

A SPECIAL REFORMATION SERIES

The downtown church which is confined to only one regularly scheduled meeting of its total congregation (i.e., Sunday morning worship) presents an educational problem for the Minister of Music. Church membership in this type of parish tends to be dominated by older people, a generation which grew up on the gospel hymn and the pseudo-grand-opera anthem. This is not to say that these members do not understand that the church needs to bring about the practice of higher standards of service music. However, opportunities to introduce and familiarize the congregation with such music are difficult to arrange. The morning service of worship certainly cannot become a music school. The children and young people are contacted through the graded choir program and the Christian Education Department, but this in our church involves only 325 families out of 1600 homes included on the church roll. I have attempted from time to time to work some sacred-music education into the morning service without disrupting the worship elements.

Our latest attempt was last fall, when for five Sundays we presented music representing various developments of the Protestant Reformation. This series began on Reformation Sunday in October and continued through November. In this period the following anthems were presented by the Adult Choir: "The Lamb That Was Slain" (Cantata 21), J. S. Bach; "Praise to the Lord" arranged by Shaw; "Turn Back, O Man" (Old 124th) by Holst; and two selections from the Moravian Series as edited by Dickinson: "Thou Hast Given Us Bread from Heaven" by Geisler; and "Praise, Thanksgiving, Glory and Honor" by Bechler. These latter two selections were accompanied by a ten-piece ensemble. The High School Choir presented "Jesu, Joy of Man's Desiring" by J. S. Bach and "Lord, We Cry to Thee," Zwingli-Dickinson. The Junior High Girls presented an arrangement by Krone of "Now Thank We All Our God." The Junior Girls sang "O Saviour Sweet," Bach-Dickinson; the Junior Boys "A Mighty Fortress" by Luther; and the Bell Choir played "O Sacred Head" arranged by Tufts. Congregational hymns included "Praise to the Lord," "Fairest Lord Jesus," and "Away in a Manger."

Each Sunday an article was included in the church bulletin dealing with the phase of Protestant music being illustrated in the service, and the same article was printed in the church paper. Since the November services were televised, this made the information available to those who watched and listened at home. I received calls from several shut-ins expressing their appreciation of this. Included in these articles were topics such as: J. S. Bach and his influence, Martin Luther and his views on music, the Metric Psalters, the German Chorale and Pre-Reformation sources (especially the Moravian Brethren) with specific information on each particular selection. Organ music during this series included four selections by J. S. Bach and two by Buxtehude to illustrate the German organ school, and arrangements of a number of chorales by various composers. There were those in the congregation who complained of this "forced feeding" but most comments were very favorable, indicating that understanding increased appreciation and acceptance of good music. Certainly this series was good for the Minister of Music who had to choose the music and do the research for the articles!

DAVID V. WILLIAMS, *Minister of Music*
First Christian Church
Tulsa, Oklahoma

THE CELEBRATION OF THANKSGIVING

Children are peculiarly responsive and sensitive to celebrations. The Thanksgiving Day festival is a heaven-sent opportunity for children's choir directors to help boys and girls learn gratitude and appreciation, thankfulness and sharing. Next to parents the church school teacher and the children's choir director bear perhaps the greatest responsibility in the teaching of sound and right attitudes. It has been well said in many different ways that Christian character and attitudes are not so much taught as caught by children. The choir director wields a powerful tool—music—in working with boys and girls. Therefore you, the director, should make the fullest use of Thanksgiving—this on-a-platter opportunity.

Too often we think of Thanksgiving as an American festival only. Our celebration, however, has Biblical background. Once a year in the autumn the Hebrews celebrated the "Feast of Booths," when they gave thanks to God for a bountiful harvest as they harvested and stored for the winter their fruits and grains.

Other Bible Thanksgiving festivals occurred when the ancient Israelites celebrated great events in their history. Bible scholars say that Deborah's song after the victory over Sisera, one of the oldest passages in the Bible, is an ode of glorious thanksgiving. (Judges 5)

When the Hebrews had crossed the Red Sea safely, they held a joyous festival, during which Miriam, Moses' sister, gathered the women together who sang and danced with timbrels. (Exodus 15)

In 2 Samuel 6 is recorded the Thanksgiving that celebrated the return of the Ark of the Covenant by David. And again, after the

263

dedication of Solomon's Temple (1 Kings 8) the people celebrated for two weeks, during which time they praised and thanked God. Another festival was held when the Temple was rebuilt in the time of Ezra. (Ezra 3)

The entire Bible, both the Old and the New Testament, is filled with words of gratitude. The people made thanksgiving a part of ordinary everyday life. Jewish people not only gave thanks before meals, but had special prayers for filling a cup, lighting a lamp, or entering a door.

The background of our own American Thanksgiving must be re-emphasized. Many youngsters have only a hazy notion of what it is all about. A big feast is naturally uppermost in their minds. The ease of present-day life means nothing to them until contrasts are made vivid to them. Make them proud of their heritage, for we are in danger of losing its sense and meaning.

THANKSGIVING FESTIVAL OF THE SINGING CHURCH

(CECIL LAPO, Minister of Music, St. Luke's Methodist Church, Oklahoma City, Oklahoma, has developed this annual Festival Service)

PART I
Choir Dedication Ceremony
Combined Choirs sing "Prayer for the Ministry of Music" by Cecil Lapo (R. D. Row Co.)

PART II
Psalm 100 in Music
MAKE A JOYFUL NOISE UNTO THE LORD, ALL YE LANDS
"O God, Our Help in Ages Past" (St. Anne) _____arr. Lapo
(Chapel Handbell Choir)
"Let All the People Praise Thee" _____Martin Shaw
(Sanctuary and Vesper Choirs)   (Oxford Press)

SERVE THE LORD WITH GLADNESS,
COME BEFORE HIS PRESENCE WITH SINGING
"Come, Together Let Us Sing" _____J. S. Bach
(E. C. Schirmer)
(Chapel, Carol, Bethlehem and Carillon Choirs)

KNOW YE THAT THE LORD, HE IS GOD
"King of Kings" _____Clokey
(Sanctuary and Vesper Choirs) (Summy-Birchard)

264

IT IS HE THAT HATH MADE US AND NOT WE OURSELVES
"Jesus Whom Thy Children Love" _____H. Elliott Button
(Bethlehem and Carillon Choirs)   (H. W. Gray)

WE ARE HIS PEOPLE AND THE SHEEP OF HIS PASTURE
"Jubilate Deo" _____Richard Purvis
(Chapel and Carol Choirs)   (Leeds Music, L143)

ENTER INTO HIS GATES WITH THANKSGIVING,
AND INTO HIS COURTS WITH PRAISE
"Rejoice, Ye Pure in Heart" _____Healey Willan
(H. W. Gray)
(Sanctuary, Vesper, Chapel and Carol Choirs)

BE THANKFUL UNTO HIM AND BLESS HIS NAME
THE PRESENTATION OF TITHES AND OFFERINGS
"Now Thank We All Our God" _____J. S. Bach
(Vesper Handbell Choir)

OFFERING RESPONSE BY CHOIRS AND CONGREGATION:
HYMN: "Now Thank We All Our God" (1st stanza)

FOR THE LORD IS GRACIOUS: HIS MERCY IS EVERLASTING
"The Christmas Bells" _____Junior Choir Anthems, Book 4
(The Mother-Ringers)   (Westminster Press)

AND HIS TRUTH ENDURETH TO ALL GENERATIONS
J. S. Bach _____   "O Savior Sweet"
(Combined Choirs)   (H. W. Gray)

ADDRESS BY THE MINISTER

HYMN: "Come, Ye Thankful People, Come" (St. George's, Windsor)

BENEDICTION

The Christmas Season

PEOPLE LOOK EAST—THE TIME IS NEAR!

Dear Friends:

This is the month when more than any other time I should like to be able to walk into your church and worship with you at one of your Christmas services.

I hope that you have planned well, so that no extra rehearsals are necessary, and no one feels harassed and resentful at the pressure of the season. *It really can be done.* That current diplomatic phrase "too little and too late" with one word changed would describe a fault common to Christmas music planning—*too much and too late.* Music that does not tax the ability of the choir makes for a much more enjoyable experience for all concerned; enjoyment should never be made a sacrifice to ambition.

Here is some timely advice on those Christmas programs:

1. Christmas is not the time to educate people musically.
2. Give them a liberal portion of familiar carols.
3. And a liberal share in participation.
4. And keep it to an hour, no longer.
5. Simplicity is the keynote.
6. And careful attention to details.
7. If the choir carries candles, then make sure that the house lights are turned off.
8. Go through every detail of the service mentally beforehand, and arrange carefully with all persons concerned.
9. Heed this advice and you will have less work.
10. And everybody will have more fun.

RUTH KREHBIEL JACOBS

267

KEEPING CHRISTMAS

Dear Guilders:

Henry Van Dyke, one of our country's truly great and inspired men of letters, wrote many years ago: "There is a better thing than the observance of Christmas Day, and that is, keeping Christmas. . . . Are you willing to forget what you have done for other people, and to remember what other people have done for you; to ignore what the world owes you, and to think what you owe the world? . . . Are you willing to stoop down and consider the needs and desires of little children? Are you willing to believe that love is the strongest thing in the world—stronger than hate, stronger than evil, stronger than death—and that the blessed life which began in Bethlehem nineteen hundred years ago is the image and brightness of the Eternal Love? Then you can keep Christmas. And if you can keep it for a day, why not always? But you can never keep it alone."

Certainly, as Children's Choir directors, you cannot keep Christmas alone! You can enjoy Christmas as can few others. The entire following section brings you suggestions, ideas, program and service plans and music selections to assist you in your Advent and Christmas plans. In recent years in our non-liturgical churches Advent has come into its own. Certainly much music labeled "Christmas" may and should be sung during Advent, which begins four Sundays before Christmas. This joyous season of anticipation of and preparation for the birth of our Lord can, by use of music, make Christmas more than a quickly passing "big" event. Help your boys and girls to grow into Christmas through the Advent season with the help of music.

So away to your joyful task—and always remember that you above all other people, not even parents excepted, enjoy greater privileges and opportunities to celebrate Christmas gloriously. And further, few people command such an unparalleled opportunity to teach sharing and unselfishness to boys and girls as does the Children's Choir director.

May your endeavors be richly rewarded!

ARTHUR LESLIE JACOBS

KEEPING THE CHRIST IN CHRISTMAS

A growing custom, and one of the loveliest, is the making of an Advent Wreath. Advent always begins four Sundays before Christmas. The following is taken from the bulletin of the First Lutheran Church, Glendale, California, where one of our original Guild members, ALICE HEWLETT, directs the Children's Choirs.

268

The Advent Wreath

Many symbols are associated with the Advent season preceding Christmas. One that seems especially appropriate, and less secular than most others, is the Advent Wreath. Used in Europe for many years, it is rapidly gaining popularity in North America in both Christian homes and churches.

The Advent Wreath is a circle of greens held together by a metal band which also provides support for candles. The wreath may rest upon a stand in the church chancel or be suspended from the ceiling by ribbon-covered wires. Usually four candles are provided for the church wreath. On the first Sunday in Advent one candle burns during the worship service. Two candles are lighted for the service on the second Sunday; three for the third; and all four for the final Sunday in Advent.

In the home the wreath may hang over the dining table, or rest upon a table or mantel. Sometimes there are candles for each day in Advent. One candle is lighted for the family devotions on the first day in Advent, an additional candle being lighted each day thereafter. Thus on Christmas Eve all the candles would be burning during the devotional period. Some families use just four candles, lighting only one for each daily worship period during the first week; two candles for the second week, and so on throughout the whole Advent season.

Advent means "coming," and the church-year season bearing that name is a time of preparation for the coming of Christ. It recalls the coming of Christ to Bethlehem as a baby; his coming into our hearts; and his coming at the end of the world. Our meditation on these comings should deepen our love for Christ and prepare our hearts to receive him. The Advent Wreath may help us to do this. The circle of greens symbolizes the earth and the need of everyone for Christ. The ribbons may be of purple, the color of royalty, and thus remind us that Christ is our King. The lighted candles remind us that Christ is the light of the world whose coming dispels the darkness of sin.

To be sure that the meaning of the wreath is understood Bible verses should always be read when it is being used. A good plan is to read Old Testament prophecies of Christ's coming together with the New Testament fulfillments of those prophecies.

Much of our modern preparation for Christmas is totally unrelated to the true meaning of the season. The Advent Wreath, properly used, may help us to keep our thoughts centered on Christ, without whom no season has either meaning or value.

* * *

Advent—the arrival of the Saviour. Since man has been yearning

269

for redemption for centuries, the Advent season was already emphasized by the early Christians. Different countries have developed their own customs for this season.

In Germany each of the four Advent Sundays is celebrated by lighting a candle on the *Adventskranz,* a wreath of evergreens and bearing four candles. On the first Sunday in Advent one candle is lighted, and each following Sunday one more, so that all four are burning on the fourth Advent Sunday.

In churches and family circles people gather around the wreath, and sing about the arrival and birth of our Saviour. The brightening candlelight shines into the hearts of people and helps them comprehend the great significance of God's gift of love at Christmas. On Christmas Eve the wreath is a glowing testament to the nearness of the Saviour.

An article in *Good Housekeeping* magazine suggests making the Advent Wreath the center of attention in the home—in the dining room, the children's room, or the hallway. Each Sunday, gather the family together to say a short prayer or read a verse from Scripture, and sing a special Advent hymn. The article also suggests tying purple ribbons around the candles for an added decorative touch, and on Christmas Eve replacing the purple ribbons and candles with red and using the wreath as part of the holiday decorations. Another suggested custom is that of making one of the four candles pink to symbolize the joy of Gaudete Sunday. This third Sunday of Advent (Gaudete means "rejoice") breaks the seriousness of the season with a glimmer of the joy to come.

For further information about Advent customs and wreaths, write the American Lutheran Publicity Bureau, 2112 Broadway, N.Y. City, which offers a 10c leaflet. The Catholic Daughters of America, 10 W. 71st St., N.Y. City, offers a similar pamphlet, together with a small metal frame and candleholder to be used as the basis for a wreath, for $1.25. From the Lutheran Church Supply Stores, 2900 Queen Lane, Philadelphia, Pa. 19129, can be secured a booklet on *The Story of the Advent Wreath* (15c) and also *A Book of Advent* (Beck-Lindberg, $3.25) a thorough treatment of the entire Advent season, its symbols and customs, with daily devotions, hymns and prayers.

"IN THY DARK STREETS SHINETH"

There's a world-wide agreement and conspiracy at Christmas time to turn gloom into gladness, to make the dark places shine. Men do not wait for God's morning to break resplendent far above their heads. No,

270

rather, in the midst of midnight blackness they set their candles alight and kindle welcoming fires on every hearth. From unshuttered windows, and from doors flung wide, yellow light streams out into the darkness. It is when the year is at its coldest and the nights are at their longest that the carolers go out to sing. The beautiful and beloved Christmas stories, too, are all set against a background of long shadows and of night; Mary and Joseph came late and weary to the inn where there was left for them "no room"; the shepherds watched their flocks "by night"; the wise men saw a star—and all men know that the stars pale out with morning. " 'Twas the night before Christmas" that men heard "the herald angels sing."

All this is but our way of confessing—whether in our glad haste of overcrowded days we stop to recall it or no—that we are aware that at this season of the year far away and long ago, God in his goodness gave us in the Babe a light to shine upon our often shadowy ways that we might walk them unafraid. Indeed, a light has shined into our darkness and no man need grope any more!

EDWARD JOHE, *Minister of Music*
First Congregational Church
Columbus, Ohio

A WREATH OF CAROLS

Here is a Christmas Candlelight Carol Service presented in the University Park Methodist Church, Dallas, Texas, the REV. ROBERT SCOGGIN, Minister of Music. Only the musical numbers are listed below, together with the publishers. The listing is given to show a fresh approach to programing a Carol Service.

CAROL OF PROPHECY
"Let All Mortal Flesh Keep Silence" _____Gustav Holst
Chancel Choir   (SATB-Galaxy)

CAROL OF JOY   "A Carol" _____Betty Jacobson
Chapel Girls Choir   (SA-Birchard)

CAROL OF THE ANGELS
"Hark! the Herald Angels Sing" _____Charles Wesley
Congregation and Choirs   (hymn)

271

CAROL OF THE SHEPHERDS
"Whence Come Ye?" _____Clarence Dickinson
(SATB-H. W. Gray)
Chancel and Chapel Girls Choirs

CAROL OF THE KINGS   "Three Kings" _____Healy Willan
Chancel Choir   (SATB-Oxford)

CAROL OF THE QUEST
"Carol of the Questioning Child" _____Richard Kountz
(SATB-G. Schirmer)
Chancel Choir and group of children

OFFERTORY   Handbell Choir playing familiar carols

CAROL OF THE BELLS   "Carol of the Bells" _____Leontovich
Chancel Choir   (SATB-Carl Fischer)

CAROL OF PEACE   "Peace on Earth" _____Austin Lovelace
(unison-Church Choral Services)
Chorister Girl and Wesley Boy Choirs

CAROL OF THE FIRST CHRISTMAS
"O Little Town of Bethlehem" _____Phillips Brooks
Congregation and Choirs   (hymn)

CAROL OF THE MOTHER   "Star Candles" _____Michael Head
Caroler Choir   (SA-Boosey & Hawkes)

CAROL AT THE MANGER   "Away in a Manger" _____Anonymous
Cherub Choir   (in most hymnals)

CAROL OF THE DRUM   "Carol of the Drum" _____K. K. Davis
Chancel Choir   (SATB-Wood)

CAROL OF THE REEDS
"Carol of the Singing Reeds" _____Alfred H. Johnson
(SSA or unison-J. Fischer)
Chorister Girls and Wesley Boy Choirs

CAROL OF THE BEASTS
    "The Friendly Beasts" _____Clarence Dickinson
                  Combined Choirs   (SATB-H. W. Gray)

CAROL OF THE NATIVITY "Silent Night" _____Joseph Mohr
            Congregation and Choirs   (hymn)

THE STORY OF CHRISTMAS IN CAROLS

Lo, How a Rose E'er Blooming—Praetorius (E. C. Schirmer)
    Scripture: Luke 2:1-5
What Strangers Are These?—Purvis (Birchard 1447)
    Scripture: Luke 2:6-7
Song of Adoration—Luvaas (Kjos 2037)
    Scripture: Luke 2:8-12
While by Our Sleeping Flock We Lay—Jungst (E. C. Schirmer 1685)
    Scripture: Luke 2:13-14
Angels O'er the Fields—French (E. C. Schirmer 1653)
    Scripture: Luke 2:15-16
Cradle-Song of the Shepherds—Davison (E. C. Schirmer 1728)
    Scripture: Luke 2:17-18
Let Our Gladness Have No End—Means (Gray)
    Scripture: Luke 2:19
The Jesus-Child My Joy Shall Be—Helder (Schmidt 1618)
    Scripture: Luke 2:20
Go, Tell It on the Mountain—Work (Galaxy 1532)
Offertory
    Scripture: Matthew 2:1-6
Happy Bethlehem—Schindler (Ricordi)
    Scripture: Matthew 2:7-10
Guiding Star Carol—Christianson (Kjos 5146)
    Scripture: Matthew 2:11
All Ye Good People—Kountz (Galaxy 2043)
    Scripture: Matthew 2:12-15
And the Trees Do Moan—Gaul (Ditson 14319)
Closing Response: Grant Us Thy Peace—Bitgood (Gray)
    (Suitable for H. S. Choir)

PHILIP BLACKWOOD, *Choir Director*
First Methodist Church
Gastonia, North Carolina

A PHOTOGRAPHIC INTERPRETATION OF THE NATIVITY

(A Carol Service with Colored Slides)

LESLIE PEART, Minister of Music of the First Baptist Church, Toledo, Ohio, started his work in this church in the late fall of 1959. Because of time and certain conditions, he felt it impossible to develop a full-scale pageant that season. He and Mrs. Peart conceived the idea of making colored slides of various church activities and of boys and girls in costume depicting the Nativity. These slides were used while the story was told by a Reader, by a Speech Choir, and through music sung by Children's Choirs. Here are excerpts from the script.

"Dear Friends:

Merry Christmas! Isn't it wonderful? Carols and candles, and everyone so happy. I wish you could see our church; it is so beautifully prepared for our worship of the Christ-Child.

"We have a special visitor with us this year; his name is Kim; he just came from Korea to live here. Kim has, of course, never been in our church for Christmas, so we took him on a tour to see how we all celebrate the birth of Jesus. The pictures will tell what happened."

Mrs. Peart had worked out the script using the entire church school and doing the entire program in colored slides. The program revolved around the story of a boy visiting the church school for the first time. The younger children are shown busy in their classes. When the boy arrived in the Junior and Senior High departments, they were enacting the Nativity scenes. For these, the youngsters had been posed in costume at various places to create exciting and suitable backgrounds. For instance: Caesar Augustus was photographed on the steps of the Toledo Art Museum, a beautiful Roman setting; the Three Kings were taken beside a picturesque small stream; the Manger Scene was set in a corner of an old barn; the Angels were taken from below while on a hilltop with the sun shining across their heads; the Shepherds were seated around a real fire on a sandy slope; and so on.

The photography was done professionally; help was sought from drama coaches and from costumers. One practical result of this experience: the professional make-up was much too heavy; with the slide process, no make-up whatsoever seemed to produce the best pictures.

"O SING A SONG OF BETHLEHEM"

MRS. LEWIS H. FIGH, First Presbyterian Church, Montgomery, Alabama, in 1958 arranged a fine service entitled "O Sing a Song of Bethlehem." The Adult and Children's Choirs were used in various

274

ways together with a *Speech Chorus*. For the speaking group the following selections were used at the end of the service:

SPEECH CHORUS:

> For Christmas is not just a moment for remembering a little Child;
> It is a movement for following a magnificent Man.

> It is not a holiday when no one works;
> It is a Holy Day when the spiritually unemployed can begin work on this Man's neglected business.

> It is not a day for a shop-keeper's gain, but for the pew-holder's gift.
> And this gift is not to be wrapped in gay ribbons;
> It is to be incarnated once more in a human body:
> The body of a shepherd, good enough to give his life for lost sheep;
> The body of a wise man, wise enough to lose his life in telling someone else what he has discovered in Bethlehem;
> The body of a refugee who sees that we are all homeless and restless until we rest in Him.

SOLO (or Choirs): "O Little Town of Bethlehem" (last stanza—tune, St. Louis)

CHRISTMAS CREED (Congregation and Choirs):
> I believe in Jesus Christ, and in the beauty of the gospel that began in Bethlehem.
> I believe in Him whose spirit glorified a little town; in Him of whose coming only shepherds saw the sign, and for whom the crowded inn could find no room.
> I believe in Him who proclaimed the love of God to be invincible; in Him whose cradle was a mother's arms, whose home in Nazareth had love for its only wealth.
> I believe in Him who looked at men and made them see what his love saw in them; in Him who by his love brought sinners to purity, and lifted human weakness up to meet the strength of God.
> I believe that only by love expressed shall the earth at length be purified.

SPEECH CHORUS: John 3:16 (printed out in Church Bulletin)

HYMN OF AFFIRMATION: "Joy to the World" (tune, Antioch)

CANDLELIGHT CAROL SERVICE

(Outline of a service presented at Broad Street Methodist Church, Kingsport, Tennessee, by JOHN W. MULLEN, Director of Music. Hymns and prayers are not given here; only the musical portions of the service are indicated.)

* * *

I. ANCIENT CHRISTIAN EXPRESSIONS OF "CHRIST'S MASS"

"Let All Mortal Flesh" (primitive Byzantine) St. James Liturgy
(arr. G. Holst; Galaxy Music Co.)

* _ _ _

"Vidimus Stellam" (Gregorian Chant) circa 800 A.D.

* _ _ _

"Angelus ad Virginem" (Sequence) 14th Century (Oxford Carol Book)

* _ _ _

II. THE JOY OF CHRISTMAS AS TOLD BY THE CAROL

"In Dulci Jubilo" (Macaronic Carol) 14th Century (Oxford Carol Book)

* _ _ _

"Wonder Tidings" (Dramatized Carol) 15th Century
(Oxford Carol Book)

"I Sing of a Maiden" (Ballad Carol) 15th Century
(arr. R. T. Gore; Chantry Press)

"Three Old English Carols" (Refrain Carols) Traditional tunes
(arr. Holst; A. P. Schmidt Co.)

"In the Town" (Dialogue Carol) 15th Century (Oxford Carol Book)

III. THE BIRTH OF CHRIST AS TOLD IN FOLK SONG

"How Far Is It to Bethlehem?" (Folk-tune "Stowey")
(Oxford Carol Book)

"I Wonder as I Wander" (Appalachian Carol)
(arr. J. J. Niles; G. Schirmer)

IV. THE NEGRO SPIRITUAL TELLS OF CHRIST'S BIRTH

"Sweet Little Jesus Boy" (Vocal Solo) MacGimsey   (Fischer)
"Go Tell It on the Mountain" _____Arranged

V. A CHRISTMAS CANTATA

"The Song of Christmas" _____Ringwald (Shawnee)

* * *

At the points marked * - - - Mr. Mullen explained what the congregation was about to hear and its place in the history of Christmas music: e.g., the Chant leads to the Sequence which leads to the

276

Macaronic Carol. Following the service the congregation was urged to assemble on the church steps for the Circle Carol Sing.

Mr. Mullen wrote: "We tried to keep it from being musical entertainment. It was a service of worship with a bit of Christian education added.

"I have been educating our people for the past few years on better music (worship), and also that the text is the important element, not the music. You will notice that the program begins with 'high church' (as they call it here) and ends with a Waring cantata (although that is nothing less than good traditional carols put together with narration).

"The program is arranged so as to climax with the cantata. We used the Children's Choirs in the cantata with the Adults. I rehearse the choirs separately except for one final rehearsal. They are so trained that at that final rehearsal the work goes together like clockwork: e.g., in an SATB number I may have a different choir singing each part; at final rehearsal they put it together at first try. This has given all my choirs great fun and challenge.

"PROCESSIONAL OF CHOIRS: One of the Handbell Choirs announces the Processional by coming down the center aisle playing a fanfare from memory. This was beautiful and effective. The singing choirs stop at a given time and sing with the congregation, then proceed.

"VIDIMUS STELLAM was sung as in a Mass. I sang the priest's parts and the men answered. I was pleasantly surprised at the reactions of our people. They are very sensitive to 'high church' (they think); however, they loved the chant, and several told me it set them in a most worshipful mood.

"WONDER TIDINGS: Here I had the Adult Choir play the part of a group of carolers who suddenly spot a Messenger coming along the crooked English street. The Messenger was costumed and carried a lantern. He entered down the center aisle. This bit of drama made a break for those who found the first part of the service beyond their understanding.

"CANTATA: I selected this one because I feel that the spirit of Christmas also calls for music in the lighter festive vein. The congregation seemed happy and touched during the Finale.

"RECESSIONAL: Lights were dimmed as we left with lit candles. The Minister then said: 'And as Tiny Tim once said . . .' and one of the smallest boy choristers had been rehearsed to say from the back of the church, 'God bless us every one.' Immediately following this, a Handbell Choir rang a fanfare from the distance, then the organ burst into a joyous Postlude."

ST. STEPHEN'S DAY FESTIVAL

(December 26)

Last year the Rector of St. Stephen's Episcopal Church invited me to work out a special program to follow a service of Holy Communion in commemoration of the church's patron saint. The Bishop of the diocese had been invited to attend and had accepted. It was the first time there had ever been an attempt in this church to make an occasion of this day, because of its proximity to Christmas Day. I agreed with the Rector that all churches bearing the name of a saint, regardless of the denomination, should do something about it.

As the result of the Rector's interest, good committee teamwork, and plenty of advance publicity, both the Service and the "St. Stephen's Day Party" were well and enthusiastically attended. The Bishop declared he had never had such a good time and stayed till the last crumb disappeared. A patronal celebration will undoubtedly become an annual event in this church.

Led by the choir, the congregation came in throngs from the sanctuary to the candlelit and green-bedecked Parish Hall. The head table, fancifully decorated, was near the base of the stage and held a large round cake and also a "Partridge in a Pear Tree." The stage itself was banked with greens, and a Christmas tree glowed in the center. The auditorium was arranged as for a theater-in-the-round. The choir encircled the piano in a corner. The Rector served as Master of the Hall.

First the choir sang several numbers including "Welcome, Yule" (with emphasis on the lines "Welcome, be ye *Stephen* or John"); then the Craighill Dancers, a local professional group especially interested in the religious dance, danced to two carols, "The Cherry Tree Carol" and "Good King Wenceslas" ("look'd out, on the Feast of *Stephen*"); next a troupe from the church presented a 20-minute medieval mummer's play "The Oxfordshire Christmas Masque" which was warmly applauded (particularly the skittish hobby-horse and the dreadful dragon); finally, everybody sang "The Twelve Days of Christmas" and other carols.

Following the program, the Bishop cut the St. Stephen's Day cake and all moved to the rear of the hall to visit the "groaning board," a long table laden with cakes, sandwiches, coffee and wassail. Pretty girls in red costumes circulated carrying trays piled with calennig.

Presenting calennig is an old English or Welsh New Year's custom, whereby children go around carrying gift apples or oranges in which

278

sprigs of evergreen and sweetmeats have been stuck. A tripod of wooden skewers enables each of these apples or oranges to stand on a table with another skewer to use as a handle by which to carry it. Originally a visit from the bearers of calennig involved largesse, invoked by a traditional song and a reply by each household visited. I enjoy making these quickly as little mementos for friends visited at Christmastime. Just stick about six small sprigs of box or holly in a bright red apple, then with toothpicks add a few dates or prunes or red cherries or what-have-you-on-hand. It's gay and Christmas-y. Sweetmeats for happy times and good fortune—evergreens for life eternal! Wassail!

NANCY POORE TUFTS

FESTIVAL OF NINE LESSONS AND CAROLS

A Christmas week service entitled "Festival of Nine Lessons and Carols," based upon the ancient service held annually in King's College Chapel, Cambridge University, England, is becoming increasingly popular. It is given each year in churches of many denominations. Here is the service as presented by DAVID PEW in Denver, Colorado.

Processional Hymn—"O Come, O Come Emmanuel"
The Bidding Prayer
The Lord's Prayer
The Grace
Invitatory Hymn—"Break Forth, O Beauteous Heavenly Light"
First Lesson—Genesis 3:8-15, 22:15-18
Carols—"Still Grows the Evening" (Bohemian)
      "In the Bleak Midwinter"
Second Lesson—A cento from Isaiah, Jeremiah, and Micah
Hymn—"God Rest You Merry, Gentlemen"
Third Lesson—Isaiah 53:3-9
Carol—"Good Christian Men, Rejoice"
Fourth Lesson—Luke 1:26-33, 38
Carol—"Softly the Stars Were Shining" (Torovsky)
Fifth Lesson—Matthew 1:18-23; Luke 2:1-7
Hymn—"O Little Town of Bethlehem"
Sixth Lesson—Luke 2:8-20
Carol—"Catalonian Christmas Song" (arr. Erickson)
Seventh Lesson—Matthew 2:1-5, 7-11
Carols—"Come Marie, Elisabette" (arr. Dickinson)
      "We Three Kings of Orient Are"
Eighth Lesson—Luke 2:22-35

279

Hymn—"Angels from the Realms of Glory"

Ninth Lesson—John 1: 1-14

The Offertory Procession—Congregation and Choirs

    Hymn—"O Come, All Ye Faithful"

    Hymn—"Angels We Have Heard on High"

Presentation—The Doxology

Exhortation and Prayers

Recessional Hymn—"Once in Royal David's City"

The music in this service, of course, may be varied to suit your situation and tastes.

This service of Nine Lessons and Carols was suggested by Ruth Jacobs in September 1958. It had been done the year previously by FOSTER HOTCHKISS, who has repeated it with changes of music each year. One year he used (exclusive of the hymns) the following:

"Good Christian Men," from *The Methodist Hymnal;* "Jesus Was Born in Bethlehem," by Jane Marshall, from *Why We Go to Church;* "What Child Is This?" English, arr. by David H. Williams, from *Junior Choir Anthems;* "Go to Sleep, O Child of Mine," by Rev. William Grime; "Thou Child Divine," American Moravian, in manuscript; "The Snow Lay on the Ground," English, arr. by Leo Sowerby; "O Come, Little Children," by Schütz, from *Our Songs of Praise* (Concordia) or from *Praise Him* (Shawnee Press); "What Can I Give Him?" from *The Methodist Hymnal;* "The Quempas Carol and Nunc Angelorum," 13th century German (Chantry Press, also Concordia).

Other directors used music not so generally known. MARY MONROE PENICK used "Unto Us a Boy Is Born," from the *Oxford Carol Book;* "The Three Wise Men," by Lang; "Jesus, Jesus, Rest Your Head," by Niles. MARVIN E. PETERSON used "The Indian Christmas Carol," arr. by Russell E. Carter; "Sing Gloria," by K. K. Davis; "Come Ye to Bethlehem," by K. K. Davis; "Sing, O Sing, This Blessed Morn," by Healy Willan; "The Coventry Carol," arr. by George Lynn. HOWARD SLENK used "The Three Kings," by Peter Cornelius; "A Carol of Adoration," by Pettman.

(*Editor's Note:* Although there is no set rule, this service is frequently given on the Sunday between Christmas and New Year's. When all or part of the choirs are on holiday, it is an easy, effective service, with much congregational participation. The custom prevails in some churches that various officers of the church read certain Lessons; sometimes the youngest chorister.)

BOAR'S HEAD AND YULE LOG FESTIVAL

Delightfully traditional English Christmastide customs come to life in the colorful "Boar's Head and Yule Log Festival," a service of drama and pageantry presented annually to "standing room only" congregations at Christ Episcopal Church, Cincinnati, Ohio, since 1940 and inaugurated at Trinity Cathedral in Cleveland in 1960. DR. PARVIN TITUS and DR. HARRY W. GAY, the respective choirmasters, have become adept at handling masses of adult and child choristers. A brief description of the service and its background follows.

Borne by a sprite into the darkened church, a burning candle symbolizes the coming of Jesus into the selfish world which awaits his advent. The light is given to the church and remains on the altar beneath his figure. Then, announced by the fanfare of a trumpet, a noble company of knights and attendants enter in procession bearing the Boar's Head.

Rooted deep in pagan times, when the boar was the first dish served at a Roman feast, the colorful ceremony of the Boar's Head became a part of the Christmas celebration in the great manor houses of the Middle Ages. The Christian church endowed the custom with symbolic meaning and elevated it to the service of God, thereby enriching the lives of all it touched. The ceremony of the Lord of the manor became a service of praise to the Lord of the Universe.

In Norman England the boar was a ferocious beast and sovereign of the forest, a danger and menace to man, was therefore the symbol of evil. The presentation of the boar's head at Christmastime signified the triumph of the Christ Child over sin. The fresh yule log, lighted by last year's ember and representing the warmth of the family fireside, has from the earliest times marked the rekindling of love as the Old Year passes and the New Year is born.

No one knows who first planned the Boar's Head procession, but it is a matter of record that it was in use at Queen's College, Oxford, shortly after the founding of the University in 1340, and there it continues to this very day.

After three or four centuries of presentation in Cambridge as well as in Oxford, to the ceremony of the Boar's Head had been added the mince pie and plum pudding, the Wise Men, the Shepherds, Good King Wenceslas and his page, sometimes the martyr Stephen, knights and beefeaters (English ceremonial guards).

In American colonial days the festival was instituted by the Bouton family of French Huguenot origin, who lived for a while in England, then settled in Connecticut, and later moved to Troy, N.Y. A scion of this family, Dr. Tibbits, became Rector of Hoosac School in Hoosick, N.Y., in 1888. There he established the traditional festival that had meant so much to his own family.

In 1940 Christ Church in Cincinnati secured the consent of Hoosac School to present the ceremony, changing it from its former style of a refectory presentation to that of the present processional in the church building.

Members of the congregation not only witness but participate, lifted out of themselves and their everyday world by joining in paeans of praise to Almighty God. As the boar's head is brought into the church, the entire congregation chants the chorus of rejoicing:

"Caput apri defero
Reddens laudes Domino."

Amid a fanfare of trumpets the beefeaters, knights, and attendants follow in a procession that includes yule pages, woodsmen, archers, shepherds, carolers, an Oriental group, and of course the boar's head and the mince pie. Down the long aisle of the cathedral the procession moves slowly, bearing the symbolic offerings of thanks, love, and allegiance. The music is also of the 14th century; at Trinity Cathedral five choirs participated.

With more than 100 costumed participants, the festival involves tremendous effort. In Cleveland it is a cooperative project by parishioners of 21 Episcopal parishes in the area. The colorful period costumes, each one an authentic copy, were made by the ladies of twelve parishes. Costumes for the Star of the East processional group were received by Bishop Burroughs as a gift from St. Andrew's Church in Ramallah, Jordan.

The gigantic mince pie was made in the church kitchen; it contained 22 pounds of mincemeat. Twenty glass lanterns were made by a friend in Oberlin. A clergyman in Wooster made the beefeaters' pipes, staffs for the shepherds, and the cart that bears the yule log. An East Indian living in Cleveland volunteered to wrap the turbans properly.

The church bulletin reads: "After all have offered their unique gifts to the Christ Child on his birthday, they go forth to the glorious strains of "Adeste, Fideles," and members of the congregation leave *silently* with hearts aglow with thanksgiving to the Lord of the Universe for his triumph over selfishness and his redemption of his children. (Your own gift, which represents you, may be left at the door when you leave the Cathedral.")

Much of the music of the Boar's Head festival can be found in most denominational hymnals or in the *Oxford Book of Carols*. The music outline is as follows:

1. "The Boar's Head Carol"
2. "Good King Wenceslas"
3. The Woodsmen—"Deck the Halls"
4. The Waits—"Wassail Carol"
5. The Shepherds—"Let us now go even unto Bethlehem"
6. Adoration of the Shepherds—"Hail to the Lord's Anointed"
7. The Kings—"Kings to Thy Rising"
8. The Star—"We Three Kings"
9. "Let All Mortal Flesh"
10. "O Come, All Ye Faithful"

"Silence is requested until the candle has been extinguished and the Minister has left the Sanctuary at the conclusion of the Service."

"GOD BLESS US ALL, BOTH GREAT AND SMALL"

(N.P.T.)

AN EPIPHANY SERVICE

To help your choirs and church friends recognize and honor the proper sequence of Christmas events and to herald the season of the Epiphany as a significant and meaningful time of the church year, I recommend the addition of this simple and colorful touch to either your Service of the Epiphany (January 6) or the regular Service on the First Sunday after the Epiphany. This practice is a tradition of St. Stephen's Episcopal Church in Washington, D.C.

During the Service of the Epiphany the Three Kings in brilliant garb march behind the clergy and the candle-bearers and ahead of the choir in a Festival Procession around the church. At the Offertory the Three Kings, bearing their gifts, come up ahead of the ushers as the offering is brought to the chancel steps and leave their gifts also. At the Recessional the Three Kings go ahead of the choir over to the Rectory next door for the "blessing of all homes at Epiphany." The congregation follows. In the Rectory the choir sings, "God Be in My Head" by Walford Davies, and also "Bless the Four Corners of This House" (tune, St. Anne). This hymn can be found in several hymnals: e.g. in *The Methodist Hymnal*, No. 433. Here is the text of this poetic benediction by Arthur Guiterman:

1. Bless the four corners of this house,
   And be the lintel blest;
   And bless the hearth, and bless the board,
   And bless each place of rest.

2. And bless the door that opens wide
   To stranger as to kin;
   And bless each crystal windowpane
   That lets the starlight in.

3. And bless the rooftree overhead,
   And every sturdy wall;
   The peace of man, the peace of God,
   The peace of love o'er all.

                                          (N.P.T.)

THE TWELVE DAYS OF CHRISTMAS

"The Twelve Days of Christmas" carol is an ancient yule song of England and is typical of many early carols. In quaint mingling of praise to the Lord with praise of feasting these early carols represent perfectly the spirit of Christmas in Tudor days: "I pray you, my masters, merry be!" This was the keynote. No work was expected. The abundance of the rich was shared with the poor, many keeping open house through Twelfth Night. The brotherhood of humanity was emphasized during this time of the year by canceling debts, setting prisoners free, and the expression of goodwill among all men.

This quaint carol is one of many "accumulative" folk songs or forfeit games which were popular with country singers who regarded them as tests of endurance, memory, and sometimes sobriety. Each person, in succession, has to repeat the gifts of the day or pay a forfeit for every mistake in the list or the order. This is a relic of certain ancient Yule or even Druid customs and ceremonies.

Nineteenth Century authors such as Halliwell and Husk and the late Cecil Sharp list other versions. One variation goes:

"The First Day of Christmas   Ten Ships a-sailing, etc.
My Mother sent to me   Eleven Ladies spinning, etc.
A Partridge in a Pear Tree.   Twelve Bells a-ringing."

Another variation has "Four Canary Birds," etc.

Yet another version, from around 1700, lists 364 gifts received by the lucky lady—one for each day in the year, save one!

A "Twelve Days of Christmas" party has always proved tremendously popular with my children's choirs and with grown-ups too, especially as a pickup for the let-down following Christmas, or as a social hour after an Epiphany Service. The entertainment and decorations center around the singing of the carol, and the children will "sing it again" until exhausted, if permitted.

Arrange the singers (or the party) into eleven teams each responsible for one section of the song: "Two Turtle Doves," "Three French Hens," "Ten Pipers," etc. Each team at the proper time must rise, sing, act out its part, then sit down. I always choose one child, often the youngest, to stand in front holding "The Partridge in a Pear Tree." (Quickly cover a small artificial Christmas tree with sprigs of laurel or other leaves; tie on artificial pears from the dime store, and top it with a fat, perky brown bird made from a roll of cotton and brown crepe-paper.) Each time the refrain "And a partridge in a pear tree" is sung, this child might be instructed to revolve like a mechanical toy or make some repetitive gesture.

Have a "dry run" of the carol to check the teamwork, then you're set for an amusing stunt. Of course a good, fast pianist and an authoritative leader are necessary. Refreshments might include wassail or hollyberry punch (fruit concoctions) and Christmas cookies. A finale with a bit of caroling and chiff-chaff will leave the children enchanted and already crying: "Are we gonna do it again next year?" Of course we are! Unless you'd rather have an Epiphany Pie Party and calennig!

NANCY POORE TUFTS

CHRISTMAS PROJECTS OF CHORISTERS GUILDERS

OPEN HOUSE AT CHRISTMAS

Wesley Methodist Church, Worcester, Massachusetts, held an "Open House" shortly before Christmas one year. The whole beautiful structure was resplendent with Christmas decorations. The traditional tree towering to the ceiling of the two-story room and the panoramic scenes on the stage transformed the social hall. Rows of evergreen trees made a fragrant avenue of the narthex. Decorations characteristic of different nations marked the various assembly rooms. Imported creches, Nativity figures, cherub-choir figures and other festive articles were gathered from other lands; carols and Christmas songs from each nation were played as background. Tea was served, and the ministers and staff were on hand to greet all guests. The invitation to "Open Church" was extended to all members to come and bring friends, as well as to the aged and shut-ins, and to shoppers who were downtown for the day.

SHADOW-BOX NATIVITY SCENE PROJECT

LINDA BAAKE, a creative member of the Junior High Department at First Methodist Church, Santa Barbara, California, made a series of shadow-box scenes of the successive events of the Nativity. With infinite patience she dressed tiny dolls, hunted for effective background material, connected Christmas-tree lights to provide the right amount of brightness or shadow, and lettered with Gothic beauty the appropriate Scripture passage. Wouldn't this be a fine Junior High project, with the shadow boxes displayed in the narthex a week or two before Christmas, and the identical scenes in tableaux for the Carol Service? The scenes, as Linda set them up, were:

1. Joseph and Mary coming down a gravel road, leading a donkey.
2. The Nativity scene.
3. Shepherds in the foreground, looking at an angel on a hill.
4. The Wise Men talking to Herod on his throne.
5. Mary, Joseph, and the Child on the way to Egypt.
6. Family scene in a typical American home.

* * *

"MESSIAH" NOTEBOOK PROJECT

We are indebted to MARGERY GOSSARD, First Presbyterian Church, North Hollywood, California, for this bright idea. If your community has a presentation of *The Messiah* in view, and you would like to arouse the interest of your youngsters in this work, give them a notebook page with several of the themes, followed by the remainder of the text of that particular number. The themes Mrs. Gossard used were: 1) For Unto Us A Child Is Born; 2) He Shall Feed His Flock Like a Shepherd; and 3) the first five hallelujahs of the Hallelujah Chorus. Each child in Junior Church was given one of these pages. The director told a little about Handel (use the Opal Wheeler biography published by Dutton) and then the choir sang these themes. The children loved it, and many attended the evening performance of the *The Messiah*.

* * *

A CHRISTMAS PRESENT OF MUSIC

Mrs. ROBERT W. FISHER of Rolling Hills, California, gives each of her choir children a copy of his or her favorite Christmas anthem. It is a welcome but inexpensive gift, and one that will, we hope, encourage playing and singing at home.

286

A CHURCH DECORATING PARTY

All-Saints-by-the-Sea, Santa Barbara, California, has in recent years arranged a potluck supper followed by the decorating of the church. A chairman plans the decorations and suggests what greens, etc., to bring. This would be a fine project for a high school choir or group. It is much better for the youth and the church as well than having the work professionally done.

* * *

A CHRISTMAS CARD CHOIR ROOM

What do you do with your most beautiful and artistic Christmas cards? I have been hoarding mine for years and can almost paper the Choir Room with them during the holiday season. KATHRYN HILL RAWLS, of St. Luke's Methodist Church in Washington, D.C., has collected a frieze of Choir Boy cards that process completely around her Music Office, and covers several doors as well. I can now arrange a Holy Family corner (those rich and colorful copies of the Old Masters from the Washington Cathedral Association and the Metropolitan Museum of Art, etc.) and a whole wall end of Christmas Bell cards. Junior choristers take great pleasure in collecting and fastening up such a display every year, as well as arranging an Advent Wreath and then a Creche.

I am satisfied that these ideas have left an indelible impression of what is good and bad taste in cards and decoration. Past church bulletins have written up my "Christmas Card Choir Room" and a number of church friends still bring me their favorite cards. I have even found piles on the organ bench following spring cleaning! Directors who have no permanent Choir Room might consider decorating portable screens, bulletin boards, or hall walls.

NANCY POORE TUFTS

A CHRISTMAS PRAYER

O Christ, grant us thankful hearts today for thee, our choicest gift, our dearest guest. Let not our souls be busy inns that have no room for thee and thine, but quiet homes of prayer and praise, where the needful cares of life are wisely ordered and put away, and wide sweet spaces kept for thee; where holy thoughts pass up and down, and fervent longings watch and wait thy coming. So when thou comest again, O Holy One, mayest thou find all things ready, and thy family waiting for no new master, but for One long loved and known. Even so come, Lord Jesus. Amen.

(ANON.)

* * * * *

"AND THE WORD WAS MADE FLESH"

HOW COULD THIS CHILD who was tiny and meek
Cause weary shepherds for him to seek?

HOW COULD THIS CHILD by cattle surrounded
Bring Wise Men to kneel as the heavens resounded?

HOW COULD THIS CHILD who on a cross was hung
Be the Promised One of whom the sages had sung?

HOW COULD THIS CHILD who did not reign as a king
This day be our Lord to whom we our offerings bring?

HOW CAN WE KNOW of God's great love
When sent of himself as this Child from above?

JANET (MRS. DANIEL) HERMANY
(Ass't. to DANIEL HERMANY, *Min. of Music*)
St. Peter's Lutheran Church,
Allentown, Pennsylvania

288

Materials

I. BOOKS

Celebrations, Festivals, Holidays

An American Book of Days. G. W. Douglas. H. W. Wilson; 1948.
Anniversaries and Holidays. Mary E. Hazeltine. American Library Assn.; 1944.
Days We Celebrate. Robert H Schauffler. Dodd, Mead; 1940.
    Vol. 1. *Celebrations for Christmas and Other High Days.*
    Vol. 2. *Celebrations for Festivals.*
    Vol. 3. *Celebrations for Patriotic Days.*
    Vol. 4. *Celebrations for Special Occasions.*
Festivals of Western Europe. Dorothy Spicer. H. W. Wilson; 1958.
Christmas — An American Annual of Christmas Literature and Art. Augsburg
    Publishing House; from 1930 on.
Come to Christmas. Anna and Edward Gebhard. Abingdon.
The LIFE Book of Christmas. 3 Volumes. Time, Inc.; 1963.
    Vol. 1. *The Glory of Christmas.*
    Vol. 2. *The Pageantry of Christmas.*
    Vol. 3. *The Merriment of Christmas.*
All About Christmas. Maymie R. Krythe. Harper; 1954.
The Twelve Days of Christmas. Hadfield. Little, Brown; 1962.
The Gifts of Christmas. Rachel Hartman. Channel Press; 1962.
The Story of St. Nicholas. Mildred Luckhardt. Abingdon.

Christian Education

A Small Child's Bible. Pelagie Doane. Walck; 1948.
Daily Life in Bible Times. A. E. Bailey. Scribner.
Junior Worship. Westminster Press.
Primary Worship. Westminster Press.
Religious Activities for Primary Children. Marion P. Baden. Concordia.
The Story of the Church. W. R. Bowie. Abingdon; 1955.
Worship Program for Juniors. Bays-Oakberg. Abingdon; 1960.

Church Music

A Comprehensive Program of Church Music. Whittlesey. Westminster; 1957.
A Guidebook to Worship Services of Sacred Music. Heaton. Bethany; 1962.

289

A Survey of Christian Hymnody. Reynolds. Holt, Rinehart and Winston; 1963.
Church Music. R. N. Squire. Bethany; 1962.
How to Lead Informal Singing. Hoffelt. Abingdon; 1963.
Hymn Tune Names. McCutchan. Abingdon; 1957.
In Every Corner Sing. J. W. Clokey. Morehouse; 1945.
Music and Worship in the Church. Lovelace and Rice. Abingdon; 1960.
Our Hymnody. McCutchan. Abingdon; 1937.
Steps Toward a Singing Church. Kettring. Westminster; 1948.
The Singing Church. Liemohn. Wartburg; 1959.
The Singing Church. C. H. Phillips. Faber & Faber, Ltd.; 1946.
The Hymn and Congregational Singing. J. R. Sydnor. John Knox Press; 1960.
The Gospel in Hymns. A. E. Bailey. Scribner; 1954.
The Organist and Hymn Playing. Lovelace. Abingdon; 1962.
The Practice of Sacred Music. Halter. Concordia; 1955.
The Story of Christian Hymnody. E. E. Ryden. Augustana; 1959.

Music and Christian Education

Make a Joyful Noise. Warren. Augsburg; 1962.
Music in Christian Education. E. L. Thomas. Abingdon; 1953.
Music in My Bible. Grauman. Pacific Press.
Music in the Religious Growth of Children. Shields. Abingdon; 1943.
The Use of Music in Christian Education. Morsch. Westminster; 1956.

Music Education

A Handbook for Music Teaching in the Elementary Grades. Kjos; 1961.
Choral Conducting: Learning and Teaching. Groom-Nordin. Fortress; 1963.
Children Discover Music and Dance. Emma D. Shehy. Holt; 1959.
How to Help Children Learn Music. Carabo-Cone & Royt. Harper; 1955.
It's Fun to Listen. Coit & Bampton. Flammer.
Keys to Teaching Elementary School Music. Thompson. Nordholm.
Learning to Read Music. Weyland. Wm. C. Brown Co.; 1961.
Music in Secondary Schools. Singleton. Allyn & Bacon; 1963.
School Music Handbook. Dykema & Cundiff. Summy-Birchard; 1955.
Sing a Song to Sight Read. Rinderer. Kjos; 1961.
Song and Play for Children. Danielson & Conant. Pilgrim.
Teaching Junior High School Music. Cooper & Kuersteiner. Allyn & Bacon; 1964.
The ABC's of the Do Re Mi's. Ruth Krehbiel Jacobs. Choristers Guild.
The Amateur Choir Director. Hjortsvang. Abingdon; 1941.
The Amateur Choir Trainer. Henry Coleman. Oxford.
The Children's Choir—I. Ruth Krehbiel Jacobs. Augustana; 1958.
The Children's Choir—II. Nancy Poore Tufts. Fortress; 1965.
The Successful Children's Choir. Ruth Krehbiel Jacobs. FitzSimons; 1948.
The True Book of Sounds We Hear. (Primary) Podendorf. Grosset; 1959.
The Wonderful World of Music. Britten & Holst. Doubleday; 1958.
This is Music. (Grades 1-8: with Recordings & Teacher's Manual). Allyn & Bacon.
YOU Can Teach Music. P. W. Matthews. Button.

Music Teaching Aids

Charts and Posters

Children's Choir Achievement Chart with Teacher's Guide. Boyter. C. Fischer.
Choir Posters. (16 Visual Teaching Aids) Montgomery. Abingdon.

Clap Phrase Poster. Boyter. C. Fischer.
Conducting Charts. Broadman Press.
Instruments of the Orchestra Charts. J. W. Pepper.
Music Made Easy Charts. Cokesbury.
Music Symbols Posters. Boyter. C. Fischer.
Rhythm Notation Posters. Boyter. C. Fischer.

FLASH CARDS

Instruments of the Orchestra Flash Cards. Boyter. C. Fischer.
Music Symbol Flash Cards. Kenworthy Ed. Service.
Music Rhythm Teaching Series. Wm. D. Lockwood, Inc.
Music Vocabulary Flash Cards. Boyter. C. Fischer.
My Look and Listen Flash Cards. Boyter. C. Fischer.

WORKBOOKS

Musical Stamp Book. (Golden Books) Westminster.
My Look and Listen Book. Boyter. C. Fischer.
My Musical Game Book. Boyter. C. Fischer.
My Musical Instrument Book. Boyter. C. Fischer.
My Musical Puzzle Book. Boyter. C. Fischer.

FUN AND GAMES

Build Your Own Orchestra. (Stand-Up Figures) Keyboard, Jr.
Maestro Game of Musical Terms. Remick.
Maestro Game of Notes. Remick.
Maestro, the Musical Bingo. Remick.
Make Your Own Musical Instruments. Mandell-Wood. Sterling; 1959.
Music Fun. Books I-IV. Activity Book. Kenworthy.
Symphony. (Game of Orchestra Instruments) Boyter. C. Fischer.

INSTRUMENTS

American Prep Tone Bells. (Deagan) Targ & Dinner; Chicago 47, Ill.
Autoharps, Bell Blocks & Rhythm Band Instruments. Cokesbury.
Autoharps. Lutheran Church Supply Stores, 2900 Queen Lane, Philadelphia,
    Pa. 19129.
Chime Bars. Lyons Band & Instruments Co., Chicago, Ill.
Harmony Band Instruments. Handy Folio Music Co.
JeNco Melody Percussion Instruments. Box 149, Decatur, Ill. 62525.
Melodica. M. Hohner, Inc., Andrews Road, Hicksville, L. I., N. Y.
Musical Bell Blocks. B. F. Kitching Co., Inc., Brookfield, Ill.
Recorders. Cokesbury.
Resonator (Tone) Bells. Harmolin. Box 244, La Jolla, Calif.
Resonator Bells. David Wexler & Co., 823 S. Wabash, Chicago, Ill.
Resonator Bells. Viking Co., 113 Edgemont St. S., Los Angeles 4, Calif.
Tuned Step Bells. Cokesbury.
Zither. (2 octaves) G. Schirmer.

Choir Training

BOYS' VOICES

Boys: Know Them, Teach Them, Lead Them. R. G. Stott. Assn. Foundation.
The Boy's Changing Voice. W. N. Mellalieu. Oxford; 1935.
The Training of Boys' Voices. Walter S. Vale. Morehouse.
Training the Boy's Changing Voice. D. McKenzie. Rutgers; 1956.
Training the Boy Chorister. T. T. Noble. G. Schirmer.

Children's Voices—General

A Child Development Point of View. J. L. Hymes. Prentice-Hall; 1955.
A Child Sings. Marie Pooler. Augsburg; 1958.
Building a Church Choir. Wilson & Lyall. Schmitt, Hall & McCreary; 1957.
Child Voice Training. Finn. FitzSimons.
Children Singing. Cyril Winn. Oxford; 1952.
Helen Kemp on Junior Choirs. Kemp. Lorenz; 1962.
How to Build a Church Choir. C. H. Heaton. Bethany; 1958
How to Get Along with Children. F. H. Richardson. (Tupper) McKay; 1954.
More Than Singing. Lotte Lehmann. Boosey; 1945.
New Ways in Discipline. Dorothy W. Baruch. McGraw; 1949.
Organizing and Directing Children's Choirs. Madeline Ingram. Abingdon; 1959.
The Children's Choir—I. Ruth Krehbiel Jacobs. Augustana; 1958.
The Children's Choir—II. Nancy Poore Tufts. Fortress; 1965.
The Singer's Manual of English Diction. Madeline Marshall. G. Schirmer; 1953.
The New Song. Leland B. Sateren. Augsburg; 1958.
The Successful Children's Choir. Ruth K. Jacobs. FitzSimons; 1948.
The Training of Church Choirs. James R. Sydnor. Abingdon; 1963.
Understanding Your Child. James L. Hymes. Prentice-Hall.
Vocal Technique for Children and Youth. Ingram & Rice. Abingdon; 1962.

Youth Choir Voices
(Junior and Senior High School Age)

A Guide for Workers with Junior Highs. Geneva Press.
A J. H. S. Music Handbook. Monsour & Perry. Prentice-Hall; 1963.
The SAB Choir Trainer. Carl Vandre. Mills.
The Youth Choir. Lovelace. Abingdon; 1964.
The Youth Choir Director. Marie Joy Curtiss. D. F. Wood; 1963.
Vocal Technic. Peter Tkach. Kjos.
Youth Choirs. Paul J. Miller. Flammer; 1953.

Dress and Deportment

Altogether Lovely. Charlene Johnson. Fortress; 1960.
(Advice to teen-age girls on Christian attitudes)

Speech Choirs and Choral Speaking

Speech Training

Art of Interpretive Speech. Woolbert & Nelson. Appleton-Century.
Oral Interpretation. Charlotte Lee. Houghton-Mifflin; 1959.
Reading Aloud. Wayland M. Parrish. Ronald Press.
Reading the Bible Aloud. J. E. Lantz. Macmillan; 1959.
The Speech Choir. Marjorie Gullan. Harper; 1937.

Choral Readings

Choral Readings for Junior Worship and Inspiration. Westminster.
Choral Readings for Fun and Recreation. Westminster.
Choral Readings for Worship and Inspiration. Westminster.
Choral Readings from the Bible. Westminster.
Great Bible Stories for the Verse Speaking Choir. Westminster.
Psalms for Today (Meditations for Speech Choirs). L. David Miller. Muhlenberg; 1962.

POETRY

Oxford Book of Christian Verse. Oxford Press.
Prayers from the Ark. Gasztold-Godden. Viking; 1962.
The Treasury of Religious Verse. D. T. Kauffman. Revell; 1962.

Recreation

Children Discover Music and Dance. Emma D. Sheehy. Holt; 1959.
Creative Rhythmic Movement for Children. Gladys Andrews. Prentice-Hall; 1954.
Music Fun. Books I-IV. Activity Books. Kenworthy.
Music Skills for Recreation Leaders. Baird. Wm. C. Brown Co.; 1963.
Sing a Tune. (Fun Songs) American Baptist Publication.
Sing a Merry Song. Wm. Clauson. (For Young Children; Guitar Accomp.) Oxford; 1964.
Sing and Dance. (Folk Songs and Dances) Hunt & Wilson. Schmitt, Hall & McCreary.
Songs for Pre-Teen Time. Irvin Cooper. C. Fischer.
Tuning-Up Songs. Rosemary Hadler. Lorenz.
We Sing to Learn. Marshall & Montgomery. C. Fischer.
You Can Do It! (Creative Activity for Primaries) Judson Press.

Stories

And So the Wall Was Built. Imogene McPherson. Westminster; 1949.
Armed with Courage. McNeer & Ward. Abingdon; 1957.
Arturo and Mr. Bang. Fraser. Bobbs-Merrill; 1963.
   (Story of a boy whose voice changed suddenly to A, T, then Bass; and how he met "Mr. Bang" of the Met.)
Bennie the Bear Who Grew Too Fast. Fraser. Lothrop, Lee & Shepard; 1956.
   (Story of the sizes of various instruments.)
Little Visits with God. Jahsmann & Simon. Concordia; 1957.
More Little Visits with God. Jahsmann & Simon. Concordia; 1961.
Song of St. Francis. Clyde R. Bulla. Crowell; 1952.
Stories for Junior Worship. Alice Geer. Abingdon; 1941.
The Music Master (The Story of J. S. Bach). T. J. Kleinhans. Muhlenberg; 1962.

Symbolism

An Outline of Christian Symbolism. Frank E. Wilson. Morehouse; 1961.
Christian Symbols. (Workbook) Lutheran Church Supply Stores, 2900 Queen Lane, Philadelphia, Pa. 19129.
Christian Symbolism in Evangelical Churches. T. A. Stafford. Abingdon.
Seasons and Symbols. Wetzler & Huntington. Augsburg; 1962.
Singing Windows. Mary E. Young. Abingdon; 1962.
Stained Glass Color Art. (Workbook) Lutheran Church Supply Stores, 2900 Queen Lane, Philadelphia, Pa. 19129.
Symbols and Terms of the Church. Edgar S. Brown. Muhlenberg; 1958.

Worship and the Arts

Christianity in Art. Getlein. Bruce; 1959.
Christianity in Modern Art. Getlein. Bruce; 1961.
The Acolyte. Martin Ruoss. Fortress; 1957.
The Church and the Fine Arts. Cynthia Maus. Harper; 1960.
Worship Services Using the Arts. Curry & Wetzel. Westminster; 1961.

Periodicals

Choristers Guild Letters. 440 Northlake Center, Dallas, Texas. 75238.
Journal of Church Music. Fortress Press, 2900 Queen Lane, Philadelphia, Pa. 19129.
Music Educators Journal. (MENC) 1201 16th St., Washington, D. C. 20036.
Music Ministry. (Methodist) 201 Eighth Ave. S., Nashville 3, Tenn.
The Junior Musician. (Southern Baptist) 127 Ninth Ave. N., Nashville 3, Tenn.
The Journal of the Choral Conductors Guild. 5145 Eagle St., Long Beach, Calif.
The Younger Choirs. Lorenz Publishing Co., 501 E. 3rd St., Dayton 1, Ohio.

II. MUSIC

Primary Choir — Anthems

Come and Worship. Rawls. J. Fischer, 9278. (U or SA)
Christmas Long Ago. Dunhill. Edward Arnold, 470. (U)
O, I Would Sing of Mary's Child. Lovelace. Augsburg, 1247. (U)
Rocking. arr. Woodgate. Oxford, UP-U15. (U)
Sing Praises to the Lord. Jenkins. Witmark, W-3699.
The Birds. (Czech). M. Shaw. Oxford, U-30. (U)
Timothy's Christmas Song. Gay. Choristers Guild, A-4. (U)
To a Manger. Smith. Gray, CMR 2502. (U)

Primary Choir — Song Collections

A Child Sings. (20 songs for young children) Pooler. Augsburg.
Fun and Folk Songs. Westminster.
God Bless the Little Things. Hatch. Flammer, 86086.
Joyfully Sing—Book I. Concordia.
Let Children Sing. Licht. Flammer.
Let's Sing. Thompson. Augsburg.
Little Children, Sing to God. Jahsmann & Gross. Concordia.
More Songs and Carols. Grime. C. Fischer.
Music Through the Years. (Rounds and Canons) Follett.
Movement Through Song. Oxford, 68-2021.
New Songs and Carols. Grime. C. Fischer.
Our Songs of Praise. Klammer. Concordia.
Rime, Rhythm and Song. Burnett. Schmitt, Hall & McCreary.
Sing, Children, Sing. Thomas. Abingdon.
Sing Unto the Lord, Ye Children. Grime. C. Fischer.
Sing for Joy. Mealy. Seabury Press.
Sing with Chimes—Books I & II. (Also with dulcimer, recorder, percussion) Olive Rees. Oxford.
Singing Worship. Thomas. Abingdon.
Sixty Songs for Little Children. Wilson. Oxford.
Song and Play for Children. Danielson & Conant. Pilgrim Press.
Songs and Hymns for Primary Children. Westminster.
Songs for Early Childhood. Westminster.
Songs for 4's and 5's. Crowder & Reynolds. Broadman Press.
Songs for Little People. Danielson & Conant. Pilgrim Press.
Songs with Happy Thoughts for Children. Burnam. Willis Music Co.
Teaching Little Children to Pray. Grime. C. Fischer, CM 7015.
The Cherub Choir Book. Rutenbeck. Flammer.
We Are Thy Children. Lenski & Bulla. Crowell.

294

Junior Choir — Anthems

A Child's Prayer. Barthelson. Shawnee, E-35. (SA)
A Hymn for Thanksgiving. Williams. Summy-Birchard (SA)
A Prayer of St. Richard of Chichester. White. Oxford, E-43. (SA)
A Seasonal Thanksgiving. Thiman. G. Schirmer, 8740. (U)
A Song of Praise. (Brazilian) Appleby. Broadman, MF 655. (U & SA)
All Beautiful the March of Days. Lapo. Abingdon, 202. (U-SATB)
All Hail to Christ Our King. Rawls. J. Fischer 8533. (SA or SAB)
All Praise to God Who Reigns Above. Lenel. Concordia, 98-1142. (2-part)
Alleluia, Sing to Jesus. Graham. Broadman, MF 541. (U & SA)
Blessed Lord of Heaven Above. Powell. Schmitt, Hall & McCreary, 2570. (SA)
Blessed Man Whom God Doth Aid. Lovelace. J. Fischer, 9059. (U; recorders)
Built on a Rock. Lindeman-Bender. Concordia, 98-1646. (SA)
By Night and Day. Gordon. Remick, 3410. (SA or SAB)
Come, Christians, Praise God Forevermore. Kindermann. Concordia, LD 503.
Come, Holy Spirit, Come. Wolff. Concordia, 98-1356. (SS)
Come, Ye Children, Praise the Saviour. Wienhorst. Concordia, 98-1437. (SA)
Create in Me a Clean Heart. Bouman. Concordia, 98-1143. (SA)
Father in Heaven. (East Indian) Rasley. Lorenz. (U & SA)
For the Beauty of the Earth. York. C. Fischer, CM 549. (SA)
Forever Blessed Be Thy Name. Handel-Parris. Summy-Birchard, 2128. (U)
Garden Hymn (Southern Folk Hymn) Lipscomb. Presser, 312-40490. (U)
Give Ear Unto Me. Marcello. Gray, 1522. (2-part)
God Is Here with Us. Stanton. J. Fischer, 9208. (SA)
God Watches O'er All the World. Kettring. Gray, 1935. (U)
God Who Created Me. Lovelace. C. Fischer, CM 7149. (2-part for boys)
God's Open Road. Caldwell. Remick, 3315. (U)
God's World. Caldwell. Remick, 3316. (U)
Hang Up a Star for the Lord. Lynn. Golden Music Publ., G-3. (U)
Holy Ghost, With Light Divine. Warner. Concordia, 98-1363. (SA)
How Majestic Is Thy Name. Diemer. Gray, CMR-2729. (U)
I Lift My Eyes. Pfautsch. Summy-Birchard, 2101. (SA)
I Waited Patiently. Arnatt. Mercury Music, MC-419. (SS, esp. for boys)
In Heavenly Love Abiding. Pasquet. Wood, 793. (U-SATB)
Jehovah's Throne. Clokey. Flammer, 86198. (U)
Jubilate Deo. Purvis. Leeds, L-143. (U)
Let All the World in Every Corner Sing. Olds. Remick, IG-1747. (SA)
Let Us with a Gladsome Mind. Means. Gray, 2498.
Let Us with a Gladsome Mind. Warner. Summy-Birchard, B-2063. (SA)
Lord and Saviour, True and Kind. Bach-Lovelace. Flammer, 86162. (SA or U)
Lord God, We Worship Thee. Bach-Hart. Summy-Birchard, 1270. (SA)
Lord of All, to Thee We Pray. Grieg-Hirt. Witmark, W-3685. (SA or U)
Make a Joyful Noise. Marshall. C. Fischer, CM-7322. (SA or U)
My Jesus Is My Lasting Joy. Buxtehude-Bitgood. Gray, CMR 2727. (U with 2 violins)
My Shepherd. Bach-Hirt. Witmark, W-3683. (SA or U)
O Gracious King. Van D. Thompson. Lorenz. (U)
O Holy Father. Lap. Abingdon, 163. (U-SAT)
O Lord, Our Governor. Marcello. Concordia, 09-1045. (2-part)
Praise, My Soul, the King of Heaven. Clokey. Flammer, 86149. (U)
Praised Be God, Our King. Cramer-Whitford. J. Fischer, 9494. (SA)
Psalm of Praise. Darst. Gray, 2471. (SS)
Psalm 100. Marshall. Broadman, 485-36562. (U)
Sanctus. (From *Requiem*) Gabriel Fauré. FitzSimons, 5017. (2-part with violin)

Sing to the Lord of Harvest. Marshall. Broadman, 485-36570.
Soldiers of Christ, Arise. Warner. Abingdon, 347. (SA or SAB)
The God of Abraham Praise. Thiman. Broadman, MF-649. (U with descant)
The God of Love My Shepherd Is. Peek. Canyon, 5602. (SA)
The Lord My Shepherd Is. Lovelace. Augsburg, 1284. (U)
The Sanctus. Dietterich. Abingdon, 191. (U-SATB)
The Sun Shines in Splendor. Warner. Gray, 2589. (SA)
Thy Word Is Like a Garden, Lord. Rawls. J. Fischer, 9380. (U or SA)
Touch Hands Around the Rolling World. Rawls. J. Fischer, 9075. (U or SA)
Three Carols for Juniors (Christmas, Palm Sunday, & Thanksgiving) Copes.
    Canyon, 6005. (U)
Unto Thee, O Lord. Aulbach. C. Fischer, CM-6824. (U and SATB)
Wake, Awake. (Advent) Nicolai. R. D. Row, 231. (SS)
We Praise Thee, O God. Willan. Concordia, 98-1059. (U)
We Praise Thee, We Thank Thee. Magney. Summy-Birchard, 5099
We Tread Upon Thy Carpets. Whittlesey. Flammer, 86153. (SA & Speech Choir)
Wondrous Love. (Appalachian Folk Song) Thiman. Broadman, MF-593. (U with
    descant)

Junior Choir — Christmas Anthems

A Child's Noel. Beck. G. Schirmer, 10432. (SA & SATB)
A Gallery Carol. arr. Johnson. Schmitt, Hall & McCreary, SD-5901. (U-SATB;
    handbells)
A Great and Mighty Wonder. Praetorius-Kessler. Augsburg, 1243. (SA)
A Song of Christmas. Grieg. Galleon, GSC 1002. (SA)
A Thousand Christmas Candles. Kohler-Nelson. Choir School Guild. (U)
All Were There. Lynn. Ditson, 332-40083. (Combined Choirs)
As Joseph Was A-Walking. Jordan. Galleon, GSC-1008. (U)
As Lately We Watched. Ehret. Choral Art, S-142. (SA)
Away in a Manger. Giasson. Galleon, GSC 1008. (U or SA; handbells opt.)
Babe of Beauty. Boda. Concordia, 98-1656. (SA)
Beth'lem Lay A-Sleeping. (Polish) Willan. Concordia, 1410. (SSA)
Bethlehem Night Song. Tobin. Elkin & Co. Ltd. (Galaxy). (U)
Carol of the Advent. Dietterich. Abingdon, APM-216. (U-SATB)
Carol of the Birds. Kinsman. Walton, 2001. (Jr. & Adult)
Carol of the Drum. K. K. Davis. Wood, 729. (U or SA)
Carol of the Questioning Child. Kountz. G. Schirmer, 9893. (U-SATB)
Chime, Happy Christmas Bells. Hokanson. Concordia, 98-1513. (U; with flute
    or clarinet.)
Christ, the Holy Child. Frances Williams. Flammer, 86059. (U or SA)
Christmas Counterpoint. Glover. Canyon, 6224. (SA, SSAA; with instruments)
Christmas Comes in the Morning. McKay. Summy, 1597. (SA-SATB)
Christmas Morn is Dawning. (German) Luvaas. Augsburg, IC-10. (SA)
Christmas Praise. Willan. Augsburg, 1207. (U-SATB)
Christmas Song of Peace. Lovelace. Canyon, 6253. (U)
Come, Come Away. arr. Pendleton. R. D. Row, 448. (SS)
Corner's Cradle Song. (Austrian) Reuter. Concordia, 98-1529. (SA)
From Heaven High. Willan. Concordia, 98-1645. (SA)
Happy Christmas Eve. (Norwegian) Schmitt, Hall & McCreary, 2561. (SA)
Hosanna Now Through Advent. Moschetti. Presser, 312-40258. (U & SATB)
Hush, My Dear, Lie Still. Morris. Oxford, U-64. (U)
In the Dark of the Night. Halter. Concordia, 98-1661. (SA)
In the Moon of Wintertime. Sateren. Canyon, 6213. (U-SATB)
Japanese Christmas Carol. Lee. Gray, CMR-2767. (U)

296

Joy Came Softly. Brook. Oxford, 2218. (SA)
Little Jesus Sweetly Sleep. Sowerby. FitzSimons, 5018. (U)
Long, Long Ago. (*Wind Through the Olive Trees*) Rawls. Gray, 2198. (SA)
Manger Carol. Sowerby. Gray, 2419. (U)
Mary Sat Spinning. Paul Christiansen. Augsburg, 1180. (S-SATB)
Midwinter. Milford. Oxford, OXCS 161. (U or SA)
Nativity Tale. Belyea. Summy-Birchard, 5049. (Combined Choirs)
Noel, Sing We Now of Christmas. Slater. Remick. (U)
O Holy Child, We Welcome Thee. (Bohemian) Halter. Concordia, 98-1596. (SSA)
O Little One Sweet. Dressler. J. Fischer, 9154. (SA; flute)
O Little Town of Bethlehem. Hinrichs. Concordia, 98-1528. (SS)
O Men From the Fields. (Irish) Cooke. Oxford, U-87. (U)
O Morning Star. (Epiphany). Nicolai. R. D. Row, 232. (SS)
Offerings. J. Rodgers. Galleon, 1017. (U)
On Christmas Night. Ehret. Volkwein. (U or SA)
Peace on Earth. Lovelace. Choral Services, 133. (U)
Presents All, Niño Jesus. (Catalan) No. 4, Tracy Music Libr. (U-SATB)
Quempas Carol. Praetorius-Wienhorst. Concordia, 98-1518. (U)
Saw You Never in the Twilight? (Epiphany) Lovelace. Gray, 2553. (U)
See the Radiant Sky Above. Cummings. Choral Art, SO143. (SA)
Shepherds' Song. Giasson. Galleon, 1016. (U)
Silver Lamps. Brooke. Oxford, 1134. (U)
Sing We Noel. K. K. Davis. E. C. Schirmer. (SA & SATB)
Softly Falls the Snow. Ebel-Nitske. J. Fischer, 9403. (SA)
Song of an Indian Child. Lynn. Ditson, 322-40084. (U-SATB)
Still, Still, Still. (German) arr. Wetzler. Augsburg, 401. (U)
The Angels at the Manger (Swiss). arr. Luvaas. Gray, 2613. (SA)
The Austrian Manger Carol. arr. Caldwell. Schmitt, Hall & McCreary, 2555. (SA)
The Child Jesus. Graham. Abingdon, APM-219. (U-SATB)
The Christ Child. Cornelius-Heiberg. Choral Art. (U-SATB)
The Darkness Now Has Taken Flight. (Epiphany). Lovelace. Abingdon. (SA)
The Gifts a Child Can Bring. Rawls. J. Fischer, 8899. (SA)
The Holly and the Ivy. (English). arr. Russell. Oxford, T54. (SA)
The Holy Boy. (Irish) Boosey & Hawkes, 3365.
The Manger Carol. arr. Caldwell. Schmitt, Hall & McCreary, 2555. (SA)
The Morning Star. (Epiphany) Hagen-Pfohl. Brodt, 204. (U & SATB)
The Saviour Now Is Born. Williams. Gray, 2442. (SA-SATB)
The Song of Christmas. Yang. Broadman, 485-37022. (U-SATB; flute or violin.)
The Stars Shone Bright. Williams. Flammer, 86167. (SA)
To the Holy Child. Franck-Black. Gray, CMR-2705. (SA)
To Us Is Born (*I Saw Three Ships*). arr. Ehret. Marks, 4074. (SA)
When Christmas Morn Is Dawning. (German) arr. Barnard. Summy-Birchard, 5519.
Wise Men Seeking Jesus. Bitgood. Schmitt, Hall & McCreary, SD 6005. (U)
Why Do the Bells on Christmas Ring? Rinehard. Wood, 796. (U)
Zither Carol. (Czech) Sir Malcolm Sargent. Oxford, 84. (U-SATB)

Junior Choir — Lenten Anthems

All in the April Evening. Robertson. Curwen (Gray), 8837. (SA)
Ballad of the Dogwood Tree. Davis. Choristers Guild, A-7.
Behold the Lamb of God. Bouman. Concordia, 98-1088. (SA)
Eternally Rejoice. Rawls. J. Fischer, 8518.

Hosanna! Gregor-Pfohl. Brodt, 200. (2-part)
Hosanna to the Son of David. Lorenz. Abingdon, APM-266. (SA)
In Eastern Lands. Giasson. Galleon, 2002. (SA)
Our Father. (Syrian) Clokey. J. Fischer, 9218. (SA)
Our Lord Jesus Knelt in the Garden. Dickinson. Gray, 195. (U-SATB)
Prepare the Way, O Zion. Willan. Concordia, 98-1644. (SA)
Sing to the Son of David. Rawls. J. Fischer, 8277. (SA)
The Child and the Lamb. Kirk. J. Fischer, 9290. (SSA)
The Royal Banners Forward Go. Peek. Abingdon, APM-246. (U)
Thou, Lord, Art Our Shepherd. Gregor. Gray: Early American Moravian Music
    No. 14. (SA & SATB)
Two Lenten Meditations. Wetzler. Abingdon, APM 347. (U)
Wondrous Love (American Folk Hymn) arr. Thiman. Broadman, 485-36593. (U
    with descant)

Junior Choir — Easter Anthems

Alleluia to the Triune Majesty. Warner. Summy-Birchard, B-2066. (SA)
An Easter Carol. Lovelace. Abingdon, APM-204. (U & SATB)
At the Lamb's High Feast We Sing. Wadely. Oxford, E-53. (U)
Behold, God Is My Salvation. Sowerby. Gray, CMR-2712.
Christ Our Passover. Roth. Canyon, 6101. (U)
Christ the Lord Is Risen Today. K. K. Davis. Remick 10-G1855.
Christ the Lord Is Risen Today. Eichhorn. Gray, 2124. (SA)
Easter Bell Carol. Davies. Flammer, 86101. (U with descant)
Easter Day Carol. Lovelace. Canyon, 6351. (U)
Easter Flowers Are Blooming Bright. Lovelace. Gray, CMR-2513.
Here Is Spring! (Easter Carol). Paget. Elkins (Galaxy). (U or SATB)
I Know a Lovely Garden. Caldwell. Gray, 2578. (U)
It Is the Joyful Eastertime. (Cornish) arr. Burke. Flammer, 86182. (U with
    descant)
Kindly Spring Is Here Again. Lovelace. J. Fischer, 9019. (U)
Now the Green Blade Riseth. (French) arr. Fusner. Gray, CMR 2232. (U)
O Sing Ye Alleluia on This Day. Sala-Bedell. Boston, 11391. (U)
O Thou Joyful Day. Rawls. J. Fischer, 8741. (SA)
Polish Easter Carol. arr. Caldwell. Gray, CMR-2778. (U-SATB)
Round the Earth a Message Runs. (Sussex) Lovelace. Canyon, 6301. (2-part)
Song for Easter. Eichhorn. Gray, CMR-2057. (U)
Spring Prayer. Caldwell. Summy-Birchard, 2113. (U)
The Garden. Caldwell. Wood, 748. (U)
The Strife Is O'er. Vulpius-Ley. Oxford. (SA or SSA)

Youth Choir — Anthems

A Prayer for Families. Lovelace. Abingdon, APM 267. (SATB)
All Praise to Thee, Eternal God. Darst. C. Fischer, CM-7115. (Youth & SATB
    Combined).
Be Thou My Vision. arr. Carleton Young. Kjos. (SATB)
Dawn Bears the Sun. D. H. Jones. C. Fischer. (SATB)
God Is in His Holy Temple. Neander-Davis. Remick, R-3299. (SSA)
God Is My Strong Salvation. Darst. Broadman, MF-647. (2-part)
I Love Thy Kingdom, Lord. Weaver. Galaxy, 2247. (SSA)
I Thank Thee, Lord. Copes. Abingdon, APM-167 (U & SATB)
Let Earthly Choirs Arise and Sing. K. K. Davis. Broadman, MF 667. (U with
    descant)

298

My Faith Is an Oaken Staff. (Swiss) Vigeland. Gray, CMR-2698. (U with descant)
Praise, My Soul, the King of Heaven. Gilbert. Oxford. (U & SSA)
Psalm of Praise. Darst. Gray, CMR-2471. (2-part)
Rejoice, the Lord Is King. (Darwell). Winston. Broadman, MF-592. (2-part)
Sing Alleluia Forth. Marshall. C. Fischer, CM-7328. (U-SATB; handbells)
Sound the Trumpet. Purcell. E. C. Schirmer. (Treble)
The Greatest of These Is Love. Bitgood. Gray, CMR 1396. (SA)
The Lord Reigneth. Walter. Abingdon, APM-1911. (2-part).
When Jesus Christ Our Lord and King. Halter. Concordia, 98-1663. (SA, SAB, SATB)

Youth Choir — Christmas Anthems

A Babe in Bethlehem. (Corner's Cradle Song). arr. Manney. Wood, 336.
Adam Lay Ybounden. Warlock. Oxford. (SSA; strings)
Carol of the Heavenly Hosts. Kountz. Galaxy, CMC-2253. (SSA)
Glory to God in the Highest. Pergolesi-Mueller. C. Fischer, CM-6896. (SA)
Go Tell It on the Mountain. arr. Brown. Oxford. (SSA)
God Rest Ye Merry, Gentlemen. arr. Van Iderstine. Abingdon, APM-124. (U-SATB)
Let All Mortal Flesh. Holst. Galaxy, GMC-2248. (SSAA)
Shepherds, Come. Bitgood. J. Fischer, 9480. (SATB with solo & flute.)
Sing a Gay Noel. (Basque). Glaser. Wood, 816. (SSA)
Sleep, My Baby, Lovely Child. Halter. Concordia, 98-1662. (SA, SAB, SATB)
The Carolers. Matheson. Schmitt, Hall & McCreary, 330. (SSA) (Opt. part for Finger Cymbals or Tambourin)
The Bagpipe Carol. Barthelson. Skidmore. (SSA-SATB)
To Our Little Town (French Carol). Malin. Mills, 692. (SSA)
Today Our Songs of Joy Resound. Praetorius-Ehret. C. Fischer, CM-7334. (SATB)
While Shepherds Watched. Titcomb. Wood, 634. (SA)

Youth Choir — Easter Anthems

Christ the Lord Is Risen Again. Vulpius-Couper. C. Fischer, CM-7347. (SATB; handbells)
Christ Is Arisen! Schubert-Pfautsch. Abingdon. (SATB)
Litany for Easter. Young. Abingdon, APM-354. (SATB)

Youth Choir — SAB Anthems

Awake, My Heart. Marshall. Gray, 2648.
Good Folk Who Dwell on Earth. K. K. Davis. Wood, 731.
How Firm a Foundation. (Early American). arr. Walter. Abingdon, APM-103.
Immortal Love. Dietterich. Abingdon, APM-214. (Strings, trumpet, continuo)
Let All the Seas and Earth Around. (Angers) arr. Pitcher. Summy-Birchard-2056.
Like as a Father. Cherubini. Belwin.
Lord, God of Sabaoth. K. K. Davis. Summy-Birchard, 1563.
O Hear Them Marching. Haydn-Lynn. Pallma Music, 747.
O Sing Unto the Lord. Rogers. J. Fischer, 9490.
Once More, My Soul. arr. Ehret. Broadman, MF-573.
Praise to God, Immortal Praise. Darst. C. Fischer.
Resonet in Laudibus (German). Wood. Sacred Design, 6004. (U or SAB)

Song of Praise (Bryn Calfaria). Caldwell. Gray, 2661. (SAB with descant)
The Eyes of Faith. arr. Lovelace. Canyon, 6201
We Praise Thee, O God. Darst. Gray, CMR-2660.

Youth Choir — SAB Christmas Anthems

A Child of Beauty (Dutch). Ehret. Marks.
A Christmas Gift (Puerto Rican Carol). Cramer. Marks.
All Praise to Thee, Eternal God. Wienhorst. Concordia, 98-1517.
Catalonian Christmas Carol. Cramer. Marks.
Christ Came to Bethlehem. Frederickson. R. D. Row, 6103.
Christ Is Born in Bethlehem. (English) arr. Davies. Flammer, 88649.
Christmas Carol Fantasy. arr. Davies. Flammer, 88651.
Go Tell It on the Mountain. arr. Caldwell. Gray, CMR-2765.
How Lovely Shines the Morning Star. arr. Strube. Concordia, 98-1397.
O Come, O Come, Emmanuel. arr. Lenel. Concordia, 98-2022. (SAB with descant)
Sing We Noel. arr. Pitcher. Summy-Birchard, B-264.
Three Christmas Carols (Away in a Manger; From Heaven on High; Softly Sleep, Jesus) Concordia, 98-1563.
Wake, Awake, for Night Is Flying. arr. Fr. Zipp. Concordia, 98-1104.
Why Thus Cradled Here? arr. Lynn. Abingdon, APM-138.

Youth Choir — SAB Easter Anthems

An Endless Alleluia. Candlyn. J. Fischer, 8922. (SAB, opt. T)
Easter Carol. Garden. Gray, CMR-2692.
Instruments Waken and Publish Your Gladness. Buxtehude. Concordia, 98-1422.
The Whole Bright World Rejoices. (English Carol). Hill. Gray, CMR-1861.
Wake with Joy for Christ Is Risen. Graham. Abingdon, APM-342.

Junior and Youth Choirs — Anthem Collections

Anthems for the Junior Choir; Volumes I-IV. Westminster Press. (U-SA)
Chorale Anthems, Vol. I. ed. Pasquet. Augsburg. (U or varied)
Clarendon Books for Boys with Changing Voices. Oxford:
    Book I (Mezzos and Altos)
    Book II (Altos and Tenors)
    Book III (Tenor, Baritone and Bass)
"Eight" for Junior Choir. Lynn. Golden Music Co. (U or SA)
Fairhaven Junior Choir and Duet Book. E. C. Schirmer.
Five Settings of Texts by Thomas Toplady. Lovelace. Canyon, YS-6153. (U)
Great Songs of Faith: Books I and II. Krones. Kjos. (SA)
New Songs for the Junior Choir. Bristol-Friedell. Concordia, 97-7599. (U)
Responses for Treble Voices. Harold Darke. Oxford.
Sacred Songs for the Junior Choir. arr. Hoffman. Presser.
Seven Treble Choir Anthems for the Christian Year. Copley. Abingdon.
Songs and Anthems for Treble Voices. Malmin. Augsburg. (SA, SSA)
Songs for Pre-Teen Time. Cooper. C. Fischer.
Soprano-Alto Anthems. Schmitt, Hall & McCreary.
The Belfry Book—I and II. K. K. Davis. Remick. (SA)
The Chapel Choir. Couper. J. Fischer, 9098. (SA)
The Church Year for the Children's Choir. (Carols & Hymns) Gillette. Flammer.
The Junior Choir Sings. D. H. Williams. Summy-Birchard. (SA)
The Morning Star Choir Book. ed. Thomas. Concordia.

The SSA Choir. arr. Andersen. Schmitt, Hall & McCreary.
Three Treble Choir Anthems. Powell. Abingdon, APM-198. (U)
The Treble Choir. arr. Heller. Schmitt, Hall & McCreary.
Thirty-Five Sacred Rounds and Canons from Four Centuries. Bristol. Canyon.
Twelve Sayings of Jesus. Willan. Concordia. (U & SA)
Unison Songs for Teen-Age Boys. Cooper. Gordon V. Thompson, Inc.
Unison and Two-Part Anthems. Pooler. Augsburg.
Voices of Worship. Malin. Wood.
We Go to Church. Jane Marshall. C. Fischer, 0-4009. (U, SA & SSA)
We Praise Thee—I and II. Willan. Concordia, 97-7610. (U, SA, SSA)
Praise Him. ed. Ringwald. Shawnee. (SAB)
The SSAB Choir Book. arr. Tkach. Schmitt, Hall & McCreary.
The SAB Chorister. ed. Heller. Schmitt, Hall & McCreary.

Combined Choirs — Festival Anthems

A Thanksgiving Hymn. Thiman. Mills, 5018. (U with descant)
Alleluia to the Triune Majesty. Warner. Summy-Birchard, B-2066. (SA or SSA)
Chorale Concertatos. Concordia:
    All Glory, Laud and Honor. Bunjes. Concordia, 87-4513. (Organ, trumpet)
    Built on the Rock. Bunjes. Concordia, 97-4571. (Adult Choir, Congregation,
        Jr. Choir, 2 trumpets, organ)
    I Know That My Redeemer Lives. Bunjes. Concordia, 97-4434. (Organ,
        trumpet)
    Praise to the Lord, the Almighty. Rohlig. Concordia, 97-4423. (Organ, flute,
        trumpet)
Come to the Manger. Kountz. Galaxy, GMC-2252. (SA & SATB; handbells)
Easter Hymn of Praise. Lapo. Abingdon, APM-357.
Fanfare for Easter. Pfautsch. Flammer, 84727. (Youth Choirs and Brass)
How Majestic Is Thy Name. Diemer. Gray, CMR-2729. (U)
Jesus, Sun of Life, My Splendor. Handel. Concordia. (U-SATB)
Laus Deo. (Praise to God Our King) Hughes-Jones. Mills, 5019. (U)
O Saviour Blest. Havergal-Hutson. Shawnee, A-604. (2 violins or flutes)
Only Begotten, Word of God. Casner. Concordia, 98-1598. (U; 3 trumpets)
Praise, My Soul, the King of Heaven. Fryxell. C. Fischer, CM-7312. (U or 2-
    part)
Psalm 150. Pfautsch. Flammer, 84725. (Youth Choirs and Brass)
Reconciliation. Pfautsch. Abingdon, APM-345. (Speech Choirs; Instrumental
    Parts.)
Remember All the People. Baumgardner. Abingdon, APM-211.
Rise Up, O Men of God. Scull. Novello, 1140 (H. W. Gray) (U & SS)
Shout the Glad Tidings. D. H. Williams. Augsburg, 1253. (2-part)
Sing to the Lord of Harvest. Willan. Concordia, 98-1643. (U or SA with descant;
    Brass optional.)
Song of Praise. (Bryn Calfaria) Caldwell. Gray, 2661. (U, SA, SAB & descant)
The Lamb. Wood. Abingdon, APM-206.
The Sanctus. (From Martin Luther's German Mass) arr. Dietterich. Abingdon,
    APM-191.
To Shepherds Fast Asleep. K. K. Davis. Galaxy, GMC-2243. (SA & SATB)

Hymnals for Children's Choirs

Church School Hymnal for Children. ed. R. H. Terry. Lutheran Church Press.
    (In both a Children's edition and a Leader's edition)
Choristers Guild Little Hymnal. Choristers Guild.

Hymnal for Boys and Girls. Parker & Richards. Appleton-Century.
Hymns for Junior Worship. Westminster.
Hymns for Primary Worship. Westminster.
Fifty Descants for Hymns of the Church—Vol. I. L. D. Miller. Muhlenberg.
Hymn-Study Series for Young Children. Boyter. C. Fischer:
    1. *My Favorite Hymns of Praise.*
    2. *My Favorite Christmas Carols.*
    3. *My Favorite Contemporary Hymns.*
    4. *My Favorite Hymns of Nature.*
    5. *My Favorite Hymns of Watts and Wesley.*
    6. *My Favorite Hymns of Dedication and Consecration.*
    7. *My Favorite Prayer Hymns.*
    8. *My Favorite Folk-Tune Hymns.*
Our Hymns of Praise. (Mennonite) ed. Stauffer. Herald Press. (Melody line only; ages 6-11)
Pilgrim Hymnal. Porter. Pilgrim Press.
Presbyterian Hymnal for Youth. Westminster.
Singing Worship. ed. Thomas. Abingdon.
Songs of Joy Through the Church Year. Thalman. Fortress.
The Children's Hymnbook. The National Union of Christian Schools. (For ages 3-8.)
The Canyon Hymnal for Girls and Boys. Canyon.
The Youth Hymnary. Faith & Life Press.
Twenty-Six Communion Hymns for Use by Choirs. ed. Lovelace. Abingdon, APM 301.

Christmas Carol Collections

A Carol Choir. arr. Duchow. Boston Music Co.
Carols for Choirs. Jacques-Willcocks. Oxford.
Carols for the Twelve Days of Christmas. Percy Young. Dennis Dobson, Ltd.
Christmas Carols and Hymns. Hollis Dann. American Book Co.
Christmas Carols from Many Countries. Coleman & Jorgensen. G. Schirmer.
Christmas for the Very Young. (Primary) arr. Upshur. Flammer.
Christmas, Its Carols, Customs, and Legends. Heller. Schmitt, Hall & McCreary.
Christmas 'Round the World. arr. Heller. Summy-Birchard. (U or SA)
Clarendon Books of Christmas Carols and Songs. Oxford:
    Book I—Primary and Juniors.
    Book II—High School
Descants for Christmas. Krones. Kjos.
Feliz Navidad. (Spanish) arr. Edwards. Mills, 2057. (U or SA)
Four Carols from Abroad. arr. Treacher. Oxford. (U)
More Carols from Abroad. arr. Treacher. Oxford. (U)
Froehliche Weihnachten. (German) arr. Malin. Mills, 2056. (U or SA)
Joyous Carols. arr. Whitner. C. Fischer. (2-part; suggestions for instrumental parts)
Noels With Descants. (Arranged) Schmitt, Hall & McCreary.
The Oxford Book of Carols. (200 Carols). Oxford.
60 Christmas Carols. Father Finn. Summy-Birchard.
Songs for Christmas. American Book Co.
Three for Christmas. Lynn. Golden-Music Pub. (U)
Three Moravian Carols. arr. Tate. Oxford. 45-064 (U)
Uncommon Christmas Carols. Auditorium Series, No. 54. Schmitt, Hall & McCreary.
Yule Tidings. (Carols with descants) arr. Ehret. Marks.

Christmas Cantatas

A Ceremony of Carols. Britten. Boosey & Hawkes. (SSA) (Difficult)
Christmas Cantata. Rohlfing. Concordia, 97-7534. (U)
Christmas Cards for You. Kessler. Flammer. (U; 5 Tableaux for Children)
From Heaven High I Come to Earth. Bender. Concordia, 97-6399. (SA; Instruments)
From Heaven Above, Ye Angels All. Spitta. Concordia, 97-7577. (Treble, or Male, or Mixed; Strings or Woodwinds and Continuo)
Legends of the Madonna. Grant. Belwin. (SSA) (6 Episodes with Color Slides; Narrator; Girls' Chorus)
Lo! A Star. Graham. Broadman, 486-37103. (for children's voices)
Lo, I Bring Tidings. Vierdanck. J. Fischer, 9156. (SS) (2 Treble parts, 2 violins or recorders, and organ)
Petit Noel. Underwood & Perry. Chappel. (Can be dramatized)
Saint Nicolas. Britten. Boosey & Hawkes, 16469.
 (For 2 Youth Choirs, SA & SATB; Tenor & Boy Soloists. Difficult.)
What Gift Have I? Graham. Broadman, 1963. (SA) (Cantata-Fantasy)
Welcome, Thou King of Glory. Luebeck. Concordia, 97-6379. (SA)

Christmas Drama

(Check with publishers for performance permissions and fees)

A Christmas Carol Pageant. Diller-Page. G. Schirmer. (Large cast; 3 Episodes; full instructions and illustrations)
Amahl and the Night Visitors. Menotti. G. Schirmer. (50 minutes) (One-Act Opera; important boy's role. Difficult.)
Carols for Acting. London. Novello.
Herod. ed. W. L. Smoldon. Stainer & Bell. (30 minutes) (Medieval Music Drama. U with easy instruments, percussion)
O Come, Let Us Adore Him. Pooler. Augsburg. (U or SA; Narrator; Speech Choir)
On Bethlehem Hill. Crawley-Rowley. Boosey & Co., Ltd. (30 minutes) (Speaking and solo parts; Children's Chorus)
On Christmas Night. Bolm-Ralph Vaughn Williams. Oxford. (30 minutes) (A Masque adapted from Dicken's *Christmas Carol*) U; solos; part-singing. Effective. Not difficult.)
One Christmas Night. William Mayer. Galaxy. (60 minutes) (Opera based on story "Why the Chimes Rang"; 2 Boy Soprano soloists; Adult Chorus and soloists; Chimes score adaptable for Handbells. Difficult.)
The First Noel. Ralph Vaughn Williams. Oxford. (U-SATB) (Pageant production: 50 minutes; Concert version: 30 minutes) (U-SATB; Familiar and Less Known Carols. Not difficult.)
The Pilgrim Caravan. Malcolm Arnold. Oxford.
The Shepherds. arr. Inglis Gunding. Oxford. (SSA) (30 minutes) (Medieval Music Drama; Speaking parts; Instruments.)
The Twelve Days of Christmas. arr. Buttolph-Perry. Willis. (30 minutes; U Voices; Dancing; Suggestions for Clever Costuming; Play based on familiar carol.)

Cantatas — Easter

Adoremus Te. Clokey. Summy-Birchard. (SATB; children U or SA)
And Yet Have Believed. Lynn. Presser. (Junior and Adult choirs)
The Builders. Clokey. Gray. (Unison service or pageant)
The First Easter. Richter. Presser. (U or SATB; hymns and tableaux)

The Three Marys. McKinney. J. Fischer. (U or SATB with pantomime)
To Calvary. Titcomb. Gray. (SATB and Youth Choir SA or U)

Cantatas — General

Earth Shall Be Fair. Ward. Galaxy. (SA, Youth and Adult SATB)
Songs from Luke. Bristol. Canyon. (SA, 8 selections for Juniors)
Songs from Matthew. Bristol. Canyon. (SA, for Juniors)

Handbells — Books

The Art of Handbell Ringing. Nancy Poore Tufts. Abingdon.
The Story of Handbells. Scott Parry. Whittemore Associates.
The Handbell Choir. Doris Watson. Gray.
Handbell Ringing in Church. Lorenz.

Handbells — Music Collections

A Handbell Concert. Helen Runkle. J. Fischer. (23 arr. of sacred, secular and
    Christmas pieces. Range: 1½ oct.)
A Handbell Handbill. Scott Parry. Gray. (17 arr. from classics. Range: 2 to 3
    octaves.)
Album of Recital Pieces for Handbells. Wendell Wescott. J. Fischer. (12 arr.
    from classics and folk songs. Range: 2½ to 3 oct.)
Bells Around the World. Alice Bartlett. Flammer. (18 selections. Range: 2
    octaves—G to G)
Book of Handbell Music. Set I. Doris Watson. Gray. (23 arr. of hymns and
    folk music. Range: 2 octaves—G to G)
Carols and Songs for Ringing. Edward Johe. Flammer. (19 selections for vari-
    ous numbers of bells)
Christmas Music for Handbell Choirs. Norris Stephens. G. Schirmer. (50 selec-
    tions for various numbers of bells)
Familiar Melodies for Handbells. F. L. Whittlesey. Flammer. (13 selections,
    sacred and secular. Range: 3 octaves—C to C)
Handbell Ringing. (*A Musical Introduction*) Scott Parry. C. Fischer. (10 teach-
    ing pieces, instructions and exercises. Range: 2 octaves—G to G)
Hear the Bells. F. L. Whittlesey. Flammer.
I Heard the Bells. Adams-York. C. Fischer. (17 selections suitable for church.
    Range: 3 octaves—C to C)
Ringing and Singing. F. L. Whittlesey. Flammer. (23 hymns and carols for
    handbells and treble voices. Range: 2 octaves—G to G)
Ringing in the Sanctuary. Irene and Robert Stuart. Belwin. (23 arr. suitable
    for church. Range: 1½ to 2 octaves—C to G and G to G)
66 Bell Arrangements for Church. Lorenz.
Original Compositions for Handbells. Compiled by Nancy Poore Tufts. Flammer.
    (The first collection of more difficult music for advanced ringers. Range:
    3 to 5 octaves.)

For Handbells Alone

Castle Hill Suite. Alice Procter. Gray. (Range: 3 octaves)
Four Pieces for Handbells. arr. Litterst. Choral Services, (Hymn arrangements.
    Range: 2 and 2½ octaves)
Sonata for a Musical Clock. Handel-Price. Oxford. (For Carillon or 13 Hand-
    bells)

304

Ten Tunes for Clay's Musical Clock. Handel. Societas Campaniariorum. (Range: 1½ octaves)

Trilogy. Muriel Davis. Gray, HB 2. (Range: 2½ octaves)

Variations on a Nursery Rhyme. Muriel Davis. Gray, HB 1. (Range: 2½ octaves)

CHARTS: Chart Music on 20"x24" sheets issued by Lorenz Pub. Co. include "8 Famous Tower Chimes" and "Service Music for Bells," as well as separate parts for bells for use with such anthems as Stainer's *Sabbath Bells.* Write for Handbell list.

Handbell Duos

Duo for Recorder and Handbells. Helen Runkle. Gray.

Carol for the Christ Child. Marian McLaughlin. J. Fischer. (Organ and handbells; 1½ octaves.)

Easter Prelude. Alinda Couper. J. Fischer. (Organ and handbells; 1½ octaves.)

Pastorale. Alinda Couper. J. Fischer. (Organ and handbells; 2 octaves.)

Christmas Anthems with Handbells or Chimes

A Christmas Bell Song. Couper. Choristers Guild, A-14. (U)

Adoration of the Shepherds. Butcher. C. Fischer, CM 597. (U or SATB)

A Japanese Carol. Whittlesey. Choristers Guild, A-10. (U)

Bells of Christmas. Whittlesey. Flammer, 86165. (2-part Jrs.)

Christmas Song. arr. Holst. G. Schirmer, 8119. (U)

Fum, Fum, Fum. (Catalonian) arr. Nightingale. C. Fischer, 7105. (U-SATB)

Good Christian Men, Rejoice. arr. Lorenz. Lorenz, 8594. (U or SA)

Hear the Bells of Christmas. Whittlesey. Abingdon, APM, 228. (U)

Hearken All, What Happy Singing. Rawls. J. Fischer, 9474. (U or SA)

Joyous Carols. Whitner. C. Fischer, 0-4004. (2-part)

Joy to the World! Handel-Couper. Flammer, 86187. (U or SA)

Let All Mortal Flesh Keep Silence. (Picardy) arr. Couper. Flammer, 84657. (U-SATB)

Let the Merry Church Bells. Couper. J. Fischer. (SA)

In a Stable. Couper. Flammer, 84771.

Little Bells. (from *The Magic Flute*) Mozart-Forsblad. Pro-Art, 1844. (SA-SATB)

Merrily on High. (French Carol) Hadler. Lorenz, E-13. (SA-SATB)

Nativity Morn. LaMontaine. Gray, 2491. (SA-SATB)

Noel. Marguerite Havey. Gray.

Now Behold Our Newfound Joy. (Piae Cantiones) arr. Couper. J. Fischer, 9239. (U or SA)

Rejoice and Be Merry. Hinton. Oxford. (Round for 4 voices; bells and recorders optional)

Ring, Christmas Bells! Reinecke-Dickinson. Gray, 268. (SA-SATB)

Ring Out, Wild Bells. Couper. J. Fischer, 9477. (SAB)

Ring Out, Wild Bells. Fletcher. Novello, 1053. (SATB)

Shepherds on Watch. (Spanish) Couper. Flammer, 86188. (U)

The Bells Ring Out for Christmas. Sacco. G. Schirmer, 10772. (SATB)

The Cradle. McLaughlin. J. Fischer, 9292. (SA)

The Star Was Like a Candle. Flammer, 84685. (SA-SATB)

Ukrainian Carol of the Bells. Leontovich-Couper. Flammer, 88078. (SAB)

When Christ Was Born of Mary Free. Couper. Flammer, 84641. (SSA-SATB)

With Voices and Bells. arr. Edwards. Mills, 2051. (8 European Carols; SA, with piano or autoharp)

Yule Log Carol. Giasson. Galleon, GCS-1010. (SA-SATB)

Easter Anthems with Handbells or Chimes

A Song of Praise. Thiman. A. P. Schmidt. (U)
Bells of Spring. Rawls. J. Fischer, 9186. (SA)
Christ the Lord Is Ris'n Again. Vulpius-Couper. C. Fischer, CM 7347. (U-SATB)
Easter Bell Carol. Davies. Flammer, 88654 (SAB)
Easter Bell Carol. Pfautsch. Abingdon, APM-168. (U)
Easter Bells Are Ringing. Elmore. Galaxy, 1499. (SATB)
Hosanna to the Son of David. Lorenz. Lorenz, APM-266. (2-part)
Rejoice, Ye Heavens. Couper. Flammer, 84664. (SATB)
Three Bell Carols for Junior Choirs. Hadler. Lorenz, 8583. (SA)
    1. *The Bell Noel;* 2. *The Bell Hosanna;* 3. *Easter Bell Carol.*

General Anthems with Handbells or Chimes

A Child's Prayer. Pfautsch. Choristers Guild, A-27. (U)
A Festival Chime. arr. Holst. Stainer & Bell, Ltd. (U-SATB)
Come and Worship. Rawls. J. Fischer, 9278-2. (U or SA; Primary or Jr.)
God's World. (German Folksong) arr. Nitske. J. Fischer, 9483.
Hear the Bells. (French Carol) arr. Hadler. Lorenz.
List to the Lark. (The Norfolk Chimes) Dickinson. Gray, 68. (U-SATB)
Sabbath Bells. Stainer. Gray, CMR-1537. (U for children)
Sing Alleluia Forth. Marshall. C. Fischer, 7328. (U-SATB)
Worship in Song. G. Schirmer. (Five anthems, U or varied)

Books About Bells in General

Bells of All Nations. Ernest Morris. Robert Hale.
Bells, Their History, Legends, Making, and Uses. Satis Coleman. Rand & McNally.
Bells, Their History and Romance. G. Morrison. J. F. Rowny Press.
Cow Concert. (Story for young children). Earle Goudenow. Knopf.
Christmas in the Bell Shop. (For children) Hallmark.
Old Liberty Bell. Rogers and Beard. Lippincott.
Oranges and Lemons. (Adult) Gladys Taylor. Nevill. (Stories of old London churches and bells)
The First Book of Bells. Fletcher and Auerbach. Watts.
The Nine Tailors. Dorothy Sayers. Gollancz. (A "whodunit" with references to change ringing and bell lore)
Tintinnabula. Ernest Morris. Robert Hale. (Fascinating history of small bells of the world)

Periodicals for Bell Ringers

Choristers Guild Letters. A 10-month magazine for Directors of Children's Choirs includes a monthly feature "Tintinnabulations" by Nancy Poore Tufts. Write Choristers Guild, 440 Northlake Center, Dallas 38, Texas.
Overtones. Official Quarterly of the American Guild of English Handbell Ringers. Write Editor James R. Lawson, Carillonneur, The Riverside Church, New York, N. Y. 10027.
The Bell Tower. Official Monthly Publication of the American Bell Association (Bell Collectors). Write Secretary Louise Collins, R.D. 1, Natrona Heights, Pennsylvania.
The Ringing World. Official Monthly Magazine of the Central Council of Church Bell Ringers of England. (Tower Bell Ringing, mainly). Write Editor Thomas White, % Woodbridge Press, Ltd., Guildford, Surrey, England.

INDEX

Accompaniment, 120

Advent
see Church Year

American Guild of English Handbell Ringers, 171

Anthems
see Materials

Attendance problems, 53

Attitude and successful choirs, 26f, 40f, 125f, 152f, 165-167

Audio Visual aides
Audio Visual Resources Guide, 188-190
make own audio visuals, 188
use of recordings and tape recorders, 95, 144

Bells
see Handbells

Blind
see Handicap

Boys
changing voice—see Voice
discipline, 80, 130, 137
handbells as interest keepers, 183
importance of organization, 125f
ways to attract—to choir program, 91-93

Changing voice
see Voice

Choir
ailing—program, 38f
—as aid in leading congregations in new ideas, 225-227
as purposeful activity, 7-9, 15, 87-88, 165-167
dedication of choir, 20-21
meaning of choir membership, 21-22, 67
membership, 30f, 125f
relation to church, 2, 18-19

Choristers Guild
— Letters, 1, 55
— Office, 5
— Pin, 4
— Seminar, source of inspiration, 88, 1-2
gifts to —, 3
local chapters, 4, 45
membership, 2-3

Christmas
see Church Year

Church
a singing —, 222-224
respect of — for music program 55f
value of choir to —, 9-12

Church Year, 192f
Children's Service for Good Friday, 257-258

Christmas carol services and programs, 271f
Easter Hymn Festival, 258-259
Epiphany Service, 283-284
Festival of the Masks, 260-261
keping Christmas, 268f
Lent and Easter, 83-84, 193-194, 225-227
Reformation, 262
Thanksgiving, 263-265

Conducting
see Directing

Copyright law, 59

Discipline
aid to —, 44, 80
clues to —, 50-51, 93, 137, 153, 165-167
rehearsal —, 112f

Directing
attitudes affecting, 40f

Easter
see Church Year

Epiphany
see Church Year

English handbell
see Handbell

Evaluation
— of concept of choir work, 88-89
need for constant —, 35-36, 77-78, 80
New Year good time for —, 54-55, 178
use summer for planning and —, 90

Expression, techniques for conveying message of anthem, 93f

Festivals, 163
planning for —, 240f
see also Special Activities

Games
aids to theory, 49, 61-64, 67
based on hymn study, 215
fish pond, 70
open mouth, 70
primary choir, 61f

Handbells
as memorials, 181
care of —, 180-181
dedication of —, 172-176
English, 169f
share —, 176-177

Handicap
the blind and choir, 56f

Hymnals
as resource, 213f
use of, 17

Hymn studies
Holy, Holy, Holy, 218
If Thou But Suffer God to Guide Thee, 219-220
Our Church Proclaims God's Love and Care, 221-222

307

308

63717

MT
88
.C52
v.2

DATE DUE

MAR 20 '69			
APR 4 '69			
MAY 9 '69			
MAY 28 '69			
SEP 17 '69			
OCT 18 70			
DEC 18 74			
OCT 31 1977			
871024			
GAYLORD			PRINTED IN U.S.A.